MITCHUM

MITCHUM

The Film Career of Robert Mitchum

Bruce Crowther

ROBERT HALE · LONDON

ISBN 0 7090 4502 6

Robert Hale Limited
Clerkenwell House
Clerkenwell Green
London EC1R 0HT

Photoset in Palatino by
Derek Doyle & Associates, Mold, Clwyd.
Printed in Great Britain by
St Edmundsbury Press, Bury St Edmunds, Suffolk.
Bound by WBC Bookbinders Ltd, Bridgend, Glamorgan.

Contents

List of Illustrations

Between pages 142 and 143

PICTURE CREDITS

Some of the illustrations in this book come from stills issued to publicize films made or distributed by the following companies: Columbia: 20. EK/ITC: 25, 26. MGM: 22. Paramount: 21, 24. RKO: 1, 2, 4, 5, 6, 7, 8. Twentieth Century Fox: 9, 12. United Artists: 3, 10, 11, 13, 16, 18, 27. Universal: 17, 19. Warner Brothers: 14, 15, 23.

Pictures are reproduced by courtesy of the Stills, posters and Design Department at the British Film Institute, Derek East, Hilton Tims and Ann Caves.

Although every effort has been made to trace the copyright holders of photographs, the publishers apologize in advance for any unintentional omission or neglect and will be pleased to insert the appropriate acknowledgement to the companies or individuals concerned in any subsequent edition of this book.

Author's Note

The chronology of motion pictures is often uncertain in that a film may be released promptly after shooting has been completed or its release may be delayed due to post-production complications or it may simply, if sometimes inexplicably, be shelved for months or even years before being seen by the public. All these problems and more arise in the film career of Robert Mitchum. Generally speaking, the text follows the chronology of release date rather than the chronology of the shooting of the films. Where this may give rise to confusion, reference is made in the text.

B.C.

Acknowledgements

I am very grateful to many people for their help and encouragement during the preparation of this book, in particular my principal researcher, Dave Tuck, whose involvement since inception has proved to be a great, and at times much needed, stimulus. Additionally, special thanks must go to Dave Dalton for his assiduous researches which have greatly aided the later stages of the book and especially the preparation of the Filmography; to Jane Beckley of Worldvision Enterprises Incorporated, and Elaine Burrows of the National Film Archive at the British Film Institute, for their help in enabling me to see several otherwise unavailable films; to Jane Stewart for providing translations from French magazines; the publicity departments of several motion picture and television companies, especially the Cannon Group Inc. and Paramount Television. Needless to say, however, the opinions expressed and any factual errors which might occur are my sole responsibility.

B.C.

Foreword

Six books have been written about me, but I've only ever
met two of the authors. They get my name and birthplace
wrong in the first paragraph. From there it's all downhill.

Since he first ambled onto the screen in a string of bit parts in
Hopalong Cassidy westerns in the early 1940s, Robert Mitchum
has captured the attention and the imaginations of several
generations of moviegoers, male and female, across the world.
Yet, with such remarks as the one above, he has been
engagingly dismissive of all attempts to pin down in print just
what it is that has made him so enduringly popular.

An ability to appeal that crosses age limits is rare among
screen actors. What makes Mitchum's case even more unusual
is the fact that neither is there a sexual barrier. Men wish they
were like him, and the women in their lives agree.

Then there is the impression that he is just the same off-screen
as on; tough, hard-bitten and a loner. Those books about him,
whether or not their authors met him, gradually reveal the
inaccuracy of assumptions that the first part of his off-screen
persona is real. There is a gentleness and sensitivity about him
that many might find improbable in a movie tough guy. As to
the second part of that character assessment, despite his
enduring marriage he may well be, at heart, a solitary man.

Adding to his hard-nosed image are those eagerly reported
occasions when he has decked anyone fancying his chances at
testing the toughness of a silver-screen hero. And to complicate
matters further, there is his long-running love-hate affair with
journalists, which has often resulted in articles castigating him
for boorishness, drunkenness, sexual promiscuity, racism and
heaven knows what else.

Some of the allegations in these articles have had at least a
measure of truth at their often vitriolic hearts.

Undoubtedly, Mitchum has been deliberately rude to
interviewers and others. If the reason for his behaviour was the

1

interviewer's intrusion into his private life, this in no way lessened the impact of the resulting articles.

He also had a long and dedicated fondness for booze which climaxed in 1984 with a spell in the Betty Ford clinic at Rancho Mirage, which has become famous as a place where film and television stars go in an attempt to overcome drink- or drug-related problems.

Despite his long-lasting marriage there have been sexual encounters with the famous and the available (and sometimes with the famously available).

The allegations of racism appear, at best, to have been either a misunderstanding or a demonstration of a surprisingly naïve view of how his words might appear in print, bereft of nuance, look and gesture.

At worst, these and all the other hatchet jobs might have been nothing more than a deliberate attempt to make him look bad. Some people like movie stars to have feet of clay, even if they have to be given them.

The frequency of misinterpretations generated by his wayward sense of humour raises a question about his judgement. Mitchum has been sending up the press for decades, yet his assumption that they always know when he is joking is groundless. Too often his jokes have backfired, or have been overlooked by eager, and often understandably overawed, interviewers. By now, he should know better. Perhaps, in some cases, he does, but simply doesn't care. Curiously enough, this lack of concern for what others might think of him, instead of reacting against him, somehow adds to the aura and makes him even more interesting, even more attractive, and even more the object of admiration from his fans.

That aura existed almost from the start. When Robert Mitchum began making movies the studio publicists must have thought that their prayers had at last been answered.

By 1942, when he was twenty-five years old, Mitchum, by his own account, had already been expelled from school; worked as a deck-hand on a salvage vessel; hitch-hiked across America, riding the rods like many Depression-days hobos; served time on a Georgia chain-gang from which he escaped; worked in the Pennsylvania coalfields; boxed professionally; written songs, plays and poetry; and even played the saxophone. The studio publicists fell on these 'facts' with glee. What they didn't yet realize was that Mitchum's ability to embellish tales of his youthful exploits had already begun to have its effect upon his life story. Like most born storytellers, Mitchum's tales have a basis in fact. The problem then, as now, lay in unravelling fact from fiction. Kirk Douglas, who worked with Mitchum early in his film career, commented in his autobiography, *The Ragman's Son*, that Mitchum's 'stories about being a hobo kept changing every time he told them'.

When even the most outlandish of his tales were printed as being the gospel truth, Mitchum took pleasure in seeing just how far he could go without the press realizing he was sending them up. Inevitably, in time, the press, who must surely have spotted the fact that they were dealing with a man with an incorrigibly inventive mind, went on printing anything and everything and thus made the legend stronger than the truth.

For Mitchum, who is a far more private man than his frequently high public profile might suggest, this was good news because it helped increase the density of his private smokescreen, which allowed him to be whatever he wanted to be.

Just what he wanted to be as a child is uncertain, but if, as seems likely, he wanted to be an adventurer, in mind or body and sometimes both, then he certainly succeeded even before he arrived in Hollywood.

1 Was There Life Before Hollywood?

> We got married in the kitchen because that was the
> warmest room in the house. The place smelled of cabbage
> and the preacher kept on spitting in the sink.

Robert Charles Duran Mitchum was born in Connecticut on 6
August 1917. He was the second child of James Thomas and
Ann Harriet Mitchum. His father was half Scotch-Irish, half
Blackfoot Indian; his mother was Norwegian, having come to
America when she was still a child. James Mitchum and Ann
Gunderson were married in Bridgeport, and their early years
were spent there and in Charleston, as James, who was in the
army, was moved from place to place. When he left the army,
James took his family to Lane, South Carolina, his home town,
close to Charleston where he had found work in the railway
marshalling yards.

In 1919, when Bob was not quite two years old, and his sister,
Annette (known from an early age as Julie), was four, James
Mitchum was crushed between two boxcars in an accident at
work, dying almost instantly. His wife, heavily pregnant with
their third child, soon returned to Bridgeport and her parents,
Gustave Olaf and Petrine Gunderson.

Ann Mitchum took a lease on a house in Logan Street, found
work for herself and attempted to resume her life, receiving
much-needed moral and practical support from her parents.

The next few years brought mixed blessings to Ann's three
children. The absence of a father was clearly detrimental to their
early attitudes and behaviour, which were sometimes anti-social
and wild, although the Gundersons provided a much-needed
stabilizing influence.

Gustave Gunderson was a big, stern and muscular, merchant
seaman, while his wife was a diminutive lady with a mind of her
own and unfulfilled ambitions to be an actress either on the
stage or in silent pictures.

By the time he was six years old, Bob was already showing

signs of the adult he would become, although it was still too early for him to display many of the characteristics, physical and intellectual, of his grandparents. He was as eager as any inquisitive child to explore the smoke-covered industrial town of Bridgeport and the greener surroundings, taking along his little brother, John. Among these explorations were two which ended in near-tragedy. One, in 1924, was a simple shopping chore, but John excitedly broke free of his brother's restraining hand and was badly hurt after being hit by two street cars. The other, a mid-winter fishing expedition, came to an abrupt halt when Bob fell into the icy water from where he was hauled, soaked and freezing, by a sailor.

At the age of seven, Bob ran away from home, winding up in Hartford, Connecticut. Although only forty miles away, it was quite a distance for one so young, and it served as a foretaste of longer, grander journeys of discovery.

Young Bob constantly wove tales about his exploits, real and imagined. He also wrote poetry, something which delighted his mother, although he preferred to keep this particular activity secret.

By 1923 Ann Mitchum was working at the local newspaper, *The Bridgeport Post*, as a linotype operator, and had met, married, and divorced Bill Clay, a reporter. She then met Hugh Cunningham Morris, an Englishman who also worked at the *Post* as editor of the children's page. Morris printed some of young Bob's poems, gaining the small boy some immediate and local fame. The poems were accompanied by a feature article which highlighted the family's financial difficulties, a fact which led one of Mitchum's unofficial biographers, George Eells, to speculate that this invasion of privacy, however well-meaning it might have been, was an early warning to the boy that the press was a potential hazard, was not to be trusted, and was an institution of which he would do well to be wary.

The Mitchum children spent some of their early years in rural surroundings. Gustave and Petrine Gunderson bought a small farm at Felton, Delaware, which was run by the children's Uncle Bill and Aunt Gertrude, while another uncle and aunt, John and Jenny, farmed at Killingly, Connecticut. Julie, Bob and John spent time on both farms, not always enjoying the life, and to some extent suffering from the disruptions such moves had on their young lives.

Country life was far from being a tranquil respite from city life. The local kids took an instant dislike to the Mitchum brothers, deriding them as city slickers, and prepared to punch home their presumed superiority at regular free-for-alls. Bob and John quickly showed that city life had taught them the ropes, and proved themselves to be more than a match for their bucolic opponents. After one scrap ended with two of their attackers in hospital, the Mitchums were cautiously avoided. Unfairly, perhaps, the brothers also picked up a nickname which stuck throughout the rest of their childhood, and which John would later use as the title of his autobiography; 'them ornery Mitchum boys'.

The accidental shooting with a .22 rifle of another young boy, and the felling of a tree their uncle had already sold to the telegraph company, all helped fuel belief in Felton that the Mitchums were children to be avoided.

Ann Mitchum and Morris, 'the Major', became close, and in 1927 they were married, soon having a child of their own, a daughter they named Carol. At first the boys knew nothing of the marriage, being still in Delaware, but once they found out they gave their stepfather a hard time. Their hostility was generated in part by the impact of his publication of details of the family's economic plight. In later years, however, Mitchum acknowledged the fact that the Major had been unfairly treated by himself and his siblings. 'You know how it is with step-parents. I'm afraid we kids didn't give this one much of a break for a long time ...'

There was much more to the mild-mannered Englishman than any of the young Mitchums realized. He had served with the British army in the Boer War, when he became acquainted with Winston Churchill, and in World War One, part of which he spent in the North African desert. Morris was also a qualified sailor and had his captain's papers.

Like her brothers, Julie Mitchum had spent time with relatives, in this case another uncle and aunt, Charles and Eleanor Gunderson. Julie had developed ambitions to go on the stage, and even an early marriage, to Ernest Longaker, a medic in the US Navy, did not deter her.

Julie settled briefly in Philadelphia, and when Bob and John ran away from the farm (but only as far as nearby Bridgeville) and became involved in yet more trouble, Ann Mitchum-Morris decided that the time had come to try new pastures. The troubles had been fairly routine: fights with other kids and disruptions at school which culminated in Bob being expelled (he was blamed, wrongly as it happened, when another boy used a girl student's shower cap for purposes nature never intended).

Their mother's decision was underlined by the failure of the farm where the boys were living; just one of innumerable tiny but very real financial disasters of the economically blighted year of 1929.

Soon the family, all bar the Major, was reunited in Philadelphia. But Julie, still only in her mid-teens, was eager to pursue her theatrical ambitions. When her career took her to New York the family followed, this time with the Major, whose newspaper job had ended, coming along too.

In New York, Bob, now a young teenager, developed his outward display of aggression and hostility, mostly as a guard against the tough environment in which he found himself. This environment led to a number of scrapes with his peers, which meant more than a few bruises. According to Julie, interviewed by George Eells, this was where the classically broken nose really originated; the later tales of it being a result of a career as a professional boxer were just one of his entertaining embellishments.

It was around this time that Bob learned to play the saxophone, but his attitude toward schooling was erratic. He was expelled twice, once for firing a pea-shooter at a teacher at Haaren High School; the second time, he later claimed, for brightening up a programme by the school band by secreting a firecracker in the bell of a tuba. Giving up the unequal struggle with formal learning, he decided to seek work.

He tried his hand at a few jobs, but this was late 1931, and with the Depression biting hard, opportunities were few. Early the following year he went to Fall River, Massachusetts, where he became caretaker on a ship that was laid up there. In time this brief experience was elevated in his tales to a job as deckhand on a salvage vessel; at the most, he may have made one trip to sea.

Meanwhile, Julie's husband had been posted to Long Beach, California, and his mother and stepfather had taken John and Carol to their grandmother's home in Delaware (Gustave Gunderson had died in 1928).

With no real sense of having a home, Bob suffered an attack of wanderlust; he then began some aimless travelling, which, in 1933, was targeted on his sister's new home in California.

He was in no hurry to reach California, as Julie and Ernest and their baby son had yet to settle in. So he decided to visit Okefenokee Swamp, Georgia, hopping freight trains along with many other drifters, but quickly ran foul of the law. Picked up in Savannah, Georgia, he was accused of vagrancy, charged on a different count, and jailed.

Exactly what he did, if anything, and with precisely what he was charged, is impossible to determine after all this time and numerous recounted versions. Surprisingly variable, and impossible to confirm, is the length of his sentence. This varies from less than a week to six months and more. The reality, at least as recounted by John Mitchum, is that he was given ninety days on a prison farm.

How Robert Mitchum left his incarceration is just as variable as how he ended up there in the first place. Sometimes, he and a fellow prisoner, a giant Creole murderer, dramatically escaped together; sometimes he escaped alone. Of the escape itself variations abound; indeed, there are even versions in which he doesn't escape at all but is released after serving his time. But he certainly arrived back home suffering from an infected leg wound, probably caused by chains rubbing through the skin. The wound was healed by his mother after she had refused to let doctors amputate.

As soon as he recovered his strength he was eager to make another attempt to join his sister in Long Beach, a suburb of Los Angeles.

Once again he rode the rods, but this time made no detours on the way to Southern California. He has claimed that his first home was at the Midnight Mission in downtown Los Angeles and that he worked at various lowly jobs, including tending bar. In later years, he would recall that a customer at a bar where he worked was novelist Raymond Chandler, the creator of private-eye Philip Marlowe.

For all its apparent attractions, California was not a land of golden promise and he was soon back on the hobo express, visiting Texas (where he had another brush with the law and a short stay in prison) and Pennsylvania (where he worked in a coalmine for a week), but kept returning to the little town of Camden in Delaware. Apart from visiting his family, the attraction was a girl named Dorothy Clement Spence who, at thirteen, was a couple of years younger than Bob but was already displaying qualities of serene maturity he found deeply impressive.

He had met Dorothy through his brother, John, who recalls falling for her but making the mistake of introducing her to Bob.

On another trip to California, Bob took John along with him. They took a route unwittingly devised by the people who gave them lifts or the trains on to which they scrambled. It was a route that swung south to New Orleans and then headed west, but at Lake Charles, Louisiana, John and Bob were separated when the younger Mitchum was run out of town by railroad detectives while Bob managed to stay aboard a train. John eventually reached Los Angeles, by way of Dallas, San Antonio and other Texas towns. By then, Bob was comfortably ensconced at Julie's home.

Soon after this particular trip, one of Bob's motives in periodically returning east was removed when the rest of the family also came out to the coast. By now, the Mitchum children had accepted their stepfather, and enjoyed his tales of adventures which, like Bob's, grew better with each successive telling.

Nevertheless, Bob soon took off once more for Delaware. This time, because there was no other reason, it was obvious that his interest in Dorothy Spence was more than merely a passing infatuation.

Having elicited from Dorothy a promise that they would marry as soon as he had a regular job, and convinced her reluctant parents that he wasn't the shiftless vagabond he appeared to be, he headed west yet again.

Julie was working with the Players Guild of Long Beach, then under the guidance of Elias and Oranne Truitt Day, and she persuaded her brother to join them. The theatre at Long Beach provided early training for a number of young men and women, among them Hugh Beaumont and Laraine Day who later became featured players in Hollywood.

At first a decidedly reluctant thespian, Bob Mitchum soon displayed an aptitude for work backstage and on the boards. In 1937 he played the role of Johnny Cole in *Rebound*, and later wrote and directed two plays for children in one of which, *Trumpet in the Dark*, his brother John appeared as did his half-sister, Carol. The following year he played the role of Duke Mantee in Robert Sherwood's *The Petrified Forest* and took an important role in *Stage Door*, written by George S. Kaufman and Edna Ferber, which was directed by Larry Johns, who had taken over after Elias Day's death. In 1939 Bob appeared in *The Ghost Train*, a comedy by Arnold Ridley, managing with ease an English accent, and in 1940 he played in Dodie Smith's very English *Dear Octopus*.

During this period Bob had begun making a few dollars as a deliveryman and also by writing material for various artists who were trying to make the grade in show business as comedians or singers. Among these were Julie, whose marriage had failed, Peggy Fears, Nan Blackstone, Ray Bourbon and Benny Rubin. He also wrote for Orson Welles who was preparing a fund-raising evening at the Hollywood Bowl on behalf of the Jewish Refugee Fund. Mitchum's contribution was an oratorio for which he wrote words and music. One of the most consistent writing jobs he had was with popular astrologer

Carroll Righter, for whom he also served as assistant during tours.

It was when Mitchum was on such a tour, which included Philadelphia, where Dorothy Spence was now living, that the young couple decided to marry.

The marriage took place on 16 March 1940 in Dover, Delaware, and the young couple were soon in Los Angeles where Bob's close relationship with Righter was extended to allow them to live at his home. (In an interview with Righter, George Eells elicited the statement that Mitchum had saved the astrologer's life in a road accident. It is a significant pointer to Mitchum's personality that this incident never found its way into the tales the actor spun for interviewers.) After a while the young couple moved to the house occupied by the rest of the Mitchum-Morris clan and, in the spring of 1941, Bob decided to take a steady job to help stabilize the joint family income, a decision underscored by the fact that Dorothy had just announced that she was pregnant.

The job Bob took was at the Lockheed aircraft factory near Los Angeles, where he was an assistant to a skilled factory hand named James Dougherty whose young wife, Norma Jean, would later change her name to Marilyn Monroe.

The demands placed upon Bob Mitchum at the factory were not especially onerous but he was on permanent night shift and this began to damage his health. He suffered from insomnia and developed an eyesight problem which was diagnosed as psychosomatic blindness induced by his intense dislike of his work at the factory.

He continued working with the Players Guild, including an appearance in Maxim Gorky's *The Lower Depths*, but the long hours holding down two jobs were beginning to tell on him. The arrival in May 1941 of a baby boy, whom they named James Robin Spence, confirmed his need to have work that was more remunerative but less damaging to his health. He quit his job and began looking around for something more amenable. His health improved and so did his fortunes when he found work as a film extra.

How he got his first film job is another story that is subject to variation. Some accounts say that he and a friend from the theatre, Jack Shay, decided to look for work as extras. After a few such jobs things brightened up when Mitchum was introduced to film producer Harry 'Pop' Sherman. This came about either through an agent, Paul Wilkins, or, in a more romantic version, as a result of a chance meeting with Teddy Sherman, the daughter of the producer. Either way, he met

Sherman who was churning out a long-running series of production-line westerns.

These were the Hopalong Cassidy films, which Sherman began in 1935 after he bought the rights to the Clarence E. Mulford stories. The stories, and the films made from them, might have lacked originality but they told their tales with verve and, most important to an aspiring extra, there was always room for hefty young men who could withstand a little rough stuff, throw a realistic-looking punch, and ride a horse. This latter ability was one which Bob Mitchum did not at first possess but he insisted that he could ride, and after a few bone-shaking falls made good his claim.

The Hopalong Cassidy film in which Bob Mitchum made his screen début was *Border Patrol*, the forty-third in the series, and no one, not even a Carroll Righter, could have forecast where this opening would lead.

Not surprisingly, this first role was later melded into the self-generated Mitchum legend: 'They paid me fifty bucks and all the horse shit I could sell.'

Whatever he might later say of that first screen acting job, it was an important step. Not because he was expecting stardom; he was content to have a job that did not involve a night shift, and which paid better than factory work. As a married man with a small son he had responsibilities and, for all his outward façade of casual disregard for society's mores, it was his intention to live up to them.

2   The Apprenticeship Years: Walk-ons and Bits

I never went after a job. They just seemed to come after me. The bread kept getting better, and it sure as hell beat punching a time clock.

It would take a long library shelf to accommodate every book written about the Hollywood western. Everything from personal reminiscence to pictorial extravaganza; from casually thrown together gleanings from the bar-room floor, to detailed and intensely researched academic works.

Reruns on television suggest that the western has remained remarkably popular with audiences even if, for film-makers, the genre has proved disastrous in recent years as one high-priced failure has followed another into the setting sun.

The parade of westerns, especially the often underrated B-pictures, was at its most spectacularly golden in the late 1930s and the 1940s, a period which included the time when Robert Mitchum entered the motion-picture industry. One of the most enduring riders in that parade was an actor named William Boyd, although that long library bookshelf treats him much less generously than many of his less accomplished fellows.

Bill Boyd was a star of the silents and a favourite of director Cecil B. DeMille. He took the lead in DeMille's *The Volga Boatman* (1926) and had an important role in *The King of Kings* (1927). Boyd also worked successfully with such distinguished directors as D.W. Griffith and Lewis Milestone but his career suffered a slight hiatus when a well-known stage actor, also named William Boyd, was involved in a scandal. Bill Boyd's reputation was adversely affected by this unfortunate coincidence, but he eventually regained favour. Then, in 1935, he made a run-of-the-mill oater entitled *Hop-a-Long Cassidy*.

This was the start of a long run of success for Boyd and producer Pop Sherman, which culminated in massive popularity in the early days of television, when their old films were re-released on to the small screen. This resurgence of popular acclaim brought Boyd great wealth before his death, in 1972, at the age of 74.

The Hopalong Cassidy films (the awkward hyphens of the first one were soon dropped) were simple in story-line and low in production values. They were shot quickly and cheaply but, as with so many B-pictures, they maintained an urgent excitement belying their impoverished origins.

In all the films in the series (Pop Sherman made 54 and Bill Boyd himself produced a further 12) Hoppy was a virtuous, non-smoking, non-drinking, non-swearing hero. With Boyd's natural dignity, aided by his prematurely silver hair, Hoppy became a father-figure hero, but if there was any implied preaching it certainly didn't spoil the fun for the kids. If there was a moral it was always well buried beneath lots of fast-moving action sequences, brisk gunplay, and enough fistfights to satisfy the most demanding front-row cowboy.

Hoppy usually worked with a couple of pardners, one to handle the comedy, so that Boyd's undoubted dignity would not be strained when the need for light relief arose; the other to carry any love interest. The need for another actor to serve in any romantic clinches was a matter of popular perceptions of the time. Boyd was 37 when he made his first Hoppy, and he was 45 when he made the last for Sherman. To compound the problem of identification, Boyd's prematurely silver thatch made him look older still. While his age would not disqualify him from love interest in today's films, his principal audience of the time, young teenagers, would have taken a dim view of their fatherly hero rolling in the hay. The two pardners, comic foil and romantic juvenile, were thus essential figures in any Hopalong Cassidy western.

Additionally, there was a demand for a steady supply of 'good guys' to aid, or be aided by, the star; and 'bad guys' to be shot or otherwise made to see the errors of their ways. It was as an unshaven baddie that Robert Mitchum made his first appearance on film, unbilled, in *Border Patrol* (1943).

In all, Mitchum made seven Hoppies during 1942 and 1943, yet this represented less than half of his films in this period. It was a prolific beginning, especially as his roles did not remain at the unbilled walk-on level throughout.

His rapid promotion arose in part from the fact that he photographed well, but mostly because his tenacity appealed to both Sherman and Boyd. This tenaciousness was revealed when Mitchum, who knew considerably less about horses than he'd led his new employers to believe, was given a hard time on *Border Patrol*. Determined to make the over-confident neophyte eat his words (he'd claimed to have worked as a trail-hand on a ranch in Texas), the crew arranged for him to be given a horse with a reputation for unseating even the most skilled riders. The horse threw Mitchum, not once but twice. With his new career in the balance, Mitchum couldn't afford to take a third fall into the dust. He belted the horse on the nose, remounted, and this time stayed in the saddle and on the job.

In later years, Mitchum told an interviewer that a stuntman, observing his difficulties with horses, told him to act as if he could ride. It was advice he followed, in its broadest non-literal sense, throughout most of his subsequent career.

In his second film, *Hoppy Serves a Writ*, Mitchum received ninth billing (as Bob Mitchum), but slid off the credits for the next two, *The Leather Burners* and *Colt Comrades* (all 1943). Between these last two films, however, Mitchum slotted in some non-western roles, one of which was in MGM's sentimental drama, *The Human Comedy* (1943).

Producer-director of *The Human Comedy* was Clarence Brown, whose career began in the silent era and who had many important films to his credit. Among them were *The Eagle* (1925) with Rudolph Valentino, and seven of Greta Garbo's vehicles, including *Anna Christie* (1930) and *Anna Karenina* (1935).

The story of *The Human Comedy* originated with William Saroyan (whose work on the screenplay also formed the basis of his novel), and tells of an American small-town family, the Macauleys, whose atypicality is updated to the war years by their having a dead father and an eldest son away in the army (and who fails to survive either the war or the film). The family's future is thus left in the hands of the younger members of the clan, particularly young Homer (played by Mickey Rooney who was then MGM's top box-office attraction).

Robert Mitchum came low in the credits but enjoyed some good moments as one of a trio of soldiers on leave who encounter two 'nice' girls, one of whom is Homer's sister, Bess (Donna Reed). With almost nothing in the script to guide him, Mitchum managed to make his few moments of screentime a fascinating blend of many of the characteristics he later trademarked. He was arrogant, appealing, funny and so tightly enclosed that audiences sensed that his was a character with depth and real humanity.

Mitchum made three other non-westerns, all of which were also released in 1943. As their titles suggest, *Aerial Gunner* and *Minesweeper* (in both of which he was unbilled) are war stories.

The third of the trio was *Follow the Band* which he made for Universal.

Follow the Band falls somewhere between the two extremes into which many cheapskate musicals of the period were grouped. These came about when some 'Poverty Row' producers discovered that a quick and easy way to turn out a musical was to hire a batch of singers, dancers, musicians and speciality acts to do their stuff at intervals along a threadbare storyline. Sometimes, but not always, the acts were sufficiently popular to pull in a few extra people at the box office. The films were either execrable or tolerable depending upon whether the acts hired for the occasion were bad or good. Today, the merits of such musicals depend upon the quality of these acts, and often provide a rare opportunity to see in performance a vaudeville act which might otherwise be merely a name on a fading poster.

Follow the Band is neither sensational nor unwatchable, having as it does such singers as Frances Langford and Bob Eberle, and the bands of Skinnay Ennis and Alvino Rey. Mitchum plays Tate Winters, a rival of hopeful musician Marvin Howe (Eddie Quillan) for the affections of Juanita Turnbull (Anne Rooney). In this faintly 'cornball' comedy Mitchum's scenes are restricted to the top and tail of the film. The bulk of the action takes place in New York where Marvin, archetypal country boy making good in the big city, becomes a famous radio star. He returns home to steal Tate's girlfriend from under his nose.

Returning to the Hoppy series, Mitchum graduated to romantic lead in *Bar 20* (1943) opposite Dustine Farnum whose father was Dustin Farnum, star of many DeMille silents including the 1914 dramas *The Squaw Man* and *The Virginian*, in both of which he played the title role. In *Bar 20*, Hoppy and his friends rescue the passengers in a stage-coach from a hold-up. The passengers include Richard Adams (Mitchum), his fiancée Marie (Farnum), her mother (Betty Blythe) and cattleman Mark Jackson (Victor Jory). As Jory played the villain in numerous Hoppies, *aficionados* of the series knew what to expect, and the subsequent plot convolutions before his villainy was unmasked wouldn't have confused them for a moment.

Hoppy's sidekicks in *Bar 20* were played by Andy Clyde and George Reeves. Scottish-born Clyde was a well-known comic actor who appeared in many silent comedies and made a speciality of whiskery old-timers in B-westerns. Reeves had a few promising small parts (in 1939 he played one of Scarlett O'Hara's suitors in *Gone with the Wind*) but his career slid badly until 1952 when he became television's Superman. What seemed like a marvellous opportunity proved to be his undoing. After Superman folded in 1956, Reeves had difficulty in finding work and was reduced to bit parts once again. In 1959, at the age of 45, Reeves committed suicide.

Mitchum's continuing string of credits for 1943 included bits in *We've Never Been Licked*, a rah-rah army tale (in which one of his fellow bit-part players was Cliff Robertson), and *Corvette K-225*, a Howard Hawks production about the US Navy which starred Randolph Scott (Robertson was again among the bits as was Peter Lawford). Mitchum had sixth billing in *The Lone Star Trail*, a Johnny Mack Brown western; he played a dying soldier in MGM's *Cry Havoc*, and made a couple more Hoppies – *False Colors* and *Riders of the Deadline* (for which he drew a mention in *Variety* as being 'a tough customer who continually tangles with Boyd').

The tyro actor also appeared in *The Dancing Masters* (1943), a faintly sad comedy starring Stan Laurel and Oliver Hardy. This film was one of a small number of features made by Laurel and Hardy towards the end of their movie careers. The two stars, and particularly Laurel, an undoubted comic genius on par with Charlie Chaplin and Buster Keaton, believed that they themselves knew best how to display their great talents. They were probably right, but after severing their relationship with Hal Roach in 1940 they never really had a chance to prove it. Both MGM and Fox (who made *The Dancing Masters*) insisted on exercising control, and everyone, not least the legions of Stan and Ollie fans, suffered as a result. As *The Dancing Masters* proves, these two superb comics should have been left alone to devise their own movies and not made to suffer from the dead hand of control of a major studio.

In *The Dancing Masters*, Mitchum is Mickey, an enforcer for a protection racketeer, who helps put the arm on Stan and Ollie, the proprietors of the Arthur Hurry School of Dancing. After convincing Ollie of the virtues of insuring Stan against accidents, Mitchum bows out leaving the hapless pair to flounder through a string of well-used sight gags as Ollie tries to collect on the policy by encouraging Stan to have an accident. Reviewers, many of whom never really took to Laurel and Hardy during their lifetimes, were less than tolerant of the film's failings. For Mitchum it was just another job and, as Alvin H. Marill has commented, 'for an up-and-coming young player, any role provided needed screen exposure as well as invaluable experience'. On an even more prosaic level, the work was invaluable because it helped provide for a growing family – in October of that year Dorothy gave birth to their second son, Christopher.

The Mitchums lived in a rented single-storey house on North

Palm Avenue and soon had new neighbours when Ann Mitchum-Morris, Carol and Julie (now divorced but with a young son) came to live on the same street. By this time, America's entry into the war had meant military service for the Major and for John Mitchum but Bob was deferred, first because his job at Lockheed's was classified as essential to the war effort and now because he was principal breadwinner for the growing clan.

Although he had yet to put on a real uniform, Mitchum had another role as a film soldier in his last release of 1943. This was *Gung Ho!*, a Randolph Scott flag-waver based upon the true story of the 1942 assault on Makin Island by US Marines led by Evans S. Carlson.

The actor's first release of 1944 showed him to be pretty much where he had left off in 1943; this was another war story but this time a rather subdued affair. *Mr Winkle Goes to War* is a light comedy about a middle-aged bank clerk, Wilbert Winkle (Edward G. Robinson), who is unexpectedly drafted into the army and returns home a hero. Along the way he passes through boot camp where one of the instructors is a fleetingly seen Robert Mitchum.

Mitchum's next film was his first of many for RKO. *Girl Rush* (1944) is a fairly laboured comedy vehicle for the studio's resident comedians, Wally Brown and Alan Carney, who play a couple of vaudevillians loose in the West during the Gold Rush. This production saw Mitchum as Jimmy Smith, the romantic lead opposite Frances Langford. He was now billed as Robert, instead of Bob, thus implying that someone was taking him rather more seriously than before. And *Variety* noticed him again, commenting that he 'catches the attention with a smooth performance and likeable personality'. His role in the next film to be released was little more than a bit part at the end of Monogram's *Johnny Doesn't Live Here Anymore* (1944), but the attention he was now getting encouraged RKO to give him his first leading role.

Based on a story by Zane Grey, *Nevada* (1944) was a remake of two earlier movies which had respectively starred Gary Cooper and Buster Crabbe. Although it might have been original when first written, the story-line sounds all too familiar: drifter rides into town, is suspected of murder, proves his innocence, unmasks the real villain (who is the town's leading citizen), and rides out of town with the murdered man's grateful daughter. For one, the creaking story-line came out all right with both press and public, who liked the style of the young actor playing the drifter. In the character of Jim 'Nevada' Lacy – a tough, monosyllabic loner who minds his own business and goes his own way until prodded into action by events and then handles himself with swift and violent effectiveness – can be seen a rough blueprint for many later Mitchum roles.

The commercial and critical success of *Nevada* encouraged RKO to make another Zane Grey story with Mitchum and also to seek for him something even better than the lead in a B-western. But before the studio could swing anything into production he made a couple more films elsewhere – one for Monogram, the other for MGM.

The Monogram picture, *When Strangers Marry* (1944), slots neatly into the early part of the cycle of *film noir* thrillers which graced the period. Churned out in ten days for $50,000 by the King Brothers (Maurice, Herman and Frank Kozinski), the story-line concerns a newly married couple, Paul and Millie Baxter (Dean Jagger and Kim Hunter), whose new life together in New York City gets off to an unpromising start when the police suspect him of murder. Millie isn't too sure of her husband's innocence either but the real villain of the piece turns out to be Millie's former boyfriend, Fred Graham (Mitchum), who is eventually trapped by the police.

Although slipping almost unnoticed past the major critics at the time of its release, this film has gained status over the years. Now it is generally regarded as a minor masterpiece of that intriguing division of the B-picture, the psychological thriller. Excellent, underplayed performances from the entire cast are all pointed up by taut direction from William Castle, then at the beginning of a long and successful career. *When Strangers Marry* (re-released as *Betrayed*) is one of the few, if not the only one of Mitchum's earliest films, which stands up to close scrutiny today. Indeed, many latter-day makers of television thrillers could learn a thing or two from it about pace and tension.

Mitchum's last film of 1944 was MGM's *Thirty Seconds Over Tokyo*, directed by Mervyn LeRoy and starring Van Johnson and Robert Walker, with Spencer Tracy in a cameo role.

During the making of the film Mitchum's reputation was enhanced when he had a run-in with a tough sergeant on Egland Field, the US Army Air Force base in Florida where part of the production was shot. The sergeant thought that outwardly fit and healthy civilians in wartime were dubious characters to begin with, and that film actors were effeminate. Not only did the soldier think it, he also made the mistake of saying so. It wasn't a mistake he made again. It took three of Mitchum's companions to pull him off the badly damaged sergeant.

Mitchum's role in the film was minor but he impressed himself upon the director who recommended MGM to sign him up. LeRoy's suggestion was rejected so he urged Paul Wilkins, Mitchum's agent, to talk with RKO. He did so and a deal was offered which, while built around the customary seven-year option that drained the enthusiasm of many actors, had several attractive clauses. Apart from the money, which began at $350 a week rising to $2000 in the final year, he would be free to make films for David O. Selznick's Vanguard, a connection which would give him valuable prestige.

Up to this point in his new but fast-burgeoning career, Mitchum had held out as a freelance, refusing contracts offered by Columbia Pictures and by the producers of *Aerial Gunner* and *Minesweeper*, Bill Thomas and Bill Pine, known as the 'Two Dollar Bills' in recognition of their cheerfully cheapskate productions.

At the end of 1944 Robert Mitchum had been in the motion-picture business for just two years yet had already made twenty-five films, even if he had played the lead in only one of them. He had every reason to be satisfied with his progress to date and the future looked good. RKO had him slated for that other western based on a Zane Grey story, but it was the second film he would make in 1945 that was destined to set him firmly on the road that would lead to international acclaim.

3   The Apprenticeship Years: Early Starring Roles

I played just about everything. Chinese laundrymen, midgets, Irish washerwomen, faggots. I even played a journalist once.

Robert Mitchum's new career dictated a change of lifestyle. This was not so much a matter of income – many of his roles had been $75-a-day hand-to-mouth exercises – but of the pseudo-glamorous occupation of film actor. The fact that he somehow managed to keep his private life on an even keel (well, most of the time) was in part a matter of his underlying sense of responsibility and partly through Dorothy Mitchum's pragmatism.

Very much the product of small-town America, Dorothy lived to a set of values that contrasted widely with her husband's, even if his origins had been very similar to her own. She was quiet, shy, always impeccably groomed and faultlessly mannered. As such she was almost the complete opposite of her husband who could be rowdy, was supremely self-confident, untidy and, when he felt it appropriate, downright rude. In private, the contrast was much less apparent. As Dorothy and a handful of others knew, some of Mitchum's public display was merely that, put on to conceal aspects of a personality he considered was nobody's business but his own.

Very much his own man, he took his resolve into his work, and when RKO announced that they wanted to change his name he dug in his toes.

Among the curiosities of the motion-picture business is the manner in which 'unsuitable' names were changed. In earlier years this meant names that were of obviously ethnic origin or that were inappropriate to the romantic image of Hollywood. RKO executives decided that Robert Mitchum was an unsuitable name for the man they planned to groom for stardom. They wanted to call him John Mitchell. Mitchum was furious and in favour of walking out. His agent, Paul Wilkins, calmed him down and persuaded the studio of the tactical error of changing a name that was already attracting critical attention and a following among the moviegoing public.

Inevitably, this minor contretemps entered Mitchum's growing arsenal of embroidered tales. Many years later, when BBC television produced a documentary series on RKO, he told a mystified interviewer that the studio boss had wanted to call him Marshall and was so hung up on the name that he called his son Marshall Schlom. In fact, the studio executive involved in the name change argument was Ben Piazza, not Herman Schlom, but Mitchum has never allowed accuracy to get in the way of a good story.

The remaining years of the 1940s brought Mitchum a further fourteen screen credits and the fascinated attention of an as yet unrealized number of fans.

The Zane Grey story RKO had slated for Mitchum was *West of the Pecos*. The character of Pecos Smith, the hero of *West of the Pecos* (1945), was a comparative innocent, living in a good-natured world. So innocent, in fact, is Smith (Mitchum) that in the early part of the movie he fails to observe that a young boy he is rousting is, in reality, a girl in disguise. Later in the film, Smith, now straightened out on the facts of life, becomes romantically entangled with the 'boy' who is really Chicago débutante Rill Lambeth (Barbara Hale).

Such plot clichés apart, there was enough rough, tough, two-fisted action to keep any B-western addict firmly glued to his saddle. In the light of the accolades he received for his next film, *West of the Pecos* clearly did little for Mitchum's career but he drew good notices with *Variety*, which observed that he 'does the riders of the range proud'.

RKO now loaned Mitchum out to Lester Cowan who was preparing to shoot a war story for United Artists. The impetus came from the director, William Wellman, who was eager to use Mitchum. Wellman shot a test and ever afterwards bemoaned the fact that he hadn't taken the trouble to dress the set for the test; had he done so, he later maintained, he could have used the scene in the finished film, so perfectly did Mitchum play it.

Mitchum's role was that of Lieutenant Walker in *The Story of GI Joe* (1945), a film based upon a novel by Ernie Pyle, which was built upon Pyle's experiences as a front-line war correspondent during World War Two. As a result of its pedigree, and Wellman's determination to tell a war story free of the 'gung-ho' qualities which Hollywood usually imposed, *GI Joe* has a strong documentary flavour. Without a real narrative line, yet not quite anecdotal, the movie follows the variable fortunes of an American infantry company in North Africa and Italy. Compared with the flag-waving style of so many war movies for which Hollywood has rightly become notorious, *GI Joe* is understated, laconic and honest. From time to time soldiers disappear. Their deaths are not shown; yet their unstated and sudden absence from the screen, and the elliptical conversation of their fellows, makes more impact than any number of bloodstained, slow-motion killings.

During its telling, *The Story of GI Joe* introduces the disparate members of Company C, a cross-section of Americans that is at once clichéd and real. It cannot be denied that some of the infantrymen bear the hallmarks of the standard Hollywood war epic: the tough, unsentimental sergeant who displays an unexpected streak of tenderness for his son and eventually breaks under a strain that is more self-imposed than a result of enemy action; the woman-crazy private who goofs off on tail-chasing expeditions at every opportunity; the wearily cynical, yet fundamentally compassionate, company commander. They are all here and for all their stereotypicality there is more than a mere ring of truth in them.

As for the reality of the film's setting, this was made tragically apparent to all when Ernie Pyle was killed by enemy action while *GI Joe* was still in production.

Two scenes in particular stand out, both featuring the star, Burgess Meredith (as Ernie Pyle), and Robert Mitchum (as the company commander). In the first, Pyle enters the commander's quarters, a curtained-off corner of a shell-damaged building, bringing with him a bottle of booze to share. But Lieutenant Walker has other things on his mind. Bone-weary from the efforts of the day, he is striving to write letters home to the parents of the men in his command who have died in battle. Slowly, un-emphatically, Walker diverts some of his torn emotions from the letters and puts them instead into spoken words and they still the journalist with their quiet power.

This scene, which Mitchum made as a test, and Wellman considered an inferior version, is one of astonishing strength. In the light of Mitchum's previous work it is difficult to understand why Wellman was so keen to have him in this role, yet once this quietly assured and dignified performance has been seen it is equally difficult to imagine more than a tiny handful of other actors playing it with such authority.

The second outstanding scene comes at the very end of the movie and Mitchum's part in it is totally passive. Ernie Pyle has rejoined the company after an absence. Walker, now a captain, who has become his friend, is out on patrol. Slowly, a line of mules comes down the hillside, each bearing a dead body. The body on the last mule is Walker's. One by one, wordlessly, the surviving soldiers come closer, expressing their feelings with eyes and hands, before moving off to fight the next battle. As Pyle stands looking at Walker's body, a long line of crosses is silhouetted against the skyline behind the men. For all its theatricality, it is an extraordinarily moving moment, and the sense of loss it implies owes much to the impact Mitchum made in his earlier scenes.

Mitchum's performance won him the best reviews of his career to date and from areas of the press which had previously overlooked him. Thomas M. Pryor, writing in *The New York Times*, observed that the 'meatiest role falls to Robert Mitchum who gives an excellent characterization ... William Wellman directs ... in an uncompromisingly realistic fashion and has evoked masterly performances from Robert Mitchum and co ... [this is] cinema at its adult best'.

James Agee, writing in the *Nation*, was equally fulsome in his praise. 'The picture contains, for instance, the first great triumphs of the kind of anti-histrionic casting and acting which I believe is indispensable to most, although by no means all, kinds of greatness possible to movies. It would be impossible in that connection to say enough in praise of the performances of Bob Mitchum as the Captain and Freddie Steele as the Sergeant, or of Wellman for his directing and, I suppose, casting of them.'

The motion picture community agreed and Robert Mitchum was nominated for an Academy Award as Best Supporting Actor. He didn't win and has never since been nominated for any Oscar in any category. Characteristically, he has been dismissive of this, remarking, 'You notice the Academy hasn't messed with me since.' Despite such comments, individuals close to him have suggested that he was genuinely disappointed not only then but also in later years when he made other award-worthy performances.

During the filming of *GI Joe* Mitchum was drafted but allowed to continue working until his commitment to the movie was fulfilled.

On 11 April 1945 he entered the US Army at Camp Roberts, later undergoing infantry training at Fort MacArthur. His actual duties were afterwards adjusted to suit the needs of the circumstances in which they were recounted. Sometimes he claimed to be a drill instructor, on other occasions he asserted he was an assistant to the medical examiner whose responsibility was to inspect draftees for haemorrhoids. Not surprisingly, he could coarsen the account and did so in a television interview with David Frost when he declared that he had been a member of the 'keister police'.

In fact, he served eight months in the army, part of the time being spent on retakes for *The Story of GI Joe* and on promoting the film.

The war ended in the autumn of 1945 and Mitchum was deemed eligible for early release. This was because of the hardship his absence created for his family. He was the main supporter of his wife; his two sons; his maternal grandmother; his mother and stepfather; and his divorced sister, Julie, and her small son.

Thanks to *The Story of GI Joe* his star was in the ascendant. The film's massive critical and popular success, and the quality of his performance in it, gave his career much-needed impetus. Some of his early films were re-released with his name imaginatively boosted from seventh, ninth and even lower billing into co-starring and even starring position. Of more practical benefit, his status prompted RKO to lend him $5000 as a down-payment on a house in Oak Glen Drive.

In a spirit of some euphoria he was soon back at work in the movies although remaining in uniform for his role in *Till the End of Time* (1946). The film's storyline is not dissimilar to that of *The Best Years of Our Lives* which was released in the same year to great acclaim. *Till the End of Time* traces the attempts of three returning soldiers to adjust to civilian life. The three actors portraying the soldiers all carried studio hopes of great things but only Mitchum fulfilled expectations. The others, Bill Williams and Guy Madison, never made the grade and had to be content with undistinguished careers in low-budget movies. In almost every department, certainly in writing, acting and production values, *Till the End of Time* failed to match up to *The Best Years of Our Lives* although two of the actors, Mitchum and Dorothy McGuire, were singled out for special praise by reviewers.

Commendably, *Till the End of Time* was among the earliest films to touch upon the still thorny problem of racial discrimination. In one scene Bill Tabeshaw and Cliff Harper (Mitchum and Madison) are in a bar with a black marine (Ernest Anderson). The white marines are approached by a man who exhorts them to join the American Patriots Association. Tabeshaw, already edgy and confused by his wartime experiences, learns that this is a group which is closed to all 'niggers, Jews and Catholics' and promptly explodes. 'My best friend, a Jew, is lying back in a foxhole in Guadalcanal. I'm gonna spit in your eye for him, because we don't want to have people like you in this country.'

Despite the movie's many weaknesses this tentative step towards expressing a point of view on racism was an important forerunner to a film Mitchum would make the following year. Before then, however, he had two more roles to play.

On loan to MGM, Mitchum found himself playing second male lead to Robert Taylor and with Katharine Hepburn as the female lead. Directed by Vincente Minnelli, *Undercurrent* (1946) is marginally *film noir* but suffers from a number of defects of which the most critical is the miscasting of the two men. Alan Garroway (Taylor) is a cold, emotionally unstable and neurotic murderer who has recently married Ann Hamilton (Hepburn). She discovers that Alan's brother, Michael (Mitchum), lives nearby but keeps his distance because he knows of his brother's guilt. Michael is a quiet and sensitive man who, after many plot complications, finally gets the girl. Perhaps *Undercurrent* might have been more successful had the two male leads played one another's parts but in the event no one comes off very well.

Bosley Crowther, in *The New York Times*, was less than overwhelmed by Mitchum's performance: 'You may find [him] appealing in a crumpled, modest way as the culturally orientated brother even though he only appears in a couple of scenes ...'

Off the set, Miss Hepburn expressed some displeasure at Mitchum's apparent lack of dedication to the job in hand, suggesting that he was employed for his looks, not his ability. Mitchum would later cheerfully recall his encounter with the formidable actress. While an outward display of dedication has never been Mitchum's style, this criticism was more than a little unfair. Indeed, it is rather surprising that he managed to turn up at all because he was making three films simultaneously.

During the tough shooting schedule Mitchum tried to persuade RKO to let him have a ground-floor dressing-room to save him time when he came rushing over from MGM. The request was refused and, in protest at having to climb several flights of stairs, he went into the garden outside the office block and, dressed only in a towel, prepared to take a shower with a garden hose.

The uproar this created, especially amongst the female members of staff, had its effect. He was assigned a ground-floor dressing-room, and it did no harm to his reputation.

One of the other two films he was making during production of *Undercurrent* was RKO's *The Locket* (1946) in which he was billed third after Brian Aherne and Laraine Day. A complex tale, *The Locket* centres upon Nancy Blair (Day), a psychologically disturbed kleptomaniac, whose activities drive the men in her life to distraction. In the case of a painter, Norman Clyde (Mitchum), distraction leads to suicide. The movie gained little critical acclaim and the studio executives quickly adjusted its policy towards its new star. Mitchum, as almost any casual moviegoer could have told them, was best suited for the role of the tough outsider, a loner, in gritty, realistic thrillers.

Not much in Hollywood's current production schedule had an atom of the grittiness of his next movie, even if his role was far from being the meatiest and was largely peripheral to the main thrust of the storyline.

Crossfire (1947) is outwardly a tough *noir* thriller tracing the investigation of a murder but it develops deeper undertones when it becomes apparent that the victim has been killed simply because he is a Jew. This same year also saw *Gentleman's Agreement* which received a better press at the time and was nominated for seven Academy Awards against *Crossfire's* six. When the magic envelopes were opened *Agreement* had three Oscars, *Crossfire* none. The Academy gave their votes to the lesser movie, perhaps as a result of assuming that a straightforward drama was somehow intrinsically better than a mere thriller.

Crossfire follows the attempts of police Captain Finlay (Robert Young) to unravel events leading to the death of Joseph Samuels, whose last hours were spent in the company of soldiers recently back from the war and awaiting release from the army. The soldiers, Monty Montgomery (Robert Ryan), Floyd Bowers (Steve Brodie) and Arthur Mitchell (George Cooper) are all somewhat the worse for drink and when evidence is found pointing at Mitchell he is unable to convince anyone, even himself, of his innocence. Then Mitchell's sergeant, Peter Keeley (Mitchum), takes a hand, believes his story and helps him hide out, while joining the police in an attempt to track down the real killer, Monty Montgomery, who killed Samuels in a fit of drunken rage brought on through his psychotic hatred of Jews.

The book on which the film was based, Richard Brooks's *The Brick Foxhole*, has as its central theme not anti-Semitism but society's attitudes towards homosexuality. James Agee, in the *Nation*, suggests that *Crossfire* was begun with the novel's central premise intact but the studio made a rapid shift on learning that two movies, *Gentleman's Agreement* and Sam Goldwyn's *Earth and High Heaven*, were preparing to grasp the new nettle. It seems unlikely that Hollywood should consider making a film about homosexuality as early as the 1940s but if it was a possibility then it is just as well that a shift was made. Hollywood was unlikely to have been anywhere nearly as honest about homosexuality in 1947 as it was about anti-Semitism and, despite its flaws, *Crossfire* is a remarkably honest film.

The key role in the film is that of the viciously bigoted killer, Monty Montgomery. The part is taken with both hands and evident relish by Robert Ryan. It is sad that there was no place in the screenplay for Ryan and Mitchum to play a powerful scene together. What little Mitchum does he does well but it isn't his movie – it belongs to Robert Ryan. Indeed, Edward Dmytryk later apologized to Mitchum for casting him for his box-office appeal without giving him an adequate role.

Mitchum took time off from his film career to make a handful of appearances in the theatre in a play staged at Long Beach, Catalina island and in Los Angeles. But the demands of his contract quickly brought him back on to the sound stages of Hollywood where his next role saw him back in the saddle again although this time the movie was a long way from being a routine oater. Raoul Walsh's *Pursued* (1947) is a psychological western more concerned with the motivation of its characters and with their backgrounds (explored through flashbacks) than with guns and horses. Essentially a revenge movie concerning Jeb Rand (Mitchum), a soldier returning from the Spanish-American war who hunts down his father's killer, *Pursued* is a rarity of the movies, a western *film noir*. Neither critics nor public were yet ready for psychology in buckskin but the film was reasonably well received and harmed none of its players even if it failed to provide a noticeable career boost. Bosley Crowther, in *The New York Times*, fired off another damp squib in the direction of the star: 'Robert Mitchum as the hero is a rigid gent and gives off no more animation than a fridge set to defrost.' *Esquires'* Jack Moffit was much more enthusiastic, observing, a couple of roles prematurely, that the film had placed Mitchum 'into the front ranks of stardom'.

Next to be released was MGM's *Desire Me* (1947), the third of the three films Mitchum had worked on simultaneously early in 1946. This production, in which he starred opposite Greer Garson, was dogged by misfortune from the start. Despite numerous rewrites and two directors (both of whom were later to disclaim any responsibility) the film could not be rescued. *Desire Me* is set in France and tells an improbable tale of a woman who marries the mentally unstable man who brings her the news that her husband has died in a concentration camp. On the whole reviewers were kind to Mitchum while being generally unpleasant about the production and all others who had a hand in it.

Mitchum was much more at ease in the American setting for his next role, a true classic of American *film noir*.

The crisp screenplay of *Out of the Past* (1947) is by Geoffrey Homes who, under his real name, Daniel Mainwaring, had written the novel on which it is based. (The British release bears the novel's title, *Build My Gallows High*.) Thanks to the script, excellent direction by Jacques Tourneur, and snappy editing by Samuel E. Beetley, the movie crackles along from first to last. True, there are a few minor confusions along the way but the whole is stylish and brings lasting credit to all participants.

The essential visual characteristics of *film noir*, Expressionistic camera angles, low-key lighting and much night filming, are all present and are superbly effected by photographer Nicholas Musuraca. Helping set off the moody darkness of the main body of the film are the opening and closing scenes which are shot in bright sunlight and without mannerisms.

It is from the moment of his first scene that Mitchum stamps his personality on the film. From this point onwards he is in control as an actor even if the character he is playing is being swept along as helpless as a leaf in a storm. This particular scene is set inside Jeff Bailey's (Mitchum's) motor repair shop. A visitor, tall, clad in dark clothing, and vaguely threatening despite the friendly words he speaks, paces up and down, his nervous agitation offset by Mitchum's stillness. Mitchum leans against a pillar, barely moving his eyes to follow the visitor's movements, answering him only monosyllabically; this unnerving stillness in the midst of movement commands attention.

The dialogue, much of it elliptical, demonstrates the debt such movies owe to hard-boiled writers like Dashiell Hammett, Raymond Chandler and James M. Cain.

Jeff tells Ann:

'I never saw her in the daytime. We seemed to live by night. What was left of the day went away, like a pack of cigarettes you've smoked. I don't know what we were waiting for. Maybe we thought the world would end. Maybe we thought we'd wake up with a hangover in Niagara Falls.'

This scene, and many others throughout the film (and Mitchum is on-screen in almost every scene), first establishes and then underlines the persona that had begun to emerge in some of the earlier roles he played.

The character of the cynically honest loner, so well established by Chandler and his kin, emerges in brief exchanges and throwaway lines: with Kathie (Jane Greer) and Ann (Virginia Huston.

KATHIE: I don't want to die.
JEFF: I don't want to die either but if I do, I want to die last.

and:

ANN: She can't be all bad, no one is.
JEFF: She comes the closest.

Especially in keeping with the hard-boiled characters exemplified by the authors cited, are the exchanges between Jeff and Kathie as time begins to run out for them. In one, he demands the truth even though he knows it will hurt him:

'Come on, feed my ego. Tell me he beat you. Tell me he had to drag every word out of you.'

Although uncredited, Alvin H. Marill has discovered that James M. Cain worked on the screenplay, completely revising Homes's original version. Later Homes equally thoroughly revised Cain's draft but it is tempting to think that some of Mitchum's sharpest moments benefit from Cain's acerbic touch.

In a scene highly reminiscent of the closing moments of *The Maltese Falcon* and the exchange between Sam Spade and Brigid O'Shaughnessy, Jeff tells Kathie:

'I keep thinking about you, Kathie, up there in the women's prison in Tehachapi. It won't be too bad, hills all around you, plenty of sun.'

The words may hurt Kathie but their recoil is equally damaging to the speaker.

It is at moments such as this that the entire motivation for the film, Jeff's inability to withstand Kathie's fatal charms even though he knows that she is bad for him and that their relationship is doomed, is admirably conveyed.

In one notable moment, so fleeting it might almost be overlooked were it not for its impact, Mitchum conveys pages of exposition with one glance. This is when Kathie kills his partner, Fisher, and his eyes flicker towards her and in that instant it is clear that he has suddenly realized the true nature of the woman with whom he is obsessed.

Not many women like Kathie Moffett may exist outside the

pages of a hard-boiled novel and its *film noir* counterpart but here, thanks to Jane Greer, one of them becomes flesh-and-blood real. The actress exudes a powerful sexuality which suspends disbelief that a man like Jeff would fall victim to her. She is infinitely more convincing than was Mary Astor in *The Maltese Falcon* and, indeed, was rarely matched except by such *grande dames* of *film noir* as Barbara Stanwyck or until the arrival of such latter-day actresses as Kathleen Turner.

In *Out of the Past* Robert Mitchum came close to perfecting the on-screen persona he was to retain for much of his subsequent career. In later years his most interesting screen roles would prove to be an interesting mixture of those in which he honed his image as the eternal outsider to even better effect and those in which he was cast completely against this type.

He was back in the saddle for his next film, *Rachel and the Stranger* (1948), an unpretentious, amiable story about folksy people who are faster with a song and a smile than with a gun. Surprisingly, even for his fans, Mitchum was called upon to sing a song or two in a pleasing baritone. The storyline came from a tale by Howard Fast, a writer whose novels usually had a strong political core even if their surfaces were richly varied. Hollywood made frequent use of his work but usually with non-radical stories, such as *Rachel and the Stranger*, or removed the teeth of those that did carry a message, as with *Spartacus* (1960).

For the studio, *Rachel and the Stranger* was a tentative toe in the water to test public attitudes towards its star's brush with the law over possession of marijuana.

The drugs bust had occurred on 1 September 1948 when Mitchum was arrested for possession along with an acquaintance named Robin Ford and two young women who lodged together, Lila Leeds, a would-be actress, and Vicki Evans, a dancer.

At the end of the subsequent court case, Mitchum was sentenced to a year in jail which the judge suspended against two years probation, of which two months were to be spent in Los Angeles County Jail.

It is remarkable how Robert Mitchum's conviction for possession of marijuana has stayed in the public memory for so long. Even today, when occasional pot-smoking (and worse) is almost *de rigueur* in certain ultra-respectable, middle-class circles, Mitchum's brush with the law is still remembered. Conversely, few people remember, if they ever knew, that in 1951 his conviction was set aside following submission of evidence that the arrest was a set-up.

The Mitchums' marriage had been undergoing some testing. He enjoyed a good time, which translated to include fair helpings of wine and women, and barely noticed the hard time Dorothy was having in making ends meet. A new manager had set up a deal which ostensibly kept their heads just above water while the bulk of his income was invested. In fact, the manager was quietly embezzling every cent he could get his hands on.

At one point Dorothy insisted on a break with Hollywood and they spent some time back in Delaware but eventually Mitchum had to go back to work on the coast. He went alone. Boredom drove him into more drinking with his cronies, dating passing females, and smoking grass (with which he'd had a nodding acquaintance since around 1935).

When Mitchum decided to sell the house on Oak Glen Drive, he became involved with Robin Ford, a part-time realtor, and used him in the negotiations.

One night, in Ford's company, Mitchum, who had been working hard and drinking, visited Lila Leeds' house in Laurel Canyon. The police were already in position, alerted to the fact that they had a chance of making a headline-grabbing arrest. They certainly did that.

Close observers of the events on Laurel Canyon have suggested that Ford was using the star as a means of easing his own circumstances, which were attracting the attention of the cops, and also that the girls knew rather more about the bust than perhaps they should. The fact that not only the police but also the press were alerted *before* his arrest adds to suspicions that everyone connected with the bust saw in the rising movie star a means of achieving ends that had very little to do with law enforcement.

Despite the apparent conspiracy against him, Mitchum never claimed that the charges were false and, when in later life he was asked to comment on the effect the arrest had on his career, he lightly observed that he 'couldn't play, for instance, Eagle scouts or Baptist preachers'. He also referred to prison as being like Palm Springs, 'only you meet a better class of people'.

Although content to serve out his time, Mitchum was persuaded to request a transfer to a prison farm which had the benefit of reducing his term by ten days, a period which was of great advantage to his studio who desperately wanted to finish another film, *The Big Steal*, on which he began working while awaiting trial.

The role of the studio in the drugs bust has been questioned by some observers who believe that RKO was party to the case as a means of making Mitchum more amenable to discipline.

Such suggestions appear highly speculative and gel uneasily with the fact that RKO helped him out by hiring Jerry Gisler, a top-flight lawyer with a huge reputation as 'attorney to the star'.

Additionally, on his release, Mitchum returned to RKO where the boss, Howard Hughes, had not merely promised to maintain his contract but had also loned his star almost $50,000, enough money to buy a new house.

Reaction to Mitchum's arrest and conviction was mixed but while some Bible-belt audiences responded predictably, most were surprisingly undeterred by it all. The real reasons for this are speculative but might well combine the psychological with the practical. For many fans, his lawlessness strengthened his appeal; here was one star who was as tough, outspoken and ornery as the characters he played on the screen. And, although his prison term could not be described as 'hard time', he made no complaints and served his sentence just like any other ordinary mortal. As a result, instead of distancing his fans, his imprisonment compounded their fellow-feeling for him.

It was around this time that Mitchum acquired a new secretary, Reva Frederick, who took on many of the day-to-day hassles of being a movie star and who quickly made herself indispensable in the ordering of his professional life.

The studio was relieved at the response of Mitchum's fans, who now included the bobby-soxed Bob Mitchum Droolettes, to his term in prison, and promptly released another western.

This was *Blood on the Moon* (1948), a complex tale directed with flair by Robert Wise. Mitchum's role, as Jimmy Garry, was well received by critics, with Thomas M. Pryor, in *The New York Times*, stating that the star 'carries the burden of the film and his acting is superior all the way'.

The complexities of *Blood on the Moon*, which, like the earlier *Pursued*, depends more on character development than on fast action, places it too in that hybrid genre, the *noir* western. There is little doubt that this is essentially due to Mitchum's presence, because by this point in his career he was beginning to make his mark upon certain categories of motion picture. Like so many established actors, he was already bringing to films in which he appeared personal qualities which created certain preconceptions and expectations among filmgoers. In short, he was becoming a movie icon.

On a personal level, *Blood on the Moon* introduced Mitchum to Tim Wallace who became his stand-in, drinking crony and devoted, if sharp-tongued, admirer for the next thirty and more years.

Another horse-orientated film followed but it was far from

being a routine western; indeed, in the accepted sense of the term, it was not really a western at all. The screenplay of *The Red Pony* (1949) and the original novella on which it was based were both the work of John Steinbeck. That this was seen by the studio, Republic, as a prestige picture is evident from the fact that in addition to Steinbeck's name on the credits are those of Lewis Milestone as director, Tony Gaudio as cinematographer, and Aaron Copland for the score, while the cast included Myrna Loy and Louis Calhern.

The Red Pony tells a tender tale of a small boy, Tom (Peter Miles), and his love for a pony and the manner in which the world of adults becomes increasingly foreign and disturbing to him as his parents' domestic problems develop. The inability of Alice and Fred Tilfin (Loy and Shepperd Strudwick) to understand their son is exacerbated by the yarn-spinning grandfather (Calhern) whose tales of how he guided pioneers in the great westward migration serve only to colour Tom's already vivid imagination. Only the farm's handyman, Billy Buck (Mitchum), understands the boy and hence enjoys the most sympathetic adult role in the film, especially when he risks the life of his favourite horse in an effort to provide Tom with a pony of his own.

The Red Pony, which was Mitchum's first colour film, was perhaps a shade too soft-centred for most of his fans and, despite the qualities of its participants, both on-screen and behind the scenes, it remains a minor work. However, Mitchum's performance was well in keeping with the mood of the piece and although taking second billing to Myrna Loy he was undoubtedly the film's main attraction. *Variety* commented, a little ambivalently, that 'Mitchum once again demonstrates his flair for apt characterizations without overplaying the faculty of getting at the emotional core of his audience'. Later, Mitchum was to comment upon his co-star, remarking that at one point he had asked her how she withstood the heat while remaining poised, smart, and with her make-up unblemished. Miss Loy's reply neatly summarized the difficulties movie actresses faced and how they had to be overcome (at least by anyone as professional as herself): 'There's nothing I can do about it, is there? Would you have me be unattractive?'

In *The New York Times* Bosley Crowther was, as usual, unimpressed: 'Robert Mitchum is strangely laconic – too much so – as the hired man.'

When Howard Hughes, owner of RKO, put *The Big Steal* (1949) into production before it was ready, he had hoped that when Mitchum's trial took place the judge would not jeopardize the livelihoods of all the people employed on it by jailing the star. Shooting began while Mitchum was on bail but, when Hughes's ploy failed and Mitchum was jailed, director Don Siegel was obliged to shoot around the star during his spell inside (which was reduced by those valuable ten days following the move to the prison farm).

Perhaps not surprisingly, given its hastily conceived schedule, *The Big Steal* is a patchily executed farrago. Basically a chase movie, much of it shot against unconvincing back projection, the movie is riddled with characters who are not quite what they seem at first, or even second, glance. Nevertheless, the intrigue is thinly devised and most moviegoers were able to work out what was likely to happen at the conclusion long before the end of the first reel.

The chief failing of *The Big Steal* is that it never seems to know whether it is a thriller or a comedy. With a little more time, care and finesse it might have become an adequate comedy-thriller but it fails to find a consistent level. Considering the presence of Mitchum and Greer from *Out of the Past*, together with the same editor and screenplay writer, *The Big Steal* promised a great deal more than it delivered. For Jane Greer the film was a brief escape from the tyranny of Howard Hughes. On failing to persuade her that her career depended upon co-operating with his sexual demands, Hughes had withdrawn all offers of work but simultaneously refused to release her from her contract. When other female stars refused the risk to their careers of appearing in a film with Mitchum while the court case was still unresolved, Hughes had no choice but to let Greer do it.

For all its many shortcomings, the film made a pile of money, thanks to Mitchum's new and surprisingly tolerated notoriety. Bosley Crowther, in *The New York Times*, remarked that the movie's real interest lay in its 'breathtaking scenic excursions across the landscape of Mexico', a comment which was right enough in a general sense but which ignored the sloppiness of the unconvincing back-projected panoramas.

For Mitchum's last release of the 1940s, RKO put him into light comedy, *Holiday Affair* (1949), which co-starred him with Janet Leigh. This tells a mildly whimsical tale of two people who meet and fall in love all within the space of the few days before Christmas. The casting of Mitchum as Steve Mason, a sales assistant in the toy department of a big store, was very much against the recent trend of his career but his performance was more than merely adequate. The critics were generally favourable and spoke well of his acting. Bosley Crowther was defiantly out of step with his colleagues in suggesting that

Mitchum rambled around blandly and that he was as mechanical as one of the electric trains his character was supposed to sell to the kiddies.

For Mitchum, looking back from the standpoint of the end of the 1940s, his ascent must have seemed an improbable dream. He had begun the decade trying to scrape a living, writing material for Sunset Strip night club artists and supplementing this meagre income with welfare benefit cheques. Now, ten years later, he was an internationally known star with thirty-nine movies to his credit.

Although he had merely walked on or played bits in the majority of his films to date, as the decade ended he was an automatic choice for leading roles, taking second billing only when the studio had a big, established gun as co-star. Three of his films, *The Story of GI Joe*, *Crossfire* and *Out of the Past*, had been huge commercial and critical successes and his performances in them had been excellent.

Typically, he was dismissive of his success. His distinctive, swaying walk he attributed to trying to hold his stomach in (sometimes varying the explanation to suggest it was an attempt to walk in a straight line), his hooded eyes were blamed on a combination of his 'boxing career', chronic insomnia and bad eyesight. In fact, he had looked that way from birth.

And he delighted in shocking reporters and their eager readers with his off-hand dismissal of what others regarded as the art of screen acting by steadfastly refusing to behave as if he took his craft seriously, stating, for example, 'I show up at nine and punch out at six. That's all I do. The pictures belong to other guys, and I don't care too much ...'

Despite such remarks, he was already proving to his fellow workers that when he turned up for a new film he was reliable, punctual and knew his lines. The comments for public consumption were early symptoms of what was to become a career-long fencing match with interviewers, all of whom he refused to take any more seriously than he took himself.

The future would change his public face only a little, while professionally, it held much for him to do. He could begin the new decade with the confidence of knowing that he was rapidly becoming a highly accomplished screen actor.

4   International Star

I don't know why people collect film stars' signatures;
unless it's because they're free. In most places one goes to
they can't even read.

In midsummer 1949 Howard Hughes loaned the Mitchums the
money with which to buy a new home. Official recipient of the
loan was Dorothy Mitchum, with repayments deducted from
her husband's weekly pay. The loan allowed them to move to a
house in Mandeville Canyon Road, close to where actor
Anthony Caruso and his wife, Tonia, lived. The Carusos were
among a fairly short list of close friends of the Mitchums, several
of whom also lived nearby and formed the 'Mandeville Canyon
Gang'. Others were the Widmarks, Richard and Jean; the Pecks,
Gregory and Greta; and Olive Carey, widow of early screen star
Harry Carey.

The new home and the circle of close friends who surrounded
them kept the Mitchums clear of the usual 'Hollywood set', and
these personal relationships were built not upon movieland's
values but upon earthier, simpler and more enduring standards.

Now Robert Mitchum's career entered a new and successful
chapter even if, artistically, many of the films in which he
appeared had little to commend them.

When Howard Hughes acquired RKO he brought nothing of
artistic value to his new business enterprise. Making millions in
the oil and aircraft industries was something he was good at,
and in later years he would prove to be surprisingly adept in
becoming the world's richest recluse. But to moviemaking he
could offer only limited imagination allied to a taste for obvious
sex and tawdry melodrama. These characteristics, together with
a distinct hankering after past values (in itself not necessarily a
fault), kept RKO anchored securely to formula movies.

The relationship between Hughes and Robert Mitchum held
considerable fascination for many who were able to observe it at
close hand. The consensus was that Mitchum was the kind of

man Hughes wanted to be: tough-talking, no-nonsense, hard-nosed, devil-may-care, and a wow with the women.

The likelihood that Howard Hughes wished he were Robert Mitchum probably led to his decision to team the star with several of the most attractive women under contract to RKO.

Well-substantiated claims have been made that Hughes frequently tried to exercise a latter-day form of *droit de seigneur* over his female stars and took severe steps to punish recalcitrant actresses he believed he had at his contractual disposal. Certainly, both Jane Greer and Jean Simmons suffered as a result of the steadfastness with which they resisted him, with Greer's career being most badly damaged. It is not difficult to see in the films Mitchum made during this time a sustained attempt by Hughes to enjoy a vicarious celluloid sex life through his favourite leading man's on-screen activities.

The first five movies Mitchum made for RKO in the 1950s both reflected the failings of the company's creative impulse under Hughes and teamed him with an attractive leading lady.

Where Danger Lives (1950) is a quasi-*noir* thriller in which Mitchum was cast as Jeff Cameron, a doctor who falls in love with Margo Lannington (Faith Domergue) whom he saves from suicide. When Jeff prepares to leave town with Margo he discovers that Frederick Lannington (Claude Rains), the man he has been led to believe is Margo's oppressive father is, in fact, her elderly husband. As Lannington tells Jeff, 'Margo married me for my money. I married her for her youth. We both got what we wanted – after a fashion.'

Conflict develops between the two men and, in a struggle, Jeff is knocked unconscious. When he recovers he finds that Lannington is dead. If that were not enough, he carries out a quick self-diagnosis and concludes that he is suffering from progressive concussion. He needs hospital treatment but Margo insists that they make a run for it. As they head for the Mexican border (sounds familiar?) Jeff's concussion worsens and his general state of mind is not improved when he gradually realizes that Margo is insane and that she clubbed her husband to death while both men were lying unconscious after their struggle. After several tension-building encounters along the way, most of which reveal an unsettling measure of financial corruption among small-town Americans, the fugitive couple reach the border where Margo shoots Jeff only to be shot herself by border guards – but lives long enough to clear Jeff of complicity in her husband's murder.

Directed by Australian-born John Farrow, *Where Danger Lives* is aided by Nicholas Musuraca's cinematography, which goes a long way towards creating a surface air of quality. This is especially apparent in the earlier sequences which finds the characters' personalities being explored and developed.

The performances of the two principals is never less than adequate although Faith Domergue, then being heavily but unsuccessfully promoted as a sex symbol, did not really have the range her role demands. The fact that Mitchum's character is called upon to fall in love with a potentially lethal female had worked in *Out of the Past* but there he was playing opposite the enigmatically alluring Jane Greer. Faith Domergue was not in the same league. Equally damaging to credibility is the nature of the character Mitchum plays. A down-at-heel private eye functioning on the edges of the criminal sink can be readily seen as a potential victim for traps laid by a predatory *femme fatale*; a fine upstanding young intern would have spotted a nut like Margo Lannington from the far side of a crowded ward and sent in the head nurse to carry out any necessary medical examination. He certainly wouldn't have made a run for the border with her.

Reviews were mixed but the star was mostly received favourably with even *The New York Times's* Bosley Crowther allowing that: 'Mitchum does a fairly credible job as a man operating in a vacuum and beset by unfortunate circumstances.'

Mitchum was again a doctor in *My Forbidden Past* (1951), another RKO production which lay around for a couple of years gathering dust while Howard Hughes tried to find a spare moment in which to supervise final editing. This time the setting was nineteenth-century New Orleans but the story, from Polan Banks's novel, *Carriage Entrance*, is a turgid melodrama about generally unlikeable people. Most surprising to many fans of the day was the lack of on-screen fireworks which they reasonably expected might develop between Mitchum and his co-star, Ava Gardner.

Mitchum didn't think much of *Carriage Entrance*, cheerfully telling movieland gossip columnist Hedda Hopper, 'We didn't have much of a script to start with, so I suggested the first scene be about like the climactic one in *Ecstasy* [a film notorious for its nude bathing scene]. I figured if we were going to give the public a shock, we might as well do it up brown.'

Howard Hughes disapproved and remonstrated with Mitchum who was unrepentant. Their conversation ended – according to Mitchum – with Hughes declaring, 'You're like a pay toilet. You don't give a shit for nothing, do you?'

On the whole, Mitchum appears to have been on the mark with his view of the film and, like him, reviewers were decidedly unimpressed. A.H. Weiler, standing in for an absent Bosley Crowther at *The New York Times*, commented: 'Ava Gardner, who plays the lovelorn Barbara, is quite fetching ... as the Yankee "germ detective" Robert Mitchum's characterization is somewhat wooden.'

Third to be released in the string of Howard Hughes melodramas was *His Kind of Woman* (1951). This time, following hard on the shapely heels of Faith Domergue and Ava Gardner, Mitchum's co-star was Jane Russell. The director was again John Farrow (this film was made back-to-back with *Where Danger Lives* but suffered a dust-gathering hiatus on Hughes's shelf) and with two such hot properties as Mitchum and Russell headlining it could hardly miss. At Hughes's urging, Mitchum and Russell were built up as an 'item' by means of extensive publicity. Off-screen, the relationship between the stars appears to have been one of mutual respect and comradeship.

Its potential (and realized) commerciality aside, the film didn't have too much going for it. Its storyline is markedly convoluted and the synopsis writers must have earned their pay in reducing the plot to anything under a couple of thousand words. Oddly enough, over the years this film has gained a reputation as a major *film noir*, but it is one it barely deserves.

The film's main problem stems from the decision, apparently made during production and perhaps stemming from Hughes himself, to extend the role of Mark Cardigan (Vincent Price). Cardigan is a vacationing moviestar whose activities and general demeanour provide entertainingly comic relief but whose relevance to the plot is, at best, minimal. While Mitchum, as Dan Milner, and heavyweight Raymond Burr, as Nick Ferraro, play it straight in scenes shot with interesting *noir*-ish camera angles, Price turns in a deliriously camp performance which looks and sounds as though he'd accidentally wandered in from an adjacent sound stage.

Towards the end, the intercutting of Price's scenes, as he rushes to the rescue with a team of comic-opera extras, with those in which Mitchum is facing death by injection with a brain-destroying drug, creates an uneasy imbalance. Often cited as a classic *film noir*, *His Kind of Woman* is nothing of the sort, but it is certainly good in parts. Unfortunately for its presumed *film noir* status, and that of its star, it is Vincent Price, hamming it up gloriously, who lives longest in the mind. He also has the best line when he verbally cudgels his rescue party with the cry: 'Survivors will get parts in my next picture.'

Howard Thompson, in *The New York Times*, suggested that the film was 'one of the worst Hollywood pictures in years [and] it is probably the first since the advent of Vitaphone that needs subtitles ... Robert Mitchum blinks sleepily into space and Miss Russell, strategically sheathed in some opulent gowns merely, and understandably, arches her upper lip as though smelling something awful.'

Next, Mitchum appeared in *The Racket* (1951), wherein a great deal of promise was somehow dissipated by the time this gloomily slow-moving production reached the screen. A remake of a story Hughes had first made in 1928, the new version of *The Racket* was originally written by Sam Fuller. However, when his screenplay was seen to have largely ignored the original, new writers were called in. William Wister Haines, later joined by W.R. Burnett, tussled with the script but once again what may have looked good on paper failed to materialize on the screen. Just as *Crossfire* had missed an opportunity to pit the powerful talents of Mitchum and Robert Ryan against one another, so *The Racket* also failed to capitalize upon the dramatic potential of their joint presence.

Joe Pihodna wrote in the *New York Herald* that Mitchum's was 'the sort of part that dominates the screen and helps make the picture seem better than it really is'.

Although he had several more films to make before his RKO contract expired, Mitchum's next, *Macao* (1952), was the last of a string of five almost-*noir* thrillers that Howard Hughes stored away, then brought out in quick succession. *Macao* was directed by Joseph von Sternberg who was expected to do for Jane Russell what he'd done a generation earlier for Marlene Dietrich. It wasn't to be and neither the film nor Miss Russell came off very well. Continuity of purpose was sabotaged by Hughes when, late in production, von Sternberg was replaced by Nicholas Ray who tried to breathe life into von Sternberg's weightily baroque settings by re-shooting substantial sequences with his own sharply realistic vision. It was too late, however, and despite Ray's determined efforts the joins still show.

From time to time Mitchum has felt disposed to express displeasure (usually politely) with some of his female co-stars, but he clearly liked working with the strong-willed Miss Russell. Of her, he remarked that she 'was a very strong character. Very good humoured when she wasn't being cranky'.

In *One Minute to Zero* (1952) Mitchum was back in uniform for the first time since *GI Joe*. This time the setting was the Korean 'police action' which was currently enjoying limited popularity among Hollywood's moviemakers as a setting for their routine action-men. Starting out as a colonel, named Steve Janowski, Mitchum makes general by the end and after many tribulations also wins the hand of Ann Blyth. Any lessons Hollywood might have learned from films like *GI Joe* were forgotten and with one minor exception the movie is standard Hollywood cannon-fodder replete with stereotypes. The exception to predictability comes in a sequence in which the colonel orders the shelling of a party of refugees because he believes, rightly as it turns out, that they conceal North Korean soldiers. Officialdom, in the shape of the US Department of Defense, opposed this touch of realism and refused to co-operate with exhibitors in the promotion of the film.

As if in sympathy, Mitchum's promotion of the film was less than enthusiastic and, according to legend, he enlivened one interview by telling a young, inexperienced reporter that his favourite sport was hunting 'poontang'.

According to the legend Mitchum's account of where poontang could be found, what it looked like, and whether or not it made good eating, actually found its way into print. The legend doesn't really suffer from the fact that no one has been able to produce a copy of a newspaper or magazine with the account in it. Like most Mitchum stories, it doesn't need hard evidence to keep it alive.

The legend was further enhanced when, during filming at Colorado Springs, Mitchum had a bar-room brawl with a soldier who not only lost but turned out to be an ex-heavyweight boxer.

It was in his seventh film of the 1950s that, for the first time since *Out of the Past*, Mitchum struck artistic pay-dirt.

The Lusty Men (1952) was made under his RKO contract but none of the usual Howard Hughes touches is in evidence. Instead of his customary imposition of arty crudities and synthetic sex, Hughes seems to have left director Nicholas Ray to get on with his job. The result is a masterly evocation of the world of the rodeo rider.

In *The Lusty Men* the life of the rodeo rider is depicted without frills and with none of the artificial romanticism Hollywood tended to bring to tales of the West. There were to be other attempts at realism in the 1950s and again in the 70s and 80s, but Ray was the first to see the setting's potential for an action-filled movie that could also explore complex physical and psychological human relationships under stress.

The storyline tells a simple yet effective tale of an ex-champion rodeo star, Jeff McCloud (Mitchum), who returns to his home state, Oklahoma, after almost twenty years on the rodeo circuit during which he has earned bruises and a reputation but has saved no money. He meets a young married couple, Wes and Louise Merritt (Arthur Kennedy and Susan

Hayward), and strikes up a friendship with them. Wes joins the narrow world of the professional rodeo rider, seeing the circuit as a means by which he can quickly earn money to buy the small ranch on which he and his wife have set their hearts.

With Jeff as his trainer and manager, Wes Merritt is soon earning big money, but his successes go to his head. Forgetting his plans, Wes squanders his money, fending off his wife's pleas that he should quit. Louise tries to persuade Jeff to straighten Wes out but, instead, the veteran suggests that she should ditch her husband and take up with him. When Louise rejects him Jeff agrees to try and save Wes from himself. But Wes taunts Jeff with accusations of cowardice, provoking him into taking to the saddle again. Intent on proving that he still has what it takes, Jeff's return ends in tragedy when he sustains a fatal injury. His eyes opened and his sanity restored, Wes quits this most dangerous game and he and Louise prepare to settle down at the ranch they have been hoping to buy.

The film's opening moments, the noise and excitement of a rodeo in which Jeff McCloud is slightly injured, are contrasted with harsh reality by a sudden cut to the windswept area outside the stadium after the show has closed. The crowd that had roared and cheered a short while before has gone. The only life amidst the swirling dust and litter is the lonely figure of the injured rider, moving slowly and painfully along until he disappears through a gate marked 'Stock Exit', a neatly understated touch which reduces the hero of the hour to the same level as the animals.

McCloud visits the house where he grew up. The place is falling apart, its chimney stack propped up with timbers. The door is locked, so he crawls under the house to where, long ago, he left some personal belongings: an old dismantled gun, a creased and fading rodeo programme, and a tin containing two nickels. It is here that he is found by the present owner, Jeremiah Watrus (Burt Mustin), an old man who is hoping to sell the house and land to Wes and Louise Merritt.

The dialogue exchanges between Jeff and the old man eloquently reveal that two decades bouncing around the rodeo circuit has done little for the rider:

JEREMIAH: You got anything you own?
JEFF: What I started out with. A strong back and a weak mind.

Uncomplainingly, Jeff makes it clear that there was never very much choice for him:

JEREMIAH: You a thinking man?
JEFF: Oh, I can get outta the rain. That's about all.

Later, as Jeff's growing attraction towards Louise becomes clear, he tries to indicate his feelings for her. When she asks him if he never wanted anything in the same way that she wants the ranch for herself and her husband, Jeff tells her, 'The only way I could tell how much a thing was worth was by how bad I wanted it.'

The quietly resigned cynicism with which Jeff views his life is expounded in his phlegmatic answer to Louise's demand to know what happened to all the money he has made over the years: 'I made a thousand bartenders rich in my time.'

Towards the film's end, after Jeff is thrown and dragged by a horse, he lies dying with a busted rib through his lung. Outside, Wes is taking his next ride and Louise comes to Jeff to ask him, 'What were you trying to prove?' He tells her, 'I used to make my own money. I used to buy my own whiskey, take my own falls. Thought I'd like to know if I could still do it.'

The affinity of the attitude of Jeff McCloud, rodeo rider in *The Lusty Men*, with that of Jeff Bailey, ex-private eye in *Out of the Past*, is unmistakable. Although very different roles, in films which have little in common apart from Mitchum's presence, the common thread of the alienated individual is very strong. The comfortable togetherness of Wes and Louise in the early scenes, which returns after their problems are solved through Jeff's sacrifice, contrasts vividly with the image Mitchum imparts as the eternal outsider.

This impression of a man outside the mainstream of normal domestic life is enhanced by the mood Mitchum brings to almost every screen role he has portrayed. Here, in *The Lusty Men*, it is no less in evidence than in many of his more overtly 'outsider' roles. His restraint and the sad-eyed longing with which he looks on at the Merritt's marriage, effectively underlines his emotions even though the character himself is never aware of them.

Mitchum's performance is as solid as any he had made up to this stage in his career. Equally impressive are the performances of his co-stars, Susan Hayward and Arthur Kennedy. Perhaps Miss Hayward was, outwardly at least, a shade too elegant for the role of the wife of a hired hand, albeit one with ambitions, but her acting ability and strong screen presence carry her safely over any such minor reservations the audience might have.

The film's qualities were instantly observed by critics of the time and on this occasion at least some of them got the measure of a Mitchum performance from the start. In *The New York Times* Bosley Crowther capitulated when he commented that 'Robert Mitchum is most authentic as a hard-bitten rodeo tramp.' Crowther was similarly complimentary about Nicholas Ray's direction, declaring that he 'has really caught the muscle and thump of rodeos'.

Of lasting importance in an overview of Hollywood's treatment of the West is the fact that *The Lusty Men* does not display a glossy view of what was essentially a dirty, dangerous, and frequently depressing, way of life. Despite the surface glamour of the rodeo scene, when observed from a seat high in the bleachers, there is a pervading harsh ordinariness about the rodeo rider's chosen lifestyle. In choosing to display this on the screen, director Nicholas Ray helped make *The Lusty Men* one of Robert Mitchum's best movies of the decade.

Mitchum's next film release was another determinedly grim offering from Howard Hughes's RKO studies. *Angel Face* (1952) teamed Mitchum with British actress Jean Simmons in a turgid psychological melodrama. Although many of the necessary elements for good suspenseful *film noir* are present, the heavy hand of director Otto Preminger oppresses the film's more static moments. Unfortunately, there are rather more of such moments than of those which might have allowed him to zip the action along.

In *Angel Face*, Mitchum takes the role of Frank Jessup, an ambulance driver, who becomes amorously entangled with Diane Tremayne (Simmons), a beautiful young woman with homicidal tendencies. Diane's repeated attempts to kill her stepmother bring the unwitting Frank into her baleful orbit. Eventually Diane is successful when she devises a way to cause her stepmother's car to crash backwards over a cliff beside the family home. Diane's father is also in the car and soon Frank and the girl are charged with the double homicide. The couple are pressured into marriage by their lawyer, who plans to use this formalization of their relationship to win an acquittal. The ploy is successful and they get off, but recent events have lifted the veil from Frank's eyes and he can now see Diane's true, malevolent nature and he tells her he is leaving. Frank is foolhardy enough to trust Diane to drive him to the depot from where he plans to take the bus to Mexico. Both Frank and the audience were understandably surprised by the shock ending: Diane throws the car into reverse and drives them both off the cliff edge.

The origins of *Angel Face* are almost Machiavellian. Howard Hughes had tried unsuccessfully to impose himself upon Jean

Simmons. With less than three weeks to run on her contract the actress was determined never to work again for Hughes and, knowing of his obsession with beautiful women with long dark hair, she deliberately hacked off her own to make her appearance unsuitable for filming. Hughes retaliated by urging Preminger to complete the film, despite an originally unsatisfactory script, in the available time and to conceal Miss Simmons's personal depredations with a long, black wig.

Not surprisingly, given the surrounding circumstances, tension afflicted the set and a fracas occurred when Preminger, perhaps encouraged by Hughes's demands and anger, insisted that a scene in which Mitchum has to slap his co-star's face be taken over and over again and that there should be none of the customary faking of the blow. Eventually, with Miss Simmons in some understandable distress, Mitchum decided to show the director how painful the process really was and slapped *him*. Harmony suddenly reigned (although given what was to happen between Mitchum and Preminger some 20 years later, it would seem that neither man succeeded in completely banishing feelings of acrimony).

After *Angel Face*, and now on loan to Fox, Mitchum made *White Witch Doctor* (1953) with Susan Hayward. Set in Africa (location shooting was done separately, allowing the actors to work in the comparative comfort of the back-lot for as many scenes as possible), the film tells a tale of dangerous natives beset by equally dangerous and mercenary white men in the early years of the twentieth century. Mitchum, playing white hunter Lonnie Douglas, with Susan Hayward as a selfless nurse, win the confidence of the natives by simultaneously rescuing them from the hands of the bad guys and saving them from all manner of appropriate African ailments. This kind of story had been done before and was to be done again (and again) and *White Witch Doctor* was somewhat below par for this particular course.

Mitchum's performance was ill-received by the critics but his growing reputation among his Hollywood peers was further enhanced by the response of director Henry Hathaway who commented that Mitchum was the most phenomenal actor he had ever seen. Even allowing for traditional Hollywood hyperbole this was praise indeed. In fact, Hathaway's enthusiasm had developed after a frosty start which was largely overcome by one of Mitchum's practical jokes. The actor walked on to the set, pretended to be unprepared for a long (six-page) scene, glanced at a script and promptly delivered a perfect take, complete with English and Swahili dialogue.

A publicity pose from Mitchum's days at RKO tries to promote a boy-next-door look that doesn't quite come off.

Preparing for a fishing trip with sons Chris (left) and Jim.

'Lieutenant Walker' pitches a grenade at the enemy in *The Story of GI Joe* (1945).

Kirk Douglas is a racketeer about to make 'Jeff Bailey' an offer he really should refuse in *Out of the Past* (1947) under the watchful eye of strongarm man Paul Valentine.

The door might be open for 'Duke Halliday' in *The Big Steal* (1949) but during its making an iron-barred gate slammed behind the actor.

'Jeff Cameron' is still unaware that his attraction to Faith Domergue is likely to prove fatal in *Where Danger Lives* (1950).

'Dan Miller' likes to keep his money well-ironed, especially when confronted by an eager Jane Russell who is obviously *His Kind of Woman* (1951).

'Jeff McCloud' unhorsed but still on his feet in *The Lusty Men* (1952).

The scenes between 'Matt Calder' and Marilyn Monroe in *River of No Return* (1954) led to one of the actor's typical remarks: 'How the hell can I take aim when she's undulating like that?' But here Tommy Rettig gets all his attention.

Love and hate spelled out on the fingers of 'Preacher Harry Powell' in *The Night of the Hunter* (1955), Charles Laughton's chilling masterpiece.

When Mitchum heard of Hathaway's enthusiasm he reportedly remarked, 'What did he expect at these prices? A bum?'

Mitchum's increasing reputation as an actor of stature and one with a high degree of professionalism (even if he refused to display any outward sign of taking anything seriously) helped strengthen his position in Hollywood which, as his contract with RKO expired, proved decidedly advantageous.

The Mitchums had eased themselves out of their indebtedness to Howard Hughes by remortgaging their Mandeville Canyon home with the bank. With his RKO contract fulfilled, and out of debt to Hughes, Mitchum was in a good position to consolidate the current success of his career.

It was a good time to be in such a position because, on 3 March 1952, Dorothy gave birth to a daughter they named Petrina.

For an actor, any time was a good time to be able to deal from strength in his negotiations with the studios but in the early 1950s this was even more valuable. This was a period when Hollywood was undergoing one of its occasional bouts of self-induced panic. This time it was because the motion-picture industry believed itself to be under threat from television.

Instead of looking for improvements in standards and seeking ways of countering the upstart entertainment medium with artistically superior offerings, the studio heads looked for gimmicks to help them attract audiences. *White Witch Doctor* was Fox's last normal-sized screen production before launching CinemaScope with which they hoped to keep the bailiffs at bay. Over at RKO similar thinking resulted in 3-D movies, one of which was Robert Mitchum's last under his contract with the company (although another dust-gatherer still lay on Howard Hughes's groaning shelf).

A straightforward action yarn, *Second Chance* (1953) features Mitchum as Russ Lambert, a boxer working the minor circuits and attempting to expunge from his memory the fact that he caused the death of an opponent in the ring. The psychological implausibility of trying to forget such a thing while continuing to fight is not explored by the screenplay which concentrates instead on a burgeoning relationship between the fighter and a gangster's girlfriend (Linda Darnell) who is on the run from a hired killer (played by former real-life boxer Jack Palance).

The final scrap between Mitchum and Palance takes place on a cable-car marooned between mountains and fully exploits the 3-D gimmick. Conversely, the greater part of the slight story failed to benefit appreciably from the device and none of the participants fared particularly well.

When the last remaining RKO movie of Mitchum's finally came

off the shelf it revealed that it hadn't really been worth waiting for. *She Couldn't Say No* (1953) once again teamed Mitchum with Jean Simmons (it was made before *Angel Face*) and is a slight comedy with failings that lie not so much with the players (the lower ranks include such stalwarts as Edgar Buchanan, Arthur Hunnicutt and Wallace Ford) but with an improbable storyline ill-treated by a team of writers who were not up to the task placed before them.

Perhaps it was inevitable that the film's publicists made optimistic comparisons with those slight and fluffy tales produced in earlier decades which managed to overcome candy-floss origins through the twin arts of witty writing and deft playing. Unfortunately, the era of screwball comedy had passed and even if it had not, RKO, under the dead thumb of Howard Hughes, was in no position to attempt a revival.

Free of his RKO contract at last, Mitchum's next film teamed him with the young woman who had once been married to James Dougherty, his factory mate at Lockheed a dozen years earlier, but who had now changed her name to Marilyn Monroe.

The intervening period had brought her as much public attention as it had brought Mitchum, but Marilyn Monroe's fame was of a very different order.

Despite Monroe's popularity, and in 1954 she was Fox's top moneyspinner, Mitchum, now freelancing, had sufficient box-office muscle to be granted top billing.

The simple storyline of *River of No Return* (1954) is dwarfed through being played out against spectacular scenery which is wonderfully captured by the CinemaScope lens.

Matt Calder (Mitchum), recently out of prison, turns up in the Canadian Rockies in 1875 intent on collecting his young son, Mark (Tommy Rettig), from a prospecting town. The lad has been cared for by saloon girl Kay Weston (Monroe) and now, anxious to build a new life for himself and his son, Matt returns to his farm. The farm stands on the banks of a river and one day who should come floating along, on a raft, but Kay and her no-good gambler husband, Harry (Rory Calhoun). After rescuing the pair from the rapids, Matt is attacked by Harry who makes off alone to register a claim to a gold mine he has won playing poker. Matt has been injured and Kay stays behind to care for him but then he has to defend the woman and his son against marauding Indians. Even the river, along which they try to escape, becomes a threat. If that isn't enough trouble for any man to cope with, Matt also has to protect himself from Kay whose behaviour swings wildly from off-handedness to deep affection. Matt's personal problems multiply when Mark learns something of his father's seamy past from Kay, and the boy is especially disturbed by the accidental homicide which sent his father to prison. This knowledge alienates Mark from his father but, later, the young boy shoots the villainous gambler when Harry attacks Kay, who manages to justify to Mark all that has happened. All their problems thus conveniently, if improbably, sorted out, Matt carries Kay and Mark off to the farm to start a new life together.

Directed by Otto Preminger, the movie is never too certain whether it is about people or panoramas. Moments of doubt are often settled by the careful posing of Marilyn Monroe against a suitably dramatic rocky outcrop.

River of No Return was Monroe's twenty-second film role (including bits) and came immediately after a trio of box-office hits that had boosted her to top place at Fox, the studio which had muffed an earlier opportunity to make anything of her.

Monroe completed seven more films after *River of No Return* of which three, *The Seven Year Itch, Bus Stop* and *Some Like It Hot*, are perhaps her best. In most respects, *River of No Return* is the odd-one-out of her career. Mostly, her other films had contemporary urban settings. The late nineteenth-century American wilderness was not the ideal background for Monroe's wayward talent. Her acting ability, usually submerged by artifice or neurotic instability, stood little chance in the great outdoors. Those seeking enlightenment as to just what made her special magic work need to look elsewhere than *River of No Return*.

Robert Mitchum's performance in *River of No Return* drew no raves. Indeed, what with having to fight off Indians, Rory Calhoun, and Marilyn Monroe, to say nothing of steering a raft through rapids (often without benefit of stuntmen or doubles, thanks to the highly observant CinemaScope lens), he had his work cut out just keeping clear of trouble. He seems to have held his co-star in some affection, remarking that she 'was really a sweet, marvellous, funny girl. She thought the dumb sexpot role she played was ridiculous. She was bothered by all the attention, and she got upset every time anyone so much as opened a door for her. Every time a director yelled "Action!" she'd break out in a sweat ... She was scared'.

Although set in the West, *River of No Return* was not really a western, and the same comment can be applied equally to *Track of the Cat* (1954), his next film. This was a long-dreamed-of project of director William Wellman. Although using colour and wide-screen photography, the film, set in snow-covered mountain territory, is largely white with trees and rocky outcrops standing out in sharply relieved black. Only a rare splash of colour intrudes upon this prevailing monochromatic scenery. Similarly, important sections of the story are set in the cabin in which the characters live and, despite the size of the screen available to the film's makers, these passages are oppressively confined.

The story tells of a grim, embittered family, the Bridges, who live in northern California. Beset by hardships, they have turned in against one another in hatred. The arrival in the area of a black panther which begins killing off the family's cattle affords a focus for their unreasoning anger.

The Bridges family are an unlovely and unloving bunch. Ma (Beulah Bondi) is a commanding matriarchal figure who dominates her eldest son, Curt (Mitchum), having already driven her husband (Philip Tonge) to drink. Also trapped into the household, both figuratively and as the snow deepens literally too, are two more sons, Arthur and Harold (William Hopper and Tab Hunter); and a daughter, Grace (Teresa Wright).

Curt and Arthur decides to hunt down the black cat before it kills off all their cattle, and when his brother is killed Curt decides that it is his duty to continue the pursuit. Eventually, the cat kills Curt before being killed in its turn by Harold, the youngest member of the Bridges family.

The cat is never seen on the screen, yet it pervades the film. In such scenes as where Curt has run out of matches and tries to huddle beside a dying fire in the fading light, the cat's unseen presence assumes almost tangible proportions.

The cat is used in the film as a representation of fear. Each of the men, hunters and hunted alike, 'sees' the cat in his own way. Indeed, the animal's real purpose has little significance to the plot, rather it is an unseen *deus ex machina*. The two men it kills could just have readily died in accidents without affecting the storyline but, by their use of the unseen cat as evil protagonist, director Wellman and screenwriter A.I. Bezzerides bring to the story qualities of a psychological allegory. In fact, the storyline and much of the dialogue is unwieldy but Wellman's visual interpretation, aided by superb photography from William Clothier, compensates for much of the film's failings and help account for its slow rise to cult film status.

Inevitably, the actors in a film conceived in such imaginative visual terms tend to become incidental. Few critics approved and the audience of the day was unimpressed. The passage of time has changed this view; Wellman's conception has achieved recognition for his boldness in eschewing the inherently false values of an industry gripped by feverish determination to fight off the television bogeyman with wide screens, lavish colour, and all the many tricks of the cinematographer's trade. Wellman's decision to concentrate his attention, and hence his audience's, upon an unseen and largely unspoken conflict with a mythic representation of man's internal fears was courageous. Later, Wellman expressed the view that the film was, in all respects, a flop. A more detached view, aided by distance in time, suggests that he achieved considerably more than he was prepared to grant himself.

It was while he was promoting *Track of the Cat* at the Cannes Film Festival that Mitchum had an encounter with the media that made headlines around the world.

A young starlet, Simone Silva, presumably desperately in need of publicity, rushed up to him on the beach and posed for several dozen photographers who just happened to be standing idly around at the time with loaded cameras at the ready. Responding to the encouragement of the cameramen, Miss Silva dropped the top of her swimsuit so that she could nestle up to Mitchum's chest with her bare bosom. The resulting pictures appeared just about everywhere, although in most 'family' newspapers they were suitably touched-up to meet the double standards of the day. Dorothy Mitchum, who was with her husband at the festival, was understandably irritated by the affair while he was phlegmatically unconcerned. Later, he wryly observed, 'I never saw her coming. She must have been lowered by helicopter.'

With the end of his occasionally stifling contract with RKO, Robert Mitchum could look forward to a degree of artistic freedom he had not so far enjoyed. Halfway through the 1950s his audience-pulling power was high yet it must be conceded that, *The Lusty Men* apart, none of the films of this half-decade came up to the standards of *The Story of GI Joe* or *Out of the Past*. His own view of the films he made was expectedly typical, 'I wear the same suit, speak the same lines, throw the same punches. All they do is change the girl.'

Nevertheless, as an actor he had made tremendous gains in ability and technique, although he remained (and still remains) eager to deny he has a conscious technique, a term which implies artifice. Without these qualities he would not have been able to tackle what was to be his most demanding role to date. This was the lead in a film which, as so often was the case in Hollywood, failed to impress studio, critics or audiences of the day. As with so many of these commercial and artistic 'failures', the film was destined to become a classic which would far outlast most other dream-factory products of its time.

5 The Night of the Hunter

Charles loathed those children. He made *me* direct them.

Given the kind of film popular amongst audiences for
Hollywood's products at the time, it is not surprising that on its
release in 1955 *The Night of the Hunter* mystified many. The film
met with only cautious critical response and failed to find an
adequate popular audience. Drawing heavily upon German
Expressionist cinema of the 1920s, with all the elements implied
by that genre's gothic morbidity, it did not fit into preconceived
notions of what Hollywood movies of its own era should be.

With the always comforting benefit of hindsight it is possible
to see *The Night of the Hunter* as one of the finest examples of
film-making, not just of the 1950s, but in the entire history of
popular cinema.

The principal quality of Davis Grubb's novel, upon which *The
Night of the Hunter* is based, is its well-planned, strongly
constructed story. It is a fable of sexual alienation within a
family, religious hypocrisy, fear and greed. This powerful core
formed a clean-limbed frame for the screenplay upon which it
was possible for the director to build a haunting film. Although
screenplay credits are given exclusively to James Agee, who was
one of the outstanding film critics of his day, much was changed
after his draft of the screenplay was submitted and clearly Davis
Grubb contributed many suggestions.

Ultimately, however, the film stands as a testimony to the fine
performances in all its central roles, to its superior design,
brilliant cinematography, and inspired musical score. Most of
all, however, the film brings enormous credit to the visual
imagination and artistic integrity of its director, and in so doing
goes a long way to giving credence to the often misguided and
frequently improbable 'auteur' theory of film-making.

When all this is allied to that original storyline, with its
universal and timeless appeal, it is not surprising that *The Night*

of the Hunter is as vital today as when it was made almost forty years ago.

The director was Charles Laughton, at the time noted as a stage and screen actor, who had never before directed a motion film.

Born into a hotel-keeping family in Scarborough, England, in 1899, Laughton went on to the London stage shortly after the end of World War One. He made his first films in 1928 with Elsa Lanchester whom he married the following year. The couple appeared on the New York stage in 1931 and then went to Hollywood. There, Laughton made *The Old Dark House* (1932) which was directed by James Whale who was fresh from his success with *Frankenstein* (1931). Laughton and Whale had previously acted together on the stage in England and it is highly probable that the Expressionistic vision Laughton brought to *The Night of the Hunter* was influenced by his fellow-countryman who displayed similar preoccupations in some of his work.

From 1931 to the end of his film career Laughton moved back and forth between Hollywood and England playing an astonishing variety of roles. His most memorable performances show the infinite range of his talent: *Island of Lost Souls* (1932), *The Private Life of Henry VIII* (1933), *The Barretts of Wimpole Street* (1934), *Ruggles of Red Gap*, *Mutiny on the Bounty* (both 1935), *Rembrandt* (1936), *The Hunchback of Notre Dame* (1939), *Hobson's Choice* (1954), *Advise and Consent* (1962). The manner in which Laughton immersed himself completely in his roles, and the flamboyant relish with which he tackled them, concealed a tortured private life. Unable to accept certain realities, especially his physical appearance and his sexual proclivities, he fought against them. A side-effect of this consuming if misdirected effort was that Laughton could seldom enjoy the fame and reward his professional life justly brought him.

A positive effect of his deep-seated psychological unrest was that he was able to bring to some of his projects a measure of understanding few others could command. This is especially true of *The Night of the Hunter* with its complex psychology and undercurrents of hidden impulses which drive men and women to acts that appear outwardly to be beyond all reason.

James Agee's version of the screenplay for *The Night of the Hunter* emphasized the Depression setting of the novel, concentrating on conditions of the unemployed and hungry and taking up political issues implicit in the novel's background. Given the emotional depth of Agee's journalistic writing on the Depression, this slanting of the screenplay is thoroughly understandable even if it took the tale away from its true heart. Laughton, aware that the screenplay was neither the true core of the novel nor of the film he wanted to make, set about a massive editing job in which he was aided by Davis Grubb whose visual image of how the finished film should look fitted in well with the director's preconceptions. The end result owed much to their collaboration and, aware of this, Agee asked that he should not be credited. His wishes were overruled by producer Paul Gregory who knew the value of having Agee's name on the credits. George Eells, in his biography of Robert Mitchum, quotes Gregory as remarking that Agee 'was rolling around on the floor drunk most of the time', and that Laughton sought help from Dennis and Terry Saunders but, ultimately, 'Charles ended up doing most of it.'

Laughton's vision eschewed reality in favour of deliberate non-naturalistic stylization. Where Agee opted for an accurate visual comment upon Depression life, Laughton chose artistic devices which contrive simultaneously to be astonishingly simplistic. Laughton also made use of unfashionable technical devices. Wipes and iris-outs, for example, had long-since ceased to be normal Hollywood practice.

The setting for *The Night of the Hunter* is Cresap's Landing, a small town on the banks of the Ohio River, which has recently been shocked by a killing during a robbery carried out by Ben Harper (Peter Graves) who now awaits execution, meanwhile sharing a cell with Preacher Harry Powell (Mitchum).

After the execution the Preacher arrives in Cresap's Landing where he ingratiates himself with the townspeople and attempts to charm his way into the Harper family. The intrusion of the Preacher into the emotionally distraught Harper household generates powerful sexual impulses. The newly widowed Willa Harper (Shelley Winters) is still sexually vibrant and is attracted by the dominating figure of the Preacher whose pseudo-religious words and actions barely conceal a twisted psychotic who has already murdered several women in his personal, heaven-sent campaign to rid the world of sexual undesirables. To the Preacher's deranged mind this includes any woman possessing natural sexual needs and following his marriage to Willa he cruelly rejects her tentatively loving approaches. As a result of the Preacher's behaviour towards her Willa begins to retreat into a private fantasy world in which Biblical stories mix uneasily with the reality of hunger and deprivation in Depression-hit America.

Willa's children, John and Pearl (Billy Chapin and Sally Jane Bruce), are less sure of the Preacher's intentions. John especially mistrusts him, sensing his innate evil.

The $10,000 stolen by the children's father is hidden in Pearl's doll, but before he was arrested their father swore them to secrecy, even from their mother. The Preacher however intuitively guesses that they hold the secret he seeks. He attempts to persuade John and Pearl to tell him where their father hid the money but they resist him. Willa, who has turned to fundamentalist religion in her fear and frustration, overhears the Preacher's efforts and becomes a danger to him. He murders her, disposing of the body in the river. With no one to defend them against the Preacher, the children are helpless and young John tries to make him believe that the money is hidden in the cellar but his trick is soon discovered. The Preacher's anger is diverted only when Pearl tells him the truth. Before the Preacher can seize the doll the children manage to make their escape and take to the river.

Sheltering with an old woman, Rachel Cooper (Lillian Gish), who is already caring for a number of homeless waifs, John and Pearl experience an interval of security and happiness but this is dispelled when the Preacher tracks them down. Old Miss Cooper recognizes his true nature and defends the children against him when he desperately tries to enter her house and take the money. In the course of a night of psychological harassment Miss Cooper shoots and injures the Preacher and next day he is arrested. For a brief moment John experiences the hallucination that it is his father's arrest all over again and in a sudden, hysterical outburst he throws himself on the Preacher, belabouring him with the doll until dollar bills float all around. 'I can't stand it, Dad,' he yells. 'It's too much, Dad. I don't want it.'

Later, at the trial, John refuses to testify against the Preacher and as a lynch mob gathers Miss Cooper scurries home with her brood while the police smuggle the murderer away to another town where he may expect a fair trial. With the threat to their happiness and their lives removed, John and Pearl are able to settle down with Miss Cooper.

It was Charles Laughton's preoccupation with the films of D.W. Griffith (he and James Agee screened several of them at New York's Museum of Modern Art while preparing *The Night of the Hunter*) that led him to cast Lillian Gish, the First Lady of the Silent Screen. In her autobiography, *Mr Griffith the Movies and Me*, Miss Gish comments only briefly about her role in *The Night of the Hunter*. She suggests that the film's theme, which she describes as a 'battle between good and evil', was undercut by Laughton's decision not to risk ruining 'Robert Mitchum's image by having him play a thoroughly wicked man. In the earlier days of film it would have been considered a triumph to play evil convincingly.' This description of the theme of the film seems to be oversimplified, and her implication that Mitchum made the Preacher anything less than wholly wicked does not sit easily with most perceptions of his performance. In the event, Lillian Gish's own performance, by contemporary standards a too good, almost sugary interpretation, fits the overtly simplistic tone of the central struggle.

As Willa Harper, who misguidedly marries the Preacher, Shelley Winters has a part which perfectly matches her ability to project characters possessing an intriguingly balanced mixture of warmth and redolent sexuality. Here, with the fearful sexual repression inflicted upon the character through her association with the malignant psychopath, she has a role which allowed her fully to exploit her talent. Only rarely in later years did she have opportunities like this, often being reduced to caricaturing the person moviemakers seem to think she is.

In deciding to cast Robert Mitchum in the central role of Preacher Harry Powell, Laughton raised a few eyebrows. On his record up to this time Mitchum had certainly shown enough signs of his ability, given an adequate script, to turn in an excellent textured performance. This, however, was something well outside any role he had tackled so far. In some respects it could be seen as a risk to his career but it was also a challenge and one to which he rose magnificently. His decision to play the role may be seen as a practical example of an assertion he once made in an interview with Hedda Hopper: 'If you want my interest, interest me. If you just want my presence, pay me.' Undoubtedly, the role of the Preacher interested him.

Mitchum's first appearance in the film, as he drives along a country road, immediately establishes the psychotic Preacher's character. He is talking to God; it is a friendly conversation in which the tone of voice contrasts sharply and uneasily with the words being spoken. Words, spoken softly with alarming matter-of-factness, which acknowledge the fact that the Preacher is a multiple-murderer:

'Well, now. What's it to be, Lord, another widow? How many's it been, six? Twelve? I disremember. Lord, I am tired. Sometimes I wonder if You really understand. Not that You mind the killings.'

But then the evil shows through, building in a speech which ends on a note of lip-curling, disgusted viciousness:

'But there are things You do hate, Lord: perfume-smelling things – lacy things – things with curly hair.'

Later, the Preacher is in a burlesque theatre watching a stripper performing in the spotlight. Now, without words, the vengeful maniacal hatred of the man spills out on to his face. A hand, with the letters H-A-T-E tattoed on the fingers, clenches in anger before sliding into a pocket. A second later, with orgasmic violence, the blade of a switchknife cuts through the cloth of his parson-black coat. Head angled upwards, the Preacher pleads that 'there are jes' too many of 'em, Lord. I can't kill 'em all.'

When the Preacher is briefly incarcerated for car theft, he shares a cell with Ben Harper and in a melodramatic moment his reptilian head appears upside down at the top of the screen as he stares from the top bunk at his cellmate who lies sleeping below. It is in these moments, talking in his sleep, that Ben reveals the existence of the money and sets in chain the grim events that follow.

James Agee's concern for the millions of Depression-hit Americans had formed the impulse for his best-known literary work, *Let Us Now Praise Famous Men*, which movingly chronicles their plight. It appears probable that he saw the film in terms akin to the photographs taken by Walker Evans which hauntingly illustrate this book. Although Laughton's vision removed almost all such images, a speech by Ben Harper as he lies on his bunk talking more to himself than to the Preacher, ably expresses Agee's preoccupation:

> 'That's right, Preacher. I robbed that bank because I got tired of seeing children roaming the woodlands without food, children roaming the highways in this year of Depression; children sleeping in old abandoned car bodies on junk heaps; and I promised myself I'd never see the day when *my* younguns'd want.'

The religious motif of the film's many threads makes its first strong appearance as Ben Harper dies on the scaffold at the end of the hangman's rope. A bell tolls and the prison tower is silhouetted like a church against the sky. The Preacher stands at his cell window, hands clasped around his switchknife as if holding a crucifix as he prays:

> 'Lord, You sure knowed what You was doing when You put me in this very cell at this very time. A man with ten thousand dollars hid somewheres, and a widow in the making.'

Mitchum's ability to convey great depths of meaning with nothing more than a flicker of the eyes is very well in evidence on several occasions. Most telling, perhaps, are the moments when the Preacher engages the boy John in a battle of the will.

When they first meet and John tries to discover if his father told the Preacher the truth about the money, his mere questions reveal his knowledge to the Preacher who lets the boy know he is on to him with a sardonically amused glance. Again, on the river bank at the town picnic, when the Preacher sets out to charm the vulnerable Willa, he and the boy battle for possession of the secret. The Preacher announces that the children's father told him where the money is, all the time watching the boy's face:

'That money's at the bottom of the river, wrapped around a twelve-pound cobblestone.'

As John inadvertently reacts to this statement which only he among the listeners knows to be false, the Preacher's eye gleams with the fact that now he, too, knows.

Perhaps the strongest and most telling scenes in the film are those which depict the Preacher and Willa on their wedding night. After looking at herself in the mirror, her expression full of love and warmth for the man she has married, Willa goes into the next room to where her new husband lies waiting in bed. On the way she disturbs his coat and hears a thud as something in the pocket knocks against the door. She takes out the switchknife, looks at it in surprise, then affectionately murmurs, 'Men'. Moments later she is the horrified recipient of a merciless harangue from the Preacher who forces her to look again at herself. This time Willa sees a different reflection in the mirror; she and the nightgown she wears are shabby and the love and warmth of her expression have fled to be replaced by the first stirrings of despair as she listens to the Preacher:

'What do you see, girl? You see the body of a woman. The temple of creation and motherhood. You see the flesh of Eve that Man since Adam has profaned. That body was meant for begetting children. It was not meant for the lust of men.'

Later, when Willa has learned too much to be allowed to live, the Preacher prepares to kill her. They are in the bedroom of the Harper home and the shot is angled so that the rafters of the room form a Gothic arch over Willa as she lies on the bed, arms crossed on her chest as she awaits her fate with saint-like acceptance. At this moment, the Preacher's head turns in a gesture already becoming familiar. He is listening to God's words. The awkward angle of the head and the accompanying raised arm creates exactly the right impression of externally controlled psychosis. A similar angle of the head accompanies the moment when, after disposing of Willa's body by sinking her and her car in the river (an act which foreshadows that in Alfred Hitchcock's *Psycho* still five years away from being made), he tells her friends that she has run away from him. One of them is confident of Willa's return: 'She'll come dragging her tail back home.' The Preacher's head angles and the eyes glitter: 'She'll not be back. I reckon I'd be safe in promising you that.'

Mitchum exercises firm control over the difficult scenes he plays with John and Pearl. The dangerous game they play in the cellar, when the children escape from him and run for the stairs, is pure farce but there is a powerful undercurrent of tension created by awareness that evil lies close beneath the surface. This evil breaks out as the children trap him in the cellar and Mitchum emits a primitive moan. The moan later becomes an animal shriek of rage as the current carries the children and their boat beyond his reach.

Startlingly, the director then contrasts the evil animality of this moment by the use of real but unthreatening animals to display the children's relatively tranquil passage along the river. As they drift along the river, close up to the camera is a spider's web from which they appear to be escaping as Pearl sings:

> Once upon a time there was a pretty fly,
> He had a pretty wife this pretty fly,
> But one day she flew away, flew away.
> She had two pretty children
> But one night these two pretty children flew away,
> Into the sky, into the moon.

This scene, and subsequent moments which show a bullfrog, rabbits and sheep, underlines the traditional peacefulness of nature. The imagery is strong, almost childlike in its boldness. Yet, because this and later passages depict the world through the eyes of John and Pearl, the imagery is exactly right.

Although off-screen, Mitchum's presence menacingly over-hangs these scenes and others that trace the children's progress along the river. Even when he is on-screen it is usually in long-shot, often photographed from a helicopter (by no means as commonplace in 1955 as it was to become). And there is a famous moment when the silhouetted image of a man on a horse is framed in the opening of a barn in which John and Pearl are hiding. For this scene a midget on a pony was used to achieve the correct perspective within the confines of the studio but the camera trickery in no way diminishes the dramatic visual effect.

Thus, whether playing emotionally powerful scenes with

Shelley Winters as the doomed widow, or a comic yet dangerous game of cat-and-mouse with either Billy Chapin as the boy or Lillian Gish as the sugar-coated old lady, Mitchum dominates the film. This dominance is such that when he is not on-screen, when his presence is merely suggested, no one can be unaware of his impact and his importance to the artistic whole.

Good as the other performances are, and Shelley Winters is exceptionally fine in the role of the repressed and doomed widow, no one succeeds in diminishing Mitchum's powerful presence. That he is able to dominate the screen in the setting of Laughton's uniquely personal film, in which haunting visual images abound, is a remarkable testimony to his ability as an actor.

Laughton's regard for Mitchum was clear from remarks he made, among them the declaration, to journalist Helen Lawrenson, that 'Bob is one of the best actors in the world.' Laughton was not only deeply impressed with the actor but also with the man himself: 'All his hip talk is a blind. He's a very fine man with wonderful manners and he speaks beautifully when he wants to. He won't thank you for destroying the tough image he's built up as a defence. In fact, he's a very tender man and a very great gentleman.'

Undoubtedly, this was one of those rare occasions when a truly imaginative director was able to develop his source material, which was in this case already strong in imagery and psychological content, by going back to the roots of the original and recreating it in his own terms. There is much that is pure Laughton: his decision to include farcical moments was potentially dangerous but in the event they work beautifully and create an entirely justifiable variation upon the book. Laughton's touch remains sure throughout the film and, contrary to Lillian Gish's assertion, the humour is not allowed to deplete the overall menace. Even when there is something to laugh at on the screen, there is never any suggestion that the children find what is happening to them anything less than terrifying. At the same time, however, Laughton does not see the need for the audience to be terrified as well. It is better that the onlooker should be afraid for the characters on the screen.

Similarly, Laughton has adjusted Davis Grubb's sometimes uneasy attitude towards the sexual content of the novel. Central to the novel's theme is the implicit undesirability in society of 'clean' sexual responses. Any suggestion of enjoyment emerging in sexual relationships is artificially repressed by labelling such sexuality as 'dirty'. Unfortunately, through

Grubb's stylistic devices, much of the purity of purpose disappears. By eschewing certain elements of the novel which unsatisfactorily attempt to draw Freudian parallels, the film improves on some moments by giving them a wider range of implications. Notable among these is John's refusal to testify against the Preacher. In the novel he does this because he refuses to look at the man and thus cannot identify him. In the film, without this underlying motivation, John's action becomes positive and can be taken as a practical assertion of a Biblical text quoted at the beginning: 'Judge not, lest ye be judged.' By acting in this way John has behaved in a truly Christian manner thus counterpointing the falsity of the Preacher's use of the Bible. It is not accidental that John simultaneously uses this moment to show that he has a truer sense of right and wrong than the mob which will later try to lynch the Preacher.

Further touches of originality from the director include his introduction of recurring visual and verbal imagery of fruit, especially apples, which serve the purpose of linking the essentially sin-free quality of nature with the harbinger of evil (the apple in the Garden of Evil).

The overall impression of the film's making is one of superb command. Laughton is constantly in control of his actors and his visual effects. The use of studio sets for some of the river scenes and the occasional deliberately unconcealed artifice never detract from the forward sweep of the narrative. The pace varies but only when the director chooses to allow it to do so. The fast-paced struggle in the cellar and the urgent chase to the river are followed by moments of apparent tranquillity as the children's boat drifts away from the menacing Preacher. Yet these moments of calm are effectively undermined as Laughton cross-cuts to the pursuer. As suggested earlier, although the children might think they are safe the audience knows that they are not. The audience's concern for the safety of the children is thus redoubled.

Stanley Cortez's cinematography and Hilyard Brown's production design make full use of the director's decision to illustrate his story in a manner which derives directly from German Expressionist cinema of the 1920s. Dramatic angling of shots, the use of tilt pans, bold use of shadow in moments of tension, elegant chiaroscuro in the more tranquil moments, all enhance the director's intentions. Although Cortez was much praised for his work on *The Magnificent Ambersons* (1942), on no other film was he allowed such free rein to his considerable technical expertise as on *The Night of the Hunter*.

Walter Schumann's score similarly adds immeasurably to the

film especially through the incorporation of 'Leaning on the Everlasting Arms' which occurs at moments almost exactly matching those in the novel. Other songs are incorporated: at the picnic the townspeople and the Preacher sing 'Bringing in the Sheaves'; there is the children's nursery rhyme sung by Pearl in the boat drifting down the river; as the children take refuge in a barn an off-screen voice sings a lullaby, 'Hush, Little One, Hush'.

Schumann's original themes for Willa and the Preacher are highly effective, especially in the scene in which Willa is murdered. There, the two motifs blend together, one gentle, the other starkly dramatic and eventually overpowering. The major chords with which the movie begins and which recur on each of the Preacher's appearances also make the final aural comment on the film, thus hinting that the peace and tranquillity with which the story ends might not be the real last chapter; after all, the Preacher is still alive. In its effectiveness, and to a certain extent in its construction within the context of the film, Schumann's score foreshadows Bernard Herrmann's later score for Hitchcock's *Psycho*.

The importance of Walter Schumann's score for the film is underlined by cinematographer Stanley Cortez, reported by Paul Mayersberg in his book, *Hollywood the Haunted House*. While Cortez was preparing the lighting for the scene in which the Preacher murders Willa, Laughton asked him what was in his mind at the time. Cortez told him that he was thinking of a piece of music, Sibelius's 'Valse Triste'. Laughton was immediately inspired to convey the scene in rhythms reflecting the waltz. He sent for Schumann, told Cortez to explain to the composer what was in his mind, and as a result the music for this scene was scored in waltz time. This musical motif was developed by Schumann in the scene in which Willa's body is shown in the river, the light striking through from the surface of the water, as her hair floats eerily to and fro as if in time to the music.

For all such important contributions, however, *The Night of the Hunter* is Charles Laughton's work. Indeed, the manner in which he encouraged the involvement of cameraman and composer in the creative process enhances rather than detracts from his superb command. His vision is a powerful and unifying presence which lifts the finished product far above the norm for the period in which it was made. The attendant quirkiness and his insistence on using wipes and other techniques many thought to be outmoded helped fuel adverse criticism at the time of its release. Effects such as, for example, the use of a right to left wipe as the Preacher slashes Willa's throat, can now be seen as the hallmarks of an authentic, if eccentrically off-beat genius.

For Robert Mitchum, the part of the malevolent Preacher was an opportunity to plunge wholeheartedly into a compelling bravura performance. In the light of the manner in which Charles Laughton played so many of his own film roles there is little doubt that Mitchum was encouraged in this by his director. Adverse criticism of Mitchum's portrayal of Preacher Harry Powell, while not widespread, levelled accusations of an absence of subtlety, the performance most commonly being described as two-dimensional. Yet, as Robin Wood points out, Mitchum's 'technically brilliant two-dimensional performance is exactly what is required – a detailed psychological portrait would surely have burdened the film unnecessarily'.

One thing can be stated without reservation: Mitchum's performance in *The Night of the Hunter* overflows with instances of understatement and subtle awareness of the needs of the part.

However, as a result of the poor initial public response, the film was not widely seen and thus barely affected Mitchum's screen career. Hindsight allows the conclusion to be drawn that this was unfortunate. Perhaps a more enlightened response to *The Night of the Hunter* by the public, and especially by the film industry's moguls, might have allowed different decisions to be taken which could have directed his career away from the arid patch through which it was to pass during the 1960s.

For all the general lack of interest in the film some critics of the day offered favourable comments. Hollis Alpert, in *Saturday Review*, felt this was 'by far [Mitchum's] best role to date'. Bosley Crowther, in *The New York Times*, stated that he 'plays the murderous minister with an icy unctuousness that gives you the chills. There is more than malevolence in his character. There is a strong trace of Freudian aberration, fanaticism and iniquity'. Gordon Gow, writing in *Films and Filming* in 1975, suggests that Mitchum's portrayal of Preacher Harry Powell was 'arguably the best of his career to date'. Even with some of the remarkable performances that were to come after Gow wrote this, it is hard to completely contradict this opinion.

The status of *The Night of the Hunter* has grown steadily in recent years, earning lavish praise during revivals in the 1980s in the Los Angeles *Reader*, the *New Yorker* and the *Village Voice*, all of which is no more than its just due.

But such praise as this came too late to be of benefit to the participants in the movie's making in 1955.

Perhaps the worst after-effect of the poor initial response to the film was the fact that Charles Laughton was never again allowed to direct. Today, long after Laughton's death in 1962, this can be seen as nothing short of a major loss to motion pictures.

Occasionally films are made which fall outside any known Hollywood genre. On some of these occasions unlikely bedfellows come together largely through accident or improbable design and are helped out by good luck, with the result that a work of unique chemistry is created. It is often such creations which afford filmgoers of many generations most enjoyment. The results of these moments of genius transcend period tastes and sensibilities; they are an aspect of the film-maker's art which cannot be confined by the calendar. *The Night of the Hunter* is such a work.

6 International Superstar

I'd rather go fishing.

Following his departure from RKO Robert Mitchum took steps by which he hoped to ensure that his career would not thereafter be misdirected by outside influences. He formed a production company with himself as its sole asset.

Mitchum's Sunset Boulevard office was staffed by Reva Frederick and Gloria Westmore who helped field the numerous ideas for productions and offers of work that poured in.

Mitchum spent his early days as would-be producer looking at various projects but with the regular RKO salary no longer coming in he soon had to find a way to keep the financial wheels oiled. That meant putting the company's only asset to work.

Early in 1955, however, Mitchum found himself harassed by press reports concerning alleged off-screen activities.

Hired to play the lead in *Blood Alley*, being made by John Wayne's Batjac production company in San Francisco, he was reported to have indulged in a little over-boisterous horseplay (which is one of the ways it was described) that ended with a member of the crew taking an unscheduled swim in San Francisco Bay. It was the first week of shooting and with little footage in the can there would clearly be only minor inconvenience to the company if they asked him to leave. Apparently prompted by director William Wellman, they did, and Wayne himself stepped in to play the lead. Reality was perhaps that Wayne's contractual obligations required him to step in; a report of a Mitchum fracas was better publicity.

Headlines of a different sort surrounded Mitchum's response to an article about him which appeared in *Confidential* magazine. Specializing in scandal about the rich and famous, the magazine displayed little regard for accuracy or truth, often simply inventing stories. They printed one such fabrication about Mitchum to which he took exception and instead of lying back and letting them roll on, as had many other stars, he hit back with a lawsuit. The case took a long time to drag to a conclusion and cost both parties a great deal of money (Mitchum's lawyer was again the high-powered and high-priced Jerry Giesler), but Mitchum's angry and successful retaliation created a precedent. Other victims of this grubby little sheet took heart and sued with the eventual result that *Confidential* disappeared from the news-stands.

A 1955 film released before *The Night of the Hunter* was a version of Morton Thompson's medical novel, *Not As a Stranger*. Thompson's novel tells the story of Lucas Marsh, a young boy who grows up to become a doctor with a dedication that is simultaneously selfless and selfish.

The screenplay picks up Luke's story when he is a student at medical school. In danger of being bounced from school through lack of funds Luke Marsh (Mitchum) marries Kristina Hedvigson (Olivia de Havilland), a nurse at the hospital, not because he loves her but because she earns enough money to support them both. After graduation Luke gradually becomes fanatical in his belief that doctors are 'superbeings', capable of doing no wrong. He takes a job with a small-town general practitioner, Dr Runkelman (Charles Bickford), has a casual affair with a patient, Harriet Lang (Gloria Grahame), and during a typhoid outbreak clashes idealistically with the head of the local hospital, Dr Snider (Myron McCormick). Kristina helps out during the emergency but cannot return to full-time nursing as she is pregnant, a condition Luke knows nothing of until after his wife has asked for a separation. Kristina's doctor is an old medical school friend of Luke's, Alfred Boone (Frank Sinatra), who tries to convince Luke that he should not treat the people close to him in the way that he does. When Luke has to perform surgery on the town doctor he makes a mistake and Runkelman dies. The combination of these events forces Luke to mend his ways and concede that he is, after all, just an ordinary human being and that he needs his friends and his wife.

In its content, *Not As a Stranger* is much like any latter-day hospital-set TV soap opera but lacks the saving grace of humour which redeemed such shows as *St Elsewhere*. Unfortunately, absence of humour is not the only thing missing, and the usual chief failing of novels translated into film applies. Instead of taking the original basic premise – the story of a man obsessed with the practice of medicine to the exclusion of all else – and building upon it a believable drama, the film's makers ended up with a tale of a man who seems to be merely petulantly selfish. Although the novel has some heavy-going patches it is possible to feel genuine sympathy for a man who is dedicated to doing good, but psychologically incapable of behaving in a socially acceptable manner. In the film, the audience would have to be masochistic to feel anything but contemptuous dislike for the man.

Even when taken at the fairly simplistic level it sets for itself, *Not As a Stranger* is an unimpressive film. This was Stanley Kramer's first directorial assignment after severing his connection with Columbia where he had worked as a producer. His direction, hampered by an overblown screenplay, fails to reach to the hearts of the characters and although the star-studded cast assembled for the venture do what they can, they often appear to be merely going through the motions.

Frank Sinatra, as Lucas Marsh's med. school pal, was then in the early stages of his 'second' film career. This was his fourth straight dramatic role and although his first, *From Here to Eternity* (1953), had brought him an Oscar he is ill at ease as a 'society' doctor. Olivia de Havilland, an actress of considerable understated skill, is up against an uneasily shaped role. In the novel, Kristina is dull and unlovely but possesses great depths of inarticulate understanding. Initially, in Luke's eyes, her only attractive quality is her money; only later does he perceive her other qualities. For Miss de Havilland to appear dull and unlovely was clearly beyond the bounds of anything short of a lobotomy followed by extensive plastic surgery. Luke's attitude towards her in the film is thus less readily acceptable.

In Morton Thompson's original conception, the role of Lucas Marsh has much that is in common with some of Robert Mitchum's successful portrayals. The loner, obsessed with an idealism that is parallel to, but slightly out of step with, the rest of society, bears links with at least half a dozen of his earlier roles. Yet, in *Not as a Stranger*, his performance never quite rings true. Certain actors come to the screen burdened by an audience's preconceptions of the roles they play. Mitchum had acquired such an iconographic reference by the time of *Out of the Past* and if, as happened with *The Night of the Hunter*, a casting completely against type can occasionally work wonders, most often it is an unequal struggle. Robert Mitchum, homicidal maniac, rang true; Robert Mitchum, dedicated surgeon, did not.

Not surprisingly, Bosley Crowther, writing in *The New York Times*, found 'the central character ... stolid [and] Robert Mitchum's portrayal flat', while the film as a whole was 'loaded with hospital lore but creeping with ponderous characters'.

The third of Mitchum's 1955 releases was *Man with the Gun*, a western that marked Sam Goldwyn Jr's production debut. The director, Richard Wilson, was also making his debut (he had previously worked with Orson Welles as an actor on radio and in films and had produced a number of unimpressive second features). Despite the presence of these tyros in the driving seat (or perhaps because of them) *Man with the Gun* is several notches above routine Hollywood western fare. The film does more than merely look good, it possesses many virtues not usually granted to westerns. For one thing, it has a literate script (by director Wilson in collaboration with N.B. Stone) and, as Sam Goldwyn Jr stated in an article in *The New York Times*, it has an 'emphasis on character, mood, and suspense'.

Performances in the film were good with Mitchum a cut above the rest as befitted his new station, for this was the first time his name had stood alone above the title. His attitude towards his work on the film also came in for some comment. In interviews, Mitchum has been consistently disparaging towards scripts, yet there are many tales (some of them self-generated) of his arriving on the set knowing not only his part but everyone else's too. Whether or not *Man with the Gun* was an exception, he certainly took it seriously. As Sam Goldwyn Jr observed, he 'came to the first day's rehearsal word perfect'.

Certainly the role of Clint Tollinger in *Man with the Gun* is in line with those characters which suit Mitchum best. Tollinger is outside the law but ultimately rises above his fellow citizens by acting in accordance with his own, higher, morality.

Reviews of the film were mixed but generally most critics felt there was rather more here than in the usual western and that Mitchum's performance was among its many assets. Curiously enough, few, if any, commentators at the time appear to have noticed the script's careful observation that the decent and respectable citizens of the town Clint Tollinger cleans up are shallow, self-righteous individuals clinging on to outmoded values. They have become pernicious parasites upon a society they seek to uphold. Had this film been made ten or fifteen years later it might well have been hailed as a perceptive analogue of the times.

Mitchum's fast-growing international box-office appeal was the main reason why Sheldon Reynolds hired him for the role of Dave Bishop in the big screen version of a successful TV series. *Foreign Intrigue* (1956), which was made in Europe with a multi-national cast and an impenetrably convoluted storyline, was not good. Indeed, most critics felt impelled to pan the movie. Bosley Crowther, in *The New York Times*, was especially savage, declaring that the film is 'a stale melodrama about a man who tries to trace the background of his mysterious employer ... it is slow, dull and the acting is downright bad ... especially

Robert Mitchum as the droopy-eyed sleuth'.

Mitchum had signed for a slice of the gross together with a partnership in Reynolds's company so he didn't come out of *Foreign Intrigue* too badly. Nevertheless, the film was a sharp dig in the ribs which reminded him that in the motion-picture industry fame and fortune can be fleeting.

Neither was the star's reputation advanced by *Bandido!* (1956). Set and shot in Mexico, this is a tale of complicated goings-on between revolutionary bandits and government forces while an American mercenary, Richard Wilson (Mitchum), flits around the edges of both camps. As with so many 'Americans in foreign wars' movies, *Bandido!* subscribed to the standard assumption that there had to be more to the mercenary's involvement than mere financial reward, but no one here, least of all Mitchum, appears to take anything very seriously. Mitchum's wasn't the only talent wasted on the film. His male co-stars, Zachary Scott and Gilbert Roland, two excellent players seldom given a chance to do anything other than perform cardboard cut-out roles, once again simply had to go through the motions.

Mitchum's next role, as Corporal Allison of the US Marines in John Huston's *Heaven Knows, Mr Allison* (1957), was very different to his others in the 1950s. Essentially a two-character story (the only other performers are the faceless Japanese invaders of a small Pacific island during World War Two), the story tells of the uneasy relationship between a tough Marine and a nun marooned together and in constant danger from starvation and death. Clearly there was potential here for heavy-handed sermonizing or just plain tasteless posturing. Much of the credit for the fact that the film falls into neither of these traps must go to Huston's direction and writing (he co-wrote the screenplay with John Lee Mahin); but, even with a good script and direction, there was still potential for crassness if the manner in which the two roles were interpreted was unsuitable.

In casting Deborah Kerr as Sister Angela, the film's makers were not taking any chances as the role was one which clearly suited her usual screen personality. On the other hand, the choice of Robert Mitchum as companion to a nun might well have seemed a dangerous gamble. In the event, it was a gamble which paid off handsomely. The mutual respect and affection the two stars found for one another gleams through and helps sustain what might well have been an uncomfortable moviegoing experience.

More in keeping with Mitchum's on-screen persona (and the off-screen person many people assume him to be) was a tale of another bar-room brawl in Tobago where the filming of *Heaven Knows, Mr Allison* took place. A sailor, on liberty from an American destroyer, took a few swings at Mitchum before the star, with evident reluctance, decided that self-defence was more important than retaining good public relations. The sailor, as recounted by Deborah Kerr in her foreword to Alvin H. Marill's *Robert Mitchum on the Screen*, quickly learned that Mitchum was at least as tough off the screen as he was on.

Heaven Knows, Mr Allison has been criticized for having severely limited potential for character development. There is some justification in this criticism as the two people are presented without backgrounds. The audience is given no more information than might be the case with a man and a woman meeting casually at a bus station or in a hotel lobby. A couple of hours later, when the audience leaves them, there is no clear indication of where they are headed and what lies in store for them. Yet, just a little thought makes it clear that this is precisely the right way to view these characters. Through the carefully introspective performances of both actors, the audience is left with a sharp impression of them at this moment in their lives. A man and a woman caught in amber, perhaps, but this admirably suits the transient nature of their relationship which is similarly suspended in time and space with no beginning and no end.

Apart from the mutual admiration of the stars, a similar response developed between Mitchum and John Huston. Mitchum has observed that 'John had so much to give, it's significant to remember that, when he was directing, there were no surprises because he had been there ... He'd done just about everything he ever wanted to attempt, and he did it with grace and some triumph'. Huston was similarly fulsome in his praise of Mitchum, declaring that he thought him to be 'one of the very great actors and that his resources as an actor have never been fully tapped. He could be a Shakespearean actor. In fact, I think that he could play King Lear.' Deborah Kerr's praise for her co-star was less hyperbolic but clearly heartfelt: 'Far from being like his image of a lazy kind of character who doesn't seem to care about anything, he was in fact extremely intelligent, and cared about so many things.'

Critically, *Heaven Knows, Mr Allison* attracted considerably more plaudits than was usually the case for a Mitchum film, although there was still critical disbelief that he was not the brawling, boozing slob the gutter press liked to depict.

'Slob' was the keyword in *Time* magazine's rather grudging review: 'even though [he] does nothing but slob around the screen, [he] has succeeded for once in carrying off his slobbing with significance'. Richard Coe, in the *Washington Post*, after first admitting that Mitchum was not one of his favourites, put him near the top of his list. None of the reviews was unkind but even the most glowing of them carried the impression of surprise. Arthur Knight, in *Saturday Review*, possibly the top rave, wrote: 'One has almost come to expect subtle, fine grained characterizations from Miss Kerr. The revelation is Robert Mitchum ... Not since the dawn of his screen career, not since his portrayal of the doomed and desperate company commander in *GI Joe* has he shown such capacity for tenderness, for understatement, and the creation of a three-dimensional, believable, likeable human being.'

Believable, likeable, three-dimensional human beings were in short supply on board ship for *Fire Down Below* (1957). Shot partly at Britain's Elstree studios and partly on location in Tobago, the film teamed Mitchum with Rita Hayworth and Jack Lemmon. On paper this was an unlikely combination and to a large extent remained that way on the screen. Most reviewers were quick to point out the awkwardly unintegrated screenplay, by Irwin Shaw, which offered half a movie of torrid romantic triangle followed by half a movie of suspenseful action.

Despite the somewhat unconvincing characterizations and the imperfectly matched halves of the film there are some good moments. This was an early dramatic role for Jack Lemmon and both he and Rita Hayworth came back on shore with some credit. Hayworth's career had been in a trough which followed her voluntary retirement to marry playboy Aly Khan. While *Fire Down Below* failed to pull Hayworth out of the trough, neither did it bury her out of sight even if the remaining years of her career saw her drifting uncomfortably towards obscurity.

The making of *Fire Down Below* was bedevilled with off-screen problems which resulted when one of Mitchum's jokes backfired. On landing on the island he was asked by the assembled press if he had anything to declare: he displayed his hand luggage and said it contained 'two kilos of marijuana and a quart of Jewish blood I've taken by transfusion so I can stay even with those guys'.

The comment angered not only the film's producers. Irving Allen, Albert R. Broccoli and Harry Cohn, but also made the US State Department decidedly uneasy. Calm was restored but not before the company hovered uneasily on the edge of expulsion.

Yet another punch-up occurred in a bar when three drunken sailors set about the star. He was well on his way to hospitalizing all three when Dorothy Mitchum entered the fray, beating her husband about the head with her shoe and yelling,

'Stop it now! You're beginning to enjoy this!'

Mitchum was at sea again for his next film, *The Enemy Below* (1957), and this time to much better effect. Produced and directed by Dick Powell, who had turned to behind the camera work after long and intermittently successful careers as singer and actor, *The Enemy Below* tells the story of two men who, although opponents in war, learn to admire and respect one another. Their admiration and respect is based not on personal knowledge (they meet only briefly at the end) but upon what each deduces about the other during a lethal cat-and-mouse game they play in the North Atlantic during World War Two.

Captain Murrell (Mitchum) is in command of a US destroyer which locates and begins to hunt a German submarine. The U-Boat is commanded by Captain von Stolberg (Curt Jurgens), a military man of the old school who dislikes the Nazis but has no serious objection to fighting a total war in the service of his country. This unlikely stereotype turned up time and time again in Hollywood's (and Britain's) war movies. Here, it is a necessary requirement of the script if the audience is to develop and retain sympathy for, and empathy with, the twin protagonists. Although enemies, both men are depicted as professional sailors and, in a real sense, brothers-in-arms. The nature of their relationship is such that it allows neither to be accurately termed antagonist, unless they can be said to alternate in that role as they become in turn hunter and hunted.

Thunder Road (1958) was the first production from Mitchum's own company, DRM Productions. The screenplay, by James Atlee Phillips and Walter Wise, is based upon a story by Mitchum who also wrote the music for the song 'Whippoorwill', sung in the movie by Keely Smith, and the lyrics of title song, 'The Ballad of Thunder Road'. Mitchum's son, James, plays the role of Robin Doolin and Mitchum himself plays the leading role of older brother Lucas Doolin. His involvement on so many levels made this by far his most personal movie to date.

Lucas Doolin is a moonshiner, constantly at war with big-time gangsters, who want to take over his homely little operation, and lawmen, who take a dim view of his illegal practices. The law objects to his defrauding the US government's coffers of revenue but given the fact that most of Doolin's time is spent fighting off one or another of his adversaries the government can't have lost too much; he barely has time left for distilling the white lightning that is the cause of all the trouble.

A Korean War veteran, Doolin tries to dissuade his kid brother, Robin, from following in his footsteps, but with so much excitement around it isn't surprising that he doesn't succeed. The excitement becomes dangerous when gang boss Carl Kogan (Jacques Aubuchon) orders one of Doolin's assistants to be killed. After knocking Kogan around a little, Doolin is captured but freed by his brother. Federal agents, led by Troy Barrett (Gene Barry), weigh in and arrest Kogan, then pursue Luke who leads them on a high-speed chase through the back lanes of this backwoods territory before crashing into an electricity transformer and coming to a messy end.

In the 1970s, this moonshiner moonshine became extremely popular (particularly a couple of films which had Burt Reynolds in the starring role) and it is an indication of the quality of Mitchum's quickly dismissed film that almost nothing has been done since which improves upon the standards he set. Indeed, *Thunder Road* scores over many of its later imitators (which, in 1975, would include Mitchum's son James in the leading role of *Moonrunners*) by depicting something of the real background of these backwoods people whose country appears to be removed a century or two in time from the rest of the United States of America.

The choice of Arthur Ripley as director seems at first glance to be an odd decision on the part of producer Mitchum. Ripley was sixty-two when *Thunder Road* was made (he was to die three years later) and had been a scriptwriting colleague of Frank Capra's in his days as a writer for silent comedy star Harry Langdon. Ripley's credits as a director were sporadic in their timing and erratic in their quality. It has been suggested (notably by critic Richard Thompson) that the choice of Ripley gave Mitchum greater control over the film's eventual shape and form than if he had employed a younger, tougher director, while at the same time removing from his shoulders the responsibility of directing (or, at least, of appearing to direct). An alternative and possibly more likely view, offered by George Eells, is that Ripley's proven ability to work quickly and cheaply appealed to Mitchum. Additionally, Ripley's known preference for concentrating upon the story told in a film and his dismissive attitude towards the star system and formula movies must have touched responsive chords in Mitchum.

Interviewed by Grover Lewis for *Rolling Stone* magazine, Mitchum acknowledged the fact that *Thunder Road* had retained an audience, observing that the movie 'was received for true, for real ... That was my original design ...' He then went on to explain why he did not write the screenplay, stating that it was something he did not feel 'qualified to do, because those dissolve-cuts and all that kind of shit are largely technical. Beyond me, and boring too'.

Whatever the behind-the-scenes reasons for who did what, *Thunder Road* emerged as a highly competent thriller, well above the usual B-movie standard. Alongside many other films Mitchum made in the 1940s and 1950s, this is one which deserves the acclaim it has begun to gather with the passage of time, even if its status as a cult movie is something which brings wry amusement to its creator.

Mitchum's next release was another war story, this time set in Korea. *The Hunters* (1958) had been made back-to-back with *The Enemy Below* but despite the presence of producer-director Dick Powell and screenwriter Wendell Mayes who had been on the earlier film, *The Hunters* only gets off the ground when the actors do. The aerial combat scenes are excellently photographed and there are a few dramatic moments when Major Cleve Saville (Mitchum) and two of the men in his command, Lt Ed Pell and Lt Abbott who drinks to overcome his fear of death (Robert Wagner and Lee Phillips), have to fight their way out of North Korea on foot. The improbable love affair between Saville and Kristina (May Britt), Abbott's wife, is tacked on awkwardly and the stitches show.

Hollis Alpert, in *Saturday Review*, commented that 'the real interest in the film lies in the shots of aerial combat which are truly impressive and which manage to keep the movie off the ground'. Disappointment at the non-aerial sequences was voiced by Isabel Quigley in the London *Spectator* who observed that there are 'some tentative but unpursued thoughts on the nature of courage and cowardice and a tentative but again unpursued romance between Robert Mitchum and May Britt'.

With the 1950s almost at an end Mitchum still had a couple of films to make. The first of these was the highly forgettable World War Two drama *The Angry Hills* (1959), in which Mitchum plays the role of Mike Morrison, an American journalist who becomes involved in a somewhat desultory fashion with the Greek resistance fighters. Alvin H. Marill quotes director Robert Aldrich as accepting responsibility for Mitchum's failure to produce a performance that was even halfway to being good. Perhaps a personality clash could account for Mitchum's lack of interest although his known reluctance to work hard on a script that didn't grip him might well have been influential. Written by A.I. Bezzerides, who had done much better work on *Track of the Cat*, the screenplay suffers from its attempt to cram in too much of the Leon Uris novel on which it is based. Nor did the coherence of the finished film benefit from twenty-five minutes of largely arbitrary cuts which Aldrich claims were inflicted upon it by the studio.

Mitchum's final film of the decade was a much better effort all round. Produced by his own company, DRM Productions, *The Wonderful Country* (1959) is a western that scores in almost every department.

Based upon the novel by Tom Lea, the story tells of an American, Martin Brady (Mitchum), who is on the run from the law and is living in Mexico. He hires himself out to two brothers, the local dictator and the army chief, Cipriano and Marcos Castro (Pedro Armendariz and Victor Mendoza). While on a gun-running mission which takes him across the border into the United States, Brady is injured and becomes amorously entangled with Ellen Coulton (Julie London), whose marriage to an army officer (Gary Merrill) is disintegrating. The Texas Rangers suspect Major Coulton of trafficking with the Castro brothers in an attempt to deprive a local Indian tribe of their land. The Rangers try persuading Brady to help them and back in Mexico Brady finds he is no longer trusted by the Castros who are now at one another's throats.

Major Coulton is commander of a troop of 'buffalo soldiers' (former black slaves) and when they are ambushed by Apaches Brady helps the few survivors to safety in Mexico where Coulton dies.

Brady's conflict with the Castros leads to Cipriano ordering his death when the American refuses to kill Marcos. Whilst being pursued by Castro's men, Brady's horse 'Lagrimas' – Spanish for tears – upon which he has hitherto bestowed his affection, is injured. Forced to shoot the animal, Brady leaves his gun beside its body and returns to the United States and Ellen Coulton.

An excellent screenplay by Robert Ardrey, which gave the actors dialogue that was both literate and realistic, was well directed by Robert Parrish. Although Parrish's career as a director has been erratic, his experience as an actor and film editor, especially his work with John Ford, make it unlikely that Mitchum selected him with a similar motive to that which drew him to Arthur Ripley for *Thunder Road*. Mitchum and Parrish had worked together before, on *Fire Down Below*, but the unevenness which characterized that film is absent here.

Critical response was good, with *Variety* describing *The Wonderful Country* as a credit to the taste of its producers. Commenting on Mitchum's performance, Alton Cook, in the *New York World Telegram and Sun*, made a remark which, in varying guises, was to appear again and again: 'He is the actor who makes no apparent effort but always remains the man in close-up.' Howard Thompson, in *The New York Times* was ecstatic, calling the film 'superior' and 'intelligent' and praising Parrish's 'beautifully paced' direction and the star who was 'ideally cast as the hard-bitten derelict hero'. It was a good note on which to end the decade.

Robert Mitchum had made twenty-five films in the 1950s of which at least eight were eminently worthy of his developing talent as a screen actor of note. In the majority of this excellent handful – *The Lusty Men, Man with the Gun, The Enemy Below, Thunder Road* and *The Wonderful Country* – he had refined still further his role as the eternal outsider. A man alone, despite the presence of others around him, a man living by rules of his own devising rather than those of society at large. But he had not been content to stay within this framework. In *Track of the Cat* he played an unsympathetic character, but one in whom he was able to imbue elements which made him understandable to the audience. In *Heaven Knows, Mr Allison* he showed himself capable of bringing warmth to the role of a man whose inarticulate sensitivity is awkwardly shielded by a tough-guy exterior. But it was in *The Night of the Hunter*, a complete break with precedent, that he had lifted the corner of a self-made curtain to reveal the extraordinary depth of his ability.

Another unexpected facet of his talent emerged in 1957 when he recorded an album of calypsos which sold well at the time but was eventually deleted. Thereafter copies changed hands for exorbitant sums which suggested the demand hadn't ended simply because the record went out of print.

In the coming decade he would make fewer films but, sadly, the reduction in quantity was to be matched by a reduction in quality. Although his earning capacity continued to grow (as did his world-wide army of fans) the 1960s would not mark a noticeable advance in his career as a screen actor. But, if the fires were dampened down, they were by no means out.

7   Into the Desert

Some idiot said, 'Ask Mitchum to play it. That bum will do anything if he's got five minutes free.' Well, I had five minutes free. So I did it.

The first few years of the 1960s saw changes in Mitchum's off-screen life. He and Dorothy decided to say goodbye to Hollywood and moved back east for the first time in twenty years. Their new home was Belmont Farms, a 300-acre spread in Talbot County, Maryland, and the calm and solitude of country life proved a welcome contrast to the hassles of moviemaking. Although Dorothy Mitchum appears to have been instrumental in making the move from Mandeville Canyon to Belmont Farms, she was soon lonely and missed the proximity of neighbours. Mitchum himself appeared to enjoy life on the farm, which bordered Chesapeake Bay, although a chronic aversion to the cold meant that there were large parts of the year when he had to move out.

If the cold sent him off on sun-seeking voyages, loneliness did not seem to trouble him and he cheerfully declared, 'In Maryland, I can be as unsocial as I like and nobody gives a damn.'

He enjoyed sailing and fishing and loved close contact with horses. For all his love of the rural life, however, Mitchum spent much of his time, especially the cold winter months, away from home making films.

His production company became Talbot Productions and under the aegis of the new company he was employed at a rate of $100,000 per film, the balance of his now customary $400,000 fee being ploughed back into the business.

Mitchum's first two roles in the new decade earned him the accolade of Best Actor of 1960 from the National Board of Review of Motion Pictures' Committee on Exceptional Films.

The first of this pair was *Home from the Hill* (1960), a story set in contemporary Texas and based upon the novel by William

Humphrey. Directed by Vincente Minnelli, and taking full advantage of CinemaScope, Technicolor, and its two-and-a-half-hour running time, *Home from the Hill* is a powerful tale of believable people, even if they are not exactly the folks next door.

Wade Hunnicutt (Mitchum) is a tough, self-orientated womanizer whose family is held together only because his wife, Hannah (Eleanor Parker), refuses to leave him on the grounds that to do so would jeopardize their son's future. The son, Theron (George Hamilton), is sheltered by his mother and this, much to Wade's chagrin, attracts ridicule from the local community. Eventually tiring of this situation, Wade sets out to toughen Theron and a part of this campaign requires that his son is taught new ways by the Hunnicutts' hired hand, Rafe Copley (George Peppard), who is also Wade's illegitimate son.

The young actors playing the roles of Wade Hunnicutt's sons were both making their first important screen appearances and both gave good accounts of themselves although George Peppard, with the more interesting part to play, attracted more attention than George Hamilton. But the film rightly belongs to Robert Mitchum. He imbues the posturing, swaggering Wade Hunnicutt with all the supposed virtues of the dominant male, then exaggerates these macho characteristics just sufficiently to achieve the film's purpose which is to reveal this kind of shallow, self-deceiving braggart for what he is. This element of Mitchum's performance was underlined latterly by Martin Auty in *Movie*, who asserted that *Home from the Hill* 'was largely misunderstood in its day but in the light of its revaluation by critics like Richard Dyer, Mitchum's role as the Texan landowner Wade Hunnicutt can now be seen as one of his most mature'.

Among those misunderstanding *Home from the Hill* in its day were John McCarten in the *New Yorker* who called it 'gamey nonsense' and commented that Mitchum played his part 'with his usual manly impassivity'. Bosley Crowther, in *The New York Times*, showed that he had lost little of the acerbity with which he customarily addressed Mitchum's films by dismissing the whole thing as 'aimless, tedious and in conspicuously doubtful taste'. Arthur Knight, in *Saturday Review*, was much more in line with the views that would emerge in later years when he commented that director Minnelli 'has a keen eye for the bits and pieces of Americana that lend a sense of verisimilitude to his people'. Of the star, Knight thought that he had 'not given a performance as good for years'.

The second 1960s film which helped Mitchum win his award

from the National Board of Review was Fred Zinnemann's *The Sundowners* (1960). Of his role in this film, which is based upon Jon Cleary's novel, Mitchum is more than usually dismissive despite the high regard in which his performance is held by most observers. Perhaps his attitude towards the film lies in the fact that, although ostensibly cast well against type, certain aspects of the persona of Paddy Carmody, the feckless itinerant of the movie, occasionally come uncomfortably close to the real Robert Mitchum.

Paddy Carmody is a sheep drover, hopelessly hooked on the aimless, wandering life of Australia's outback; his wife, Ida (Deborah Kerr), really wants to settle down and live like other people; the inclinations of the Carmodys' young son, Sean (Michael Anderson Jr), lean towards his mother's ambitions. The family drift along in their horse-drawn wagon as Paddy insists on yet another sheep drive. This time, the Carmodys are joined by an English seafarer, Venneker (Peter Ustinov), and along the way they tangle with a forest fire and, far worse for Paddy, some of their contentedly domesticated friends. Such people present a far greater threat to Paddy's wandering ways than any number of natural disasters.

Persuaded by Ida to take a temporary job as a shearer on a sheep station, Paddy buckles down and earns some money. Helped out by the earnings of Ida and Sean, both employed on the same station, the Carmodys now have enough to make a down-payment on a farm but Paddy resists and, when the shearing season is over, the Carmodys take off again on their wanderings. With the family goes Venneker, despite the fact that he has become attached to the widowed hotel-keeper, Mrs Firth (Glynis Johns). The Carmodys also have a new addition to their little clan; during a lucky gambling streak Paddy has won a racehorse. Encouraged by his father, Sean becomes adept at riding and when their horse, 'Sundowner', wins a local race Paddy thinks that he has finally solved all his problems. No more will he have to work hard, he and the family will leisurely tour the country's race tracks.

After a few successes it looks as if Paddy's dream will come true but when the family's nest-egg has grown to the point where they can afford to buy that little farm outright, Paddy gambles it all away. They still have 'Sundowner' and enter him for one more race having previously agreed that if the horse wins they will sell him to recoup their loss. The horse does win but Ida has a change of heart. Giving in to the inevitable, Ida insists that Paddy keep 'Sundowner' and together with Venneker the Carmodys continue their rootless but essentially happy life drifting around the country.

Clearly a family film, in the best sense of that term, *The Sundowners* exudes warmth without ever becoming in the least cloying. Credit for this must go to both principal players and to the direction of Fred Zinnemann. Deborah Kerr's role in *The Sundowners*, as the wife whose love transcends the disappointments brought by her devotion to her feckless husband, gives one of her finest screen performances. Too often she was cast as a poised and sophisticated lady, cool on the outside and seemingly equally chilly underneath. Yet she consistently contrived to fill these frequently two-dimensional characters with a warmth and sensitivity the screenwriters themselves had failed to supply. For her portrayal of Ida Carmody she was named Best Actress of the year by the New York Film Critics, and was unsuccessfully nominated for an Academy Award.

Robert Mitchum has claimed that he took the role of Paddy Carmody simply because he would be working opposite Deborah Kerr with whom he had formed an easy-going rapport during the making of *Heaven Knows, Mr Allison*. Whatever his motivation, he entered fully into the role of Paddy Carmody, a character who could so easily have become the kind of wastrel who excites no audience sympathy. Instead, the drifter becomes a man of depth with fragile human emotions, a man who is fundamentally incapable of taking on responsibilities. In certain elements of the Carmody character it may well be that Mitchum saw reflections of himself: the closeness of the family bonds, the warmth of his relationship with wife and children, the occasional bust-outs with a bottle, and the constant struggle between a desire for footloose freedom and the pressures of a demanding stay-at-home orthodoxy. For a man who has made such a success of showing an inquiring world an enigmatic face, this might have seemed a risky business. But, for all his later dismissive attitude towards this film, it was one of his most popular screen performances.

Henry Hart, in *Films in Review*, wrote that 'Mitchum has grown as an actor ... he projects a surprising variety of emotions, effortlessly. Mitchum deserves more critical attention than he has received.' Arthur Knight, in *Saturday Review*, commented that Mitchum and Kerr 'emerge with the smell of honest sweat and the look of unglossed reality'.

With such highpoints as *Home from the Hill* and *The Sundowners* under his belt, the 1960s appeared to be off to an auspicious start, but the early promise was not to be achieved again, except in odd moments in generally inferior films.

The next release, *The Night Fighters* (1960), was well below the high standard Mitchum's own company, DRM Productions, had set for itself in the late 1950s. Any film which deals with such a contentious subject as the 'Troubles' in Ireland, and in particular with the IRA, is destined to receive ultra-cautious critical reappraisal from the standpoint of the early 1990s. Even such a superbly wrought classic of the cinema as *Odd Man Out* (1947) requires the latter-day critic to exercise the utmost care in assessing the motivation of the characters. When a film falls well short of the extremely high standards set by *Odd Man Out*, it is almost impossible to remain completely detached. *The Night Fighters* is irredeemably below this level.

Mitchum was far from blind to the film's faults. The script he saw when he agreed to make *The Night Fighters* had somehow disappeared by the time he arrived in Ireland. He disliked the new script but with the actors and crew standing ready, the businessman in him allowed financial considerations to overrule artistic judgement. This was unfortunate and Mitchum's decision to proceed can now be seen as a mistake. The revised screenplay lost sight of the intrinsic worth of Arthur Roth's *A Terrible Beauty*, the novel on which it is based.

With *The Grass is Greener* (1960), Mitchum stepped into a very different role. Indeed, this film, written by Hugh and Margaret Williams and based upon their stage play, was a new departure for him. A sophisticated, very British drawing-room comedy, *The Grass is Greener* again co-starred Mitchum with Deborah Kerr and Jean Simmons, both of whom were comfortably at home in this kind of confection. The leading role was taken by Cary Grant whose sustained elegance fitted neatly into the overall atmosphere. That Mitchum stuck out a little awkwardly, at least at first, can be gleaned from a story recounted by Mike Tomkies. When the wardrobe man began taking special care to have his shirts starched because 'Mr Grant likes them to look crisp on you', Mitchum sardonically observed, 'That's right, Cary doesn't want any dirty people in his film. I ain't neat.'

As so often happens with stage plays, *The Grass is Greener* failed to transfer convincingly to the screen. Critics and audiences alike were less than enthusiastic and of the four principals Mitchum undoubtedly came off worst, perhaps because he was the most obvious target for their displeasure. On this occasion the negative response was largely justifiable; Mitchum, the archetypal loner, really wasn't at home in a British drawing-room.

Mitchum could have gone back to more familiar territory with his next film, had he chosen to take up an interesting offer. The role he had played in *Home from the Hill* was supposedly written

with Clark Gable in mind, and Alvin H. Marill suggests that to
counter this Mitchum was offered the role Gable eventually
played in John Huston's *The Misfits* (1961). After turning this
part down, Mitchum instead made *The Last Time I Saw Archie*, a
service-life comedy, bordering on farce, which seems an unusual
preference over *The Misfits*. At script stage, however, the Huston
film had not looked right to the actor. Given the eventual nature
of *The Misfits*, the impressive manner in which it was directed,
and superb performances by Gable, Marilyn Monroe, Montgomery Clift and Eli Wallach, the chances are that Mitchum
would have blended in well. In the event, it is perhaps fitting
that Gable made the film, crowning his career with one of his
most striking roles. He died a few weeks after production ended
and before the film was released.

The Last Time I Saw Archie* (1962) casts Mitchum as Archie Hall,
a con-man who turns military bureaucracy on its head when the
US Army is foolish enough to draft him. Mitchum showed that
he had a deft touch with this kind of free-wheeling comedy.
Nevertheless, perhaps due to the improbable teaming of
Mitchum and Jack Webb, who also produced and directed, the
film met with little favourable response at either the box-office or
at the hands of the critics. A contributory factor might well have
been the ingrained stoicism of Webb (the taciturn star of US
TV's *Dragnet*); next to such granite immobility even the
customarily laid-back Mitchum looked as if he were plugged
into the light socket.

Mitchum's next film, *Cape Fear* (1962), was a psychological
shocker which simultaneously harked back to the earlier *film
noir* genre while looking ahead to the 'shock for the sake of
shocking' movies that were yet to come.

Max Cady (Mitchum) is a violent but cunning psychopath
who comes out of prison intent on revenge against the lawyer
he believes to be responsible for his incarceration, Sam Bowden
(Gregory Peck). Cady also threatens physical violence against
Bowden's wife, Peggy, and daughter, Nancy (Polly Bergen and
Lori Martin), and if rape isn't mentioned it is certainly implied.
Cady terrorizes the Bowdens but never steps outside the law
and Chief Dutton (Martin Balsam), the head of the local police
force, is unable to intercede. As a precautionary measure, Cady
has even hired another lawyer, Grafton (Jack Kruschen), to
protect his civil rights. Bowden's concern for his wife and
daughter grows and he hires private detective Sievers (Telly
Savalas) to help him. Eventually despairing that the law he
represents and has sworn to uphold is capable of protecting
himself and his family, Bowden takes direct steps to remove the

threat hanging over him. After provoking Cady into an attack, Bowden overpowers him and the psychopath is sent back to prison.

In its essence the storyline of *Cape Fear* has much going for it. There is the oft-used theme of a family under threat which is thus forced together in mutual protection from which it will supposedly gain in strength. Then there is the element of psychological disturbance available for examination and analysis. Above all there is the classic dilemma of a man who lives by the law, whose life *is* the law, but who finds himself in a situation from which escape is possible only by taking the law into his own hands. This is the most interesting of the elements in *Cape Fear*.

Today, more than a quarter of a century after *Cape Fear* was made, this dilemma is much more relevant to the times but this does not excuse the fact that here it is given only a passing nod. The film acknowledges that the dilemma is there but it offers neither a solution nor even guidance.

Unfortunately, few other aspects of the film are adequately explored. The Bowden family is insufficiently developed at the outset for total identification. They are not noticeably drawn together at an emotional level by the crisis, nor are they forced to re-examine their own motives or lifestyle, for they never appear to question their values. Neither particularly good people nor particularly bad, but just ordinary, the Bowdens come through these traumas unchanged by their experiences. They will, it seems, go on just as before.

The psychotic Max Cady is not sufficiently well developed to allow an audience to understand what drives him. The simple presentation of a totally evil character is usually an inadequate cinematic device; witness countless puerile latter-day shockers about murderous lunatics wreaking bloody havoc on small-town America. Fear through shock may be effective in the cinema but it is an effect which wears off leaving no trace. Fear created through an awareness that the evil which has caused the shock may lie buried within everyone, even oneself, remains long after the lights have gone up again.

All this, however, is what *Cape Fear* might have been. It actually *is* a gripping, occasionally shocking, tense melodrama played out against the gloomy backcloth of rural Georgia (where it was filmed). Gregory Peck's performance is adequate but he brings to any role a suggestion of command which here is slightly unsettling. Peck's production company, Melville, was in partnership with Mitchum's Talbot, a factor which perhaps encouraged Peck to play the role of the intimidated lawyer. It may be that an actor with a weaker screen presence would have served the story better; it certainly would have given the final reversion of roles greater bite had the lawyer been a meek and mild individual seemingly unlikely to respond with savage violence however much he was provoked. Here there is never much doubt that, evil and menacing though Max Cady may be, Gregory Peck's Sam Bowden will triumph in the end.

The minor roles are all performed adequately. Telly Savalas, then at the beginning of his film career (*Cape Fear* was his third screen role) does not have the same impact he had in *Birdman of Alcatraz* which was released the same year and for which he was nominated for an Oscar. A few of the actors perform with finesse. In this category falls Martin Balsam's performance. Indeed, he is an actor who, like Claude Rains, never gives a poor account of himself and who can impart reams of character description with the flicker of a shifty eye.

Given the thin development of Max Cady within the confines of the screenplay, Robert Mitchum's performance is unsettlingly intense. At a surface level, it is possible to discern similarities between this role and that of the Preacher in *The Night of the Hunter* although there is much less depth to the *Cape Fear* character. Comparisons with other roles apart, his Max Cady is always effective and there are moments, as when he crawls up the river bank towards the end, in which he exudes an almost palpable menace few other actors could achieve.

Overall, *Cape Fear* is exciting, suspenseful and brisk. Well directed by British-born J. Lee Thompson, it is the kind of film which bears favourable comparison with recent and frequent exercises in personal law enforcement and in some respects improves upon many by giving the villain of the piece as much screentime as the hero rather than leaving him a faceless cipher who is there only to be blown away in a dark alley.

Raymond Durgnat, in *Films and Filming*, called the film an 'expert impersonal American thriller ... Thompson gets a remarkably solid unsentimental performance out of Gregory Peck and Robert Mitchum ...' In *Saturday Review*, Arthur Knight wrote: 'As the vengeful killer Robert Mitchum proves again that given the opportunity he can be a resourceful performer ... his heavy-lidded eyes and petulant mouth here convey a depth of evil that is truly frightening'. Bosley Crowther of *The New York Times* remarked that 'Mitchum plays the villain with the cheekiest, wickedest arrogance and the most relentless aura of sadism that he has ever managed to generate'.

The fans liked it too, and although Gene Ringgold in *Films in Review* considered it to be a 'can of garbage', the film is one which bears re-examination today. A present-day screening of *Cape Fear* would also make the British censor's insistence on cuts before its initial screening even more impenetrable than it was at the time of the film's original release.

Next, Mitchum popped up in Darryl F. Zanuck's *The Longest Day* (1962), but with more than forty stars in the cast it isn't surprising that his portrayal of Brigadier General Norman Cota is only a cameo role. What he does with the role is effective enough but the breadth, scope and sweep of the film is too great to allow any individual to make an enormous personal contribution. Unusually enough for Hollywood's epic war movies, *The Longest Day* stays reasonably close to the facts of the real D-Day, the operation which marked the Allied armies' invasion of Europe in World War Two on that fateful day, Tuesday 6 June 1944.

The end result is not only an excellent, understated account of events in Normandy but it proved to be a hugely successful money-spinner.

There was no danger of Mitchum being lost in a crowd of extras in his next film because *Two for the Seesaw* (1962) was virtually a two-hander. Based upon William Gibson's stage play, the story tells of an out-of-town lawyer, Jerry Ryan (Mitchum), who comes to New York City when his marriage is about to end. He meets up with a dancer, Gittel Mosca (Shirley MacLaine), and the two drift into an affair which is at times more for mutual consolation than a full-blown love match. Jerry seems unable to shake his wife out of his system and drives Gittel back to an old flame. When the ensuing bust-up puts Gittel into hospital with an ulcerated stomach, Jerry is suitably dismayed, but when she suggests they should marry when his divorce is finalized he has to confess that the divorce is already final. Gittel has enough insight to realize that Jerry hasn't the conviction to carry through his affair with her and she ends the relationship. Jerry decides to return home but before he leaves New York he admits to Gittel that he loves her.

In *Two for the Seesaw*, there was no need for additional special 'screen only' techniques and director Robert Wise chose to shoot the story straight with only marginal concessions to the fact that he was working on film and not within the confines of a proscenium arch. For the most part, his decision appears to have been right.

Shirley MacLaine's performance is excellent, with the forced kookiness which mars some of her screen roles well in check. Indeed, it was the promise of her presence in the film that initially motivated Mitchum to agree to appear. In the event, rumours soon abounded that the co-stars were much more than just good friends and, for once, Dorothy Mitchum appears to have taken serious exception to her husband's periodic way-wardness.

From the account in brother John Mitchum's autobiography, the affair had affected Shirley MacLaine more deeply than Robert expected. When she later received a beautifully worded but seemingly ambiguous note from her co-star she took it to John who had seen such things before. He told her it was a kiss-off. 'That son of a bitch!' she yelled, hurling one of her shoes at the TV set on which there happened to be one of Robert's films.

Contrastingly, George Eells's account of these events, in his biography of Mitchum, suggests that the star was more deeply involved with Shirley MacLaine than was usual with his off-screen flirtations with on-screen co-stars. Conflict between Mitchum and his wife continued throughout 1963 and into the following year and overlapped several other film roles he played, including another one opposite MacLaine. But, eventually, harmony was restored to the Mitchums' remarkably durable marriage.

However hot the Mitchum-MacLaine relationship might have been, *Two for the Seesaw* was merely cool and, at best, the critical views only lukewarm. *Variety* felt that 'the basic flaws appear to be the play's innate talkiness and the unbalance of the two-way "Seesaw".' *Cahiers du Cinéma* considered that the movie brought 'no surprises but confirms the polish of Robert Wise's style (the perfect heir of the Hollywood of the Thirties). It brings to its culmination, despite the timid daring of the dialogue, a type of sentimentality which, since Griffith, has not ceased to permeate the American public. Mitchum and MacLaine really are victims and their passivity is never in doubt. One would almost think that they had been put on this earth solely to worry their heads from dawn to dusk.'

It is this indecisiveness in the character of Jerry Ryan that most critics felt to be out of keeping with Mitchum's familiar screen persona. Alton Cook, in the *New York World Telegram and Sun*, summed up for most of them: 'You can't really believe he would stand around so long with his thumb in his mouth. [He] radiates too imperious a character to have patience for this prolonged and futile discussion.'

Such comments underline the fact that at this stage of his career Mitchum was apparently too close in time to his early hard-nosed screen portrayals to permit all but the most perceptive of critics to see in him the sensitive human being he carefully concealed from public view.

Mitchum is recorded by Mike Tomkies as being particularly scathing in his view of critics, especially those based in New York City, for their generally negative response to *Two for the Seesaw*. 'They are guilty of intellectual snobbery,' he said. 'With them nothing can be done in Hollywood or anywhere as well as in their home town it seems. If you play it the same way as on stage they say the mediums are different and you should have played it with a fresh approach. If you play it with a fresh approach they accuse you of painting a rose red, especially if the stage actor received a few awards.'

Mitchum played another cameo role in *The List of Adrian Messenger* (1963), a supposedly suspenseful thriller directed by John Huston. *The List* contained a number of devices designed to keep audiences guessing although some of them served merely to irritate. Among the red herrings are guest appearances by Mitchum, Tony Curtis, Burt Lancaster, Kirk Douglas and Frank Sinatra, all of whom were made up to look as unlike themselves as the make-up department could manage. As a device, this leaves the rankling thought that if the make-up was as good as intended then there was surely no need to hire big names in the first place. Unless, perish the thought, it was just a gimmick to drag a few unsuspecting souls into cinemas.

Rampage (1963) came next and this proved to be another film well below its star's acknowledged level. Produced by Mitchum's own Talbot Productions, *Rampage* is something of a throwback to earlier days when Hollywood could get away with anything just so long as there was a lion or tiger around to convince the credulous that they were really in darkest Africa and not on a studio backlot. Actually, *Rampage* is set in Malaya and was filmed in Hawaii but, apart from the money and the trip to Hawaii, it did none of its participants much good. *Monthly Film Bulletin* was moved to comment that 'one of the remarkable things about [it] is that it is possible to see animals act badly'.

Mitchum's next role took him out of the jungles of Malaya and into British India at the end of World War Two. In real terms it took him to England's Elstree studios where *Man in the Middle* (1964) was made. The screenplay, by Keith Waterhouse and Willis Hall, was based upon Howard Fast's novel, *The Winston Affair*. A fairly orthodox courtroom drama, the story tells of a manically racist American soldier, Lieutenant Winston (Keenan Wynn), who murders a British soldier whom he believes to have 'defiled' the white race by having sex with a local girl.

The case puts American and British troops at loggerheads and a court-martial is hastily set up. General Kempton (Barry Sullivan) orders Lt.-Colonel Barney Adams (Mitchum) to defend

Winston but indicates that he expects the verdict to be guilty, and cast-iron at that. Adams soon realizes that there is no question about guilt here, his client did commit murder, but he learns that Winston is a known psychopath and that a report from an army doctor, Major Kaufman (Sam Wanamaker), which unequivocally says so has been suppressed by the top brass. Adams's hopes that he has favourable witnesses are forestalled by postings to far-distant camps but he persists with his attempts to prove his client's insanity. In the end Winston cracks up in court and although his guilt is proved, not that it was ever in doubt, so too is his insanity and he is therefore saved from execution.

The film was generally criticized for its lack of tension, a surprising failing for a courtroom drama which contains all the elements needed for a taut suspense story. Isabel Quigley, in the *Spectator*, was more amiably disposed than most, remarking that 'the film persuades us that justice alone is what counts and even keeps us in suspense and a pleasurable degree of semi-surprise'.

Changes made to the concept of the original novel cannot have helped the credibility of the screenplay. In the book Winston's bigotry is interwoven with his conviction that he is the victim of plots to demean and destroy him and the trigger which provoked the murder of which he is guilty has its origins in his latent homosexuality.

The film also changed the nature of the brief romantic liaison which Barney Adams encounters. In the novel Barney has a one-night stand with Kate Sorenson, a Swedish-American, with whom he is able to unburden himself. The relationship in the novel is awkward and barely credible (it is as if the author didn't really want such a relationship in the book but felt obliged to put it there); in the film it is no less incredible and the shift to an inter-racial affair (the girl becomes Kate Davray and is played by France Nuyen), is uneasy although in keeping with the film's theme.

Performances in the film are never less than good. The large cast contains many solid British (and British-resident) players but the acting honours go to Mitchum, Keenan Wynn and Trevor Howard as Major Kensington, a caring physician. Especially good as the deranged racist, Wynn for once had a part that used his barely suppressed volatility to good effect. As for Howard, later Mitchum would cheerfully admit that the veteran British actor stole every scene they did together right from under his nose.

Mitchum's predilection for working again with people he'd enjoyed working with in the past drew him into *What a Way to*

Go! (1964), a spoof movie which was merely splashy where it should have been frothy. Directed by J. Lee Thompson, with whom Mitchum had made *Cape Fear*, and starring Shirley MacLaine, the film is actually a six-part episodic romp through America's fantasyland. Married in turn to six husbands, Louisa Foster (MacLaine) rises from poor girl to rich widow through the plot contrivance of her husbands dying in bizarre accidents. Mitchum played Rod Anderson, husband number three (the others were Paul Newman, Dean Martin, Gene Kelly, Bob Cummings and Dick Van Dyke); Mitchum was also number three in the billing, behind MacLaine and Newman.

What a Way to Go! was never in danger of offending anyone but was out of step with what audiences wanted and consequently enjoyed only limited success.

With the 1960s half-way through, Mitchum had added a further dozen films to his screen credits. In the first two of these, *Home from the Hill* and *The Sundowners*, he performed with distinction. Of the remaining ten, only *Cape Fear* carries a performance that approached his earlier high standards. Financially, he was still big at the box-office; indeed, he was growing in stature as many of his contemporaries flagged, died, or were overwhelmed by a new, younger and different generation of actors.

In some respects the poor quality of the films of this parched period did not matter and hindsight certainly aids this view. As Roger Ebert has commented, 'You can see Mitchum in bad movies, but you can never spot him being bad'.

For all this latter-day reassurance, however, at the time he was not, artistically speaking, in the best of health. The artistic boost his career needed, and merited, was still a few years away. He still had to face the second half of a decade in which he entered the male screen actor's no-man's land. Too old to play romantic, free-wheeling adventurers, he was not yet old enough to play (or, rather, to be asked to play) character roles. As for character parts that were simultaneously leading roles, no one in Hollywood appeared to think that this was a route along which Robert Mitchum could follow in such glittering footsteps as those taken by Spencer Tracy.

As any self-respecting Mitchum fan could have told them, the Hollywood moguls were wrong – but they didn't know it yet.

Record company producers had also failed to get it right. Some time after the mild success of Mitchum's calypsos he again went into the recording studios, this time to sing some countrified music including his 'Ballad of Thunder Road'. A little while later he recorded a song he first suggested Dean

Martin should record. Martin wasn't interested so Mitchum sang the amiably nondescript song in his amiable, not-so nondescript baritone. The record was a success but the company didn't bother to promote it too much. Later still, Dean Martin changed his mind and, helped by eager promotion, 'Little Old Wine Drinker Me' became not only a big hit but synonymous with the singer.

With a little foresight Mitchum might have had a fairly successful, if short, sideline career as a singer. He certainly could have done with it because his next few years in the motion-picture studios found him still adrift in an artistic, critical and commercial wasteland.

8 Parched Times

I wouldn't give a darn if I lost my acting job tomorrow. This movie business is such nonsense.

Although the problem surrounding his friendship with Shirley MacLaine had retreated, relations between Robert Mitchum and his wife were reportedly cool. In April 1964 Dorothy announced that she wanted to sell the farm in Maryland and return to the West Coast. Mitchum didn't argue and at first they rented a house at Malibu, but also acquired a small ranch so that he could keep his quarter-horses.

It was during this period that Mitchum made the first of two visits to the troops in Vietnam. Following these visits, Mitchum expressed complex and generally enlightened views on the nature of a society which allowed its young men to be sacrificed in an unwanted (and largely unwarranted) war.

In Vietnam he talked with troops, drank with them, entertained with tall stories, sang a few songs, and generally conveyed the impression that they were not a forgotten army.

On his return to the USA he didn't simply shrug off his visit as he stepped from the plane. Instead, as George Eells recounts, despite acute physical exhaustion, he immediately began a long string of telephone calls to the relatives of many of the soldiers with whom he had spent a few moments, thus bringing them precious contact.

In his 1973 conversation with *Rolling Stone's* Grover Lewis he expounded his belief that a major contributory factor to the war was the lack of knowledge the American public had about it. 'I believe that everyone in the world should have at least the privilege of knowing what's happening all at the same time. One thing I've learned is that the greatest ... slavery is ignorance, and the biggest commodity is ignorance – the dissemination of ignorance, the sale and burgeoning marketing of ignorance.'

Clearly such thoughts were close to his beliefs and in an

interview with Dermott Purgavie of the London *Daily Mail* around the same time he repeated much of the foregoing, expanding into criticism of the imbalance in ownership of wealth: 'While the Du Pont family has a whole wing of a Washington hospital reserved for them in case any of them gets ill, humanity is facing a world crisis. Why the hell can't we get it together?'

A year later, in February 1967, he was back in Vietnam, once again visiting troops and bringing them his own brand of cheer, even though his doctor had advised against a return visit quite so soon.

Mitchum's outspoken support for the troops on the ground was later taken to indicate a right-wing attitude towards the war in Vietnam. It appears to have been yet another in a long catalogue of misunderstandings. It is possible to feel empathy with ground soldiers without supporting the political manipulations which have put them where they are.

After his first Vietnam trip Mitchum undertook a tour of a different kind. He has rarely engaged in publicity for his films (he frequently claims never to have seen the finished products of his many years in the business) but he made a rather surprising exception in the case of *Mister Moses* (1965).

This film, based on a Max Catto novel, is the tale of a quack doctor who unwillingly leads a native tribe through many hazards to a new homeland.

Joe Moses (Mitchum) is dunked in the river by some Africans who are less than delighted with the 'remedies' he has sold them. He is fished out by Julie Anderson (Carroll Baker), the daughter of a missionary (Alexander Knox). Julie takes Joe to a village that is about to be flooded during the construction of a dam which is expected to make life better for many, even if the few who live here have to suffer. The villagers, whose ancestral homeland this is, believe that they are on the raw end of the deal and refuse to move. The District Commissioner, Robert (Ian Bannen), threatens to use force whereupon the head man of the village (Orlando Martins) takes it into his head that Joe Moses will repeat his considerably more illustrious namesake's Biblical journey and lead them all to a new home, a home which will be their Promised Land.

Joe, whose character Mitchum defined as 'strictly a bum, an itinerant con-man', is somewhat less than enthusiastic at the prospect but Julie has discovered that he supplements his income with a little diamond smuggling and threatens to hand him over to the DC if he won't co-operate. Ubi (Raymond St

Jacques), an American-educated African, takes exception to Joe's intended role in his people's fate and threatens to expose him as the charlatan he really is.

Unwillingly, Joe Moses starts out on his epic journey but despite an updated parting of the waters (through crafty use of the dam's sluice gates rather than divine intervention) he encounters much less success than his ancient predecessor. Eventually, however, the natives are safely ensconced in their new lands and Joe departs with the connivance of the DC who has learned of his smuggling activities but is prepared to turn a blind eye. Julie, whose attitude towards Joe has all along been one of much less than religious awe, follows him into the bush.

Given the tale's heavy dependence upon the Africans being naïvely credulous it is hardly surprising that the movie drew attacks for its implied (and in certain scenes, explicit) racism. Paule Sengissen, writing in *Cahiers du Cinéma*, declared: 'Brutally racist, this film is an insult to every Christian and to every man with a black skin.' In condemning *Mister Moses* for its racism, Sengissen has taken exception to what appears to be a throwback to those 1930s and 1940s movies, which poured out of Hollywood (and Britain too), which saw black Africans as superstitious savages.

With *Mister Moses* out of the way, Mitchum then turned to the first of a string of westerns which would occupy most of his time during the rest of the decade.

There isn't a great deal of originality in the plot of *El Dorado* (1966); director Howard Hawks had made this same story once before, as *Rio Bravo* (1959), and would make it once again, as *Rio Lobo* (1970). In all three versions, the lead is played by John Wayne. In *El Dorado* Wayne is Cole Thornton, a gunfighter who is hired by cattle-baron Bart Jason (Edward Asner) to help out in a range war. The local sheriff turns out to be Cole's old buddy J.P. Harrah (Mitchum), who has fallen into bad ways by courtesy of the ol' demon rum. After being wounded, Cole bows out of the war but later learns that Bart Jason has hired another gunslinger (Christopher George) who is making trouble for everyone, not least Harrah who is now well and truly in his cups.

Accompanied by a gambler named Mississippi (James Caan), Cole rides to the rescue, sobers up the sheriff and with the help of old Bull Thomas (Arthur Hunnicutt) sets out to clean up the bad guys. After a couple of minor plot complications the good guys triumph over evil and the two old friends, Cole and Harrah, both half-crippled, prove that two old buddies are more than a match for any number of younger men. In the process,

Wayne and Mitchum, by now somewhat mature themselves (60 and 50 respectively), also prove a match for the younger actors in the movie.

No one takes *El Dorado* too seriously; in substantial parts of the movie fun takes precedence over action and even the action draws some intended laughs. Howard Hawks, interviewed in *Cahiers du Cinéma*, confirmed the impression of a good-humoured relationship between the two stars: 'Mitchum and Wayne hit it off together very well. They liked each other: it was easy for them to work together, there was mutual respect and they never tried to steal each other's scenes … It was the first time I'd worked with Mitchum and he's a very, very good actor. He's got no limitations – he can do almost anything. I've always thought he was droll, that he'd be good in a comic role. And he proved it to me in this film without trying to be [funny].'

Arthur Knight, in *Saturday Review*, confirms the view that the participants enjoyed a good working relationship in his review of the finished movie: 'Instead of action, the film proffers a rather pleasing, rough and ready humour – a man to man joshing – that goes on between all of the cast.'

Certainly the atmosphere of *El Dorado* is amiable and entertaining. Nothing is taken too seriously, although the mechanics of the film itself are taken very seriously indeed by a bunch of true professionals before the cameras and in all off-screen capacities.

Writing in the *Spectator*, Penelope Houston waxed lyrical, commenting at one point that while the film appeared a touch old-fashioned, 'it capitalizes superbly on the feeling that everyone around has been there before … Wayne and Mitchum ride their parts as they now do their horses – a bit of an effort to get up but once in the saddle as safe as houses … The pleasures of *El Dorado* are essentially good-tempered and reminiscent.'

Among the bit players in *El Dorado* is Mitchum's brother, John, who had also had a bit part in *The Way West*. When Hawks made the third version of *El Dorado*, as *Rio Lobo*, the part of the gambler was played by Mitchum's son, James.

After *El Dorado* Mitchum made *The Way West* (1967), a big, sprawling film which, although based upon A.B. Guthrie's Pulitzer Prize-winning novel, owes more to Hollywood's history of the great westward migration than to reality. Visually, the film is superb but the many sub-plots interwoven with the main storyline are old hat to any member of the contemporary audience who had watched a random half-dozen episodes of TV's *Wagon Train*.

The central performances are adequate, given the cardboard

The self-centred 'Lucas Marsh' in *Not as a Stranger* (1955)
ignores Frank Sinatra's advice and marries for money.

Deborah Kerr prays for survival but 'Corporal Allison' has a
more earthly solution as he prepares to defend her in
Heaven Knows Mr Allison (1957).

Only temporary, maybe, but for 'Lucas Doolin' the white lightning game is over as he is frisked by Gene Barry in *Thunder Road* (1958).

For once *The Sundowners* (1960) look like having four walls and a roof to protect them from the elements. From left: Michael Anderson Jr, Deborah Kerr, Peter Ustinov, 'Paddy Carmody', Glynis Johns.

Taking direction from Fred Zinnemann during the making of *The Sundowners* (1960) while Australian actor Chips Rafferty wonders when it will be his turn for a glass of beer.

'Dermot O'Neill' helps his wounded comrade, Richard Harris, in *A Terrible Beauty* (1960).

Back to back in *The Grass is Greener* (1960) so that Cary Grant cannot see any stains 'Charles Delacro' might have on his shirts.

Producer-director Jack Webb smiles for once at con-man 'Archie Hall', a picture of innocence that doesn't fool France Nuyen and Martha Hyer for one moment in *The Last Time I Saw Archie* (1961).

A night out at the bowling alley turns sour for Gregory Peck and Lori Martin when 'Max Cady' arrives at *Cape Fear* (1962).

cut-out nature of the roles. Although subordinate to Kirk Douglas and Richard Widmark, Mitchum's performance drew some of the better responses from critics with Bosley Crowther, in *The New York Times*, offering a left-handed compliment: 'Robert Mitchum, droopy-eyed and surly ... views the whole silly business with contempt.' Hollis Alpert, in *Saturday Review*, thought Mitchum 'the most convincing of all the players'.

Leaving the nineteenth-century wild west for a spell, Mitchum travelled to Europe to play the role of Dick Ennis, a war correspondent, in a World War Two drama, *The Battle for Anzio* (1968). Ostensibly an anti-war epic, the film suffers from a general failing to observe the fine line that must be drawn between 'gung–ho' tales and those that purport to convey a message running counter to the action taking place on the screen. Although director Edward Dmytryk should have been more than capable of finding that dividing line and staying on the right side of it, here the effect is rather cloudy. Perhaps the film's mixed origins were at fault: made in Italy, with a string of American 'names' including Robert Ryan, Peter Falk and Arthur Kennedy topping the bill with Mitchum, but with a largely Italian crew and cast, *Anzio* is always uncertain. Coming as it did at a politically crucial and delicate stage of America's involvement in Vietnam, *Anzio* tries hard to be all things to all men. This characteristic was doubtless fuelled by the Italian involvement – they were, after all, on the other side of the conflict being filmed – and ultimately succeeds in being of little meaning or value to anyone.

Mitchum did what he had to do in the film, collected his fee, and went back to America to face the cameras in another western.

Five Card Stud (1968) is more a whodunnit (or, rather, a who-gets-it-next) than an orthodox western. Mitchum, as Jonathan Rudd, a black-garbed preacher who is niftier with a gun than a Bible, comes to town soon after a man is lynched for allegedly cheating at cards. One by one, the other card-players have their aces trumped in increasingly unpleasant ways as a murderous avenger moves among them. Needless to add, things are not quite as obvious as they might seem at first sight along the barrel of the preacher's Colt ·45.

Villa Rides! (1968) was a better effort, just so long as the use of the real-life Mexican revolutionary's name didn't lead anyone into supposing this was anything more ambitious than a competent if routine western. Briskly directed by Buzz Kulik from a screenplay by Sam Peckinpah and Robert Towne, *Villa Rides!* is mostly undemanding but exciting hokum with

Mitchum cast as Lee Arnold, an aeroplane-owning gun-runner. There is much killing, most of which demands that too much attention isn't paid to the questionable morality of killing for 'good' reasons.

Mitchum strolls through the movie with his customary nonchalance but *Villa Rides!* did nothing to revive an artistically parched period in his career.

From Pancho Villa's Mexico (the film was actually shot in Spain) Mitchum travelled to England to make *Secret Ceremony* (1968) for Joseph Losey. A strange tale to begin with, several rewrites and last-minute changes failed to help matters much and this odd account of sexual relationships never really works. Sporting an improbable beard and taking third billing beneath his two female co-stars, Elizabeth Taylor and Mia Farrow, Mitchum, as Albert, has little to do and although his performance is adequate there is about him a perpetual air of puzzlement as if he is really wondering what the script is all about. This isn't too surprising as changes were made to the screenplay after shooting began and Mitchum was suddenly axed from a couple of scenes he had already made. These scenes were reshot and instead of Mia Farrow licking his neck while he lies in a bath, it is Elizabeth Taylor's neck which gets the treatment. At least these changes allowed Mitchum to add material to his ever-growing arsenal of tall tales for journalists: 'Just after we made *Secret Ceremony*, lesbianism came in. Maybe that's why they reshot the scene. I'm no damn good as a lesbian. I'll play anything else, but not that.'

By contrast with the globe-trotting presently demanded by his career, the Mitchums now settled into a new home. They had moved from Malibu to Brentwood but none of the family, least of all Mitchum, were too impressed with the new place and, as neither he nor Dorothy liked the idea of leasing, they decided to look for a house to buy. Eventually, they settled for a house on Saint-Pierre Road in Bel-Air.

Settled domestically, Mitchum also settled back into the saddle for his last two films of the 1960s.

The first of these westerns, *Young Billy Young* (1969), was routine in plot, direction (by Burt Kennedy) and performances, although the leads, Mitchum and Angie Dickinson, came out several points ahead of the rest of the cast. Film buffs had a field day spotting the offspring of several big names of past movie times as they came on to the screen, played their scenes and drifted off again. Robert Walker Jr, an uncanny look-alike of his father; Deana Martin, daughter of Dean; and David Carradine, son of John, didn't put up too much opposition to the older hands.

The second of the two westerns Mitchum made as the decade drew to a close was a much better effort.

The Good Guys and the Bad Guys (1969) was directed by Burt Kennedy (in much more confident form than he'd been on *Young Billy Young*) from a multi-layered screenplay by Ronald M. Cohen and Dennis Shryack.

Set in the early days of the automobile, when American society hoped that gunfighters were a thing of the past, the film aimed for a blend of comedy and drama by setting two ageing stalwarts of the Old West against the twin threats of a new breed of criminal and the progress of society towards twentieth-century values.

James Flagg (Mitchum) is about to be pushed into unwanted retirement from his position as marshal of Progress, a peaceful town where he has been responsible for law and order for two decades. When he learns that an outlaw gang is planning to descend on the town, and that the gang is led by his old adversary Big John McKay, Marshal Flagg tries to form a posse. The little town's mayor (Martin Balsam) is unconvinced and anxious that gunplay will damage Progress's reputation. Flagg is forced to ride out alone and when he confronts the gang, a grimy crew with blood in their eyes, he discovers that Big John (George Kennedy) is just a burned-out hanger-on. The real leader is Waco (David Carradine), a ruthless young man prepared to kill anyone who stands in his way.

Flagg is taken prisoner and Waco orders Big John to kill him. When the old outlaw draws the line at this he is left behind to guard the marshal while the rest of the gang ride into town. After a knock-down, drag-out fight, Flagg and Big John team up to confront the bad guys. By now, the mayor knows the town is in trouble and begs Flagg to come to the aid of Progress. The gang is after a bank shipment due to arrive by train so Flagg and Big John ride out and board the train before it reaches Progress in order to tell the driver to pass straight through the town without stopping. Mistaken for bandits by the train's conductors (one of whom is played by John Carradine), they had to fight their way to the engine's footplate.

When the train roars past the bemused bandits they give chase and so do the excited townspeople, led by their mayor who has visions of political greatness arising from the part he is playing in all this.

Finally, the train is wrecked and Flagg and Big John take on the bad guys and lick 'em. Flagg is offered his old job back but he declines, leaving it to his amiable but dim deputy, Howard Boyle (Dick Peabody), to look after law and order as Progress limps into the twentieth century.

The Good Guys and the Bad Guys works on many levels, and thus appeals to a wider audience than is usual for a western. On one level it is simply a good old-fashioned yarn with few pretentions towards originality; on another, telegraphed by its title, it is a comedy-western. But there are many other layers beneath the surface, all of which have comments to make upon areas of contemporary American life.

In a number of respects, storyline and general atmosphere among them, there is a passing resemblance here to Sam Peckinpah's Guns in the Afternoon (1962). That this production doesn't quite attain the extraordinarily high standards of that superb film is no great criticism.

As in Peckinpah's film, this is also a story of two old friends, the traditional 'buddies' beloved of American film and literature. The pair come together out of mutual respect for higher moral values than those which might separate them at the more mundane level of which side of the law they stand upon.

The comedy in the film is both broad and subtle. The broad laughs come from the scenes in which Flagg and Big John fight at the outlaw's camp and when they are mistaken for bandits by the guards on the train. There are even moments of outright farce when the town's mayor is literally caught with his pants down as he seduces the wife of one of Progress's leading citizens. More subtle are the scenes, again with the mayor, in which the political potential inherent in the routing of an outlaw gang becomes apparent even to those least responsible for the event.

Underneath all this, however, is an understated lament for the relative tranquillity of the past. Maybe there were outlaws and Indians and gunfights and no plumbing, but are the outward signs of progress such great alternatives? This is beautifully illuminated by the opening moments of the film which show Marshal Flagg riding his horse through a sylvan setting on a crystal-clear morning; suddenly a train passes and he vanishes in a cloud of acrid black smoke. The comfort of things that are old is expressed by Flagg's unstated preference for using his old untidy office with its creaking chair and faded 'wanted' posters instead of the shiny clean new office built for him out of hard brick and cold steel.

While missing one important element that lifted Guns in the Afternoon into its superior status, that of deep personal tragedy, The Good Guys and the Bad Guys is a much better film than was recognized on its release.

There is another historical reason for marking this film – to date it is Robert Mitchum's last western.

The 1960s had been mixed for Mitchum: despite the financial success of his films, on an artistic level they left much to be desired. Out of twenty-one films released in this period only two, *Home from the Hill* and *The Sundowners*, measured up without qualification to his best work of past decades.

His performances in *Cape Fear, El Dorado* and *The Good Guys and the Bad Guys* help lift the films to a level they might not have achieved with lesser actors in his roles. Essentially, however, the decade, while filled with hard work, lacked the zest of the 1950s and 1940s. For all that, he remained eminently watchable. As Roger Ebert has remarked, 'He has what many of the great 1930s and 1940s actors who are today's cult heroes had: a capacity to retain and even expand their dignity, their image, their self-possession, even in the midst of the worst possible material.'

Mitchum remained big at the box-office, and his popularity with audiences was reflected by the number of moviemakers who wanted to use him. As he commented in a 1969 interview with Ebert, 'I must be good at my job, they wouldn't haul me around the world at these prices if I weren't.'

By the end of the decade Robert Mitchum had passed that awkward age in any actor's life; at fifty-two even the least perceptive of moviemakers could see that he was now ready for character roles that were also above-title leads. To the surprise of the less perceptive critics who had constantly refrained from granting unqualified praise for his performances, he was about to enter a decade of film-making which, while far less prolific, would bring some of his greatest screen roles.

9   Out of the Desert

I learnt early in life that by telling a story far more colourfully
than the truth, one's truth would be let alone. I like to be let
alone.

Twice in recent years Robert Mitchum had talked of retirement.
The time he and Dorothy had lived in the seclusion of Belmont
Farms had prompted such thoughts but regular trips to
Hollywood and for location filming had drawn him back into
activity. Now, the run of indifferent films had again prompted
an urge to retire. Comfortable in his new home and with the
ranch at Atascadero, a couple of hours' drive north of Los
Angeles on which he could immerse himself in the day-to-day
problems of keeping quarter-horses, he no longer had to put up
with the much more demanding everyday hassles of making
films.

Despite his growing displeasure with the business of motion
pictures, and undeterred by the fallow period through which he
had just passed, film-makers still wanted him.

Amongst the offers were four films, eventually released in the
first half of the 1970s, in which the wide range of his roles
proved an irresistible attraction. On completion, his characterizations in this quartet went a long way towards silencing those
critics who still thought him a one-role player.

The first of this richly varied quartet was perhaps the most
off-beat of his career to date, and doubtless there were many
who thought British director David Lean had taken leave of his
senses when he cast Mitchum as the gentle, impotent
schoolteacher, in *Ryan's Daughter* (1970).

Ryan's Daughter had initially appealed to Mitchum because of
its literate screenplay which was by Robert Bolt who had written
only three screenplays before this. However, the three, *Lawrence
of Arabia* (1962), *Dr Zhivago* (1965) and *A Man for All Seasons*
(1966), were all nominated for Academy Awards, the last two
winning coveted Oscars.

It was Bolt who was largely responsible for persuading Mitchum to make the film after the actor had peremptorily hung up on David Lean during a telephone conversation that was getting nowhere. Mitchum's main objection to making the film was the fact that, much as he liked the script, it demanded his presence almost continuously throughout an extensive shooting schedule. Bolt called the actor to announce that the six-month schedule had been revised to allow him a few periods when he could take some days off. Mitchum refused, drily remarking that he was planning to commit suicide. Bolt was a match for him, eagerly declaring, 'If you'd do us a favour and appear in the picture, I'll take on the expense of the burial.'

Mitchum showed his appreciation of the jest by agreeing to make the film and the impressively massive logistics that surrounded *Ryan's Daughter* were coaxed into gear.

David Lean had first directed in 1942 and until the late 1950s was noted for small scale, intensely characterized productions. Among them were the notable *Brief Encounter* (1945) and *Hobson's Choice* (1954). His style underwent a marked change with *The Bridge on the River Kwai* (1957) and from then on his name became synonymous in the filmgoing public's mind with super-productions of grandly staged dramatic tales. In fact, between *Kwai* and *Ryan's Daughter* he made only two films, but the impact of *Lawrence of Arabia* and *Dr Zhivago* was such that casual hindsight carries the impression that he was always a maker of films of epic proportions.

Ryan's Daughter, which is set in Ireland during the 1916 Troubles, brings together the two sides of David Lean: intense personal emotion told on an epic scale. It is at once a sweeping story that appears to need its massive scope and long running time (almost three and a half hours), and a tightly observed tale of frustrated passion and unstated love. It is this apparent dichotomy that makes *Ryan's Daughter* a difficult film to assess and perhaps accounts for the broad range of critical opinion it generated.

The eponymous heroine is Rosy Ryan (Sarah Miles), a sexually frustrated and emotionally immature young woman struggling to avoid the physical entrapment of life in a small village. She marries the shy, intellectual schoolteacher, Charles Shaughnessy (Mitchum), who is several years her senior but quickly finds that although he can offer her love and tenderness, he is incapable of satisfying her overpowering sexual needs.

To the village comes Randolph Doryan (Christopher Jones), the new commander of the garrison of British soldiers located nearby. Randolph is wounded and shell-shocked following his

experiences in the trenches in France but he and Rosy are
mutually attracted and soon begin a wild love affair. The
villagers are shocked by the relationship; some because it is
against God's laws, others because she is Irish and he a member
of the hated occupying force.

Rosy's husband is caught between an angry urge to leave her
and a desire to help her overcome this deep emotional crisis.
Rosy's father, Tom Ryan (Leo McKern), is a weak man, despite
an outward aura of toughness, and can do nothing to improve
the situation; the village priest, Father Collins (Trevor Howard),
tries browbeating the young woman into mending her ways but
is as ineffectual as her father. Even the village idiot, the mentally
and physically damaged Michael (John Mills), becomes involved
in the tortuous events surrounding Ryan's daughter. Having
long adored Rosy, Michael believes that her relationship with
the crippled soldier means that he now stands a chance with
her.

While the doomed triangle of Charles-Rosy-Randolph is
played out, the political background of the times begins to
impinge. A ship carrying arms from Germany arrives off the
coast but a severe storm threatens to send it to the bottom. Led
by Tim O'Leary (Barry Foster) the villagers go down to the
beach and instigate a dangerous but ultimately successful
operation to rescue the weapons. As they return to the village
British soldiers bar the way. The villagers, knowing as they do of
Rosy's involvement with the British commander, believe she
has betrayed them. She is attacked, stripped, and her hair is cut
off. Father Collins tries to help and succeeds in preventing the
villagers from taking even more violent measures against Rosy.
Only Charles understands and is able to offer her any comfort.
She is at last aware that, despite the disparity in their ages and
the problems of their sexual relationship, Charles is the right
man for her. They leave the village, hopeful that they will be
able to rebuild a life together.

Ryan's Daughter was superbly photographed by Freddie Young,
a veteran of the British film industry with many credits for his
excellent work, especially his sumptuous colour cinematography on two of David Lean's earlier movies, *Lawrence of Arabia*
and *Dr Zhivago*, for both of which he won Academy Awards. He
won a third Oscar for *Ryan's Daughter*.

All the supporting players give excellent performances with
John Mills winning an Oscar as Best Supporting Actor for his
role as the inarticulate Michael. Leo McKern's interpretation of
the role of Tom Ryan has great depth and insight, especially
apparent in the scene where he turns his back as his daughter is

mobbed by the angry villagers. The manner in which he contrives to make it appear that this is because he endorses their actions when in fact it is because he is afraid is a splendid example of this superb actor's craft. Christopher Jones does reasonably well with his part but the interpretation suffers from dubbing. As Mitchum would later recall with glee, David Lean had hired Jones because he liked his accent in another film, not knowing that he had been dubbed because, Mitchum declared, 'Jones was off a Cherokee reservation in North Carolina.'

Outwardly, the character of Rosy bears all the marks of an unsympathetic and spoiled young woman. That it is possible to understand and ultimately sympathize with someone whose physical needs constantly battle with, and usually defeat, the artificial constraints of an imposed morality is largely thanks to the strength of Sarah Miles's interpretation. Enhancing her powerful performance is her contrastingly fragile physical appearance. Mitchum saw through this fragility, remarking, 'She's a monster. If you think she's not strong, you'd better pay attention.' For her performance as Rosy Ryan, Sarah Miles was unsuccessfully nominated for an Oscar.

As the self-effacing, lovingly tender schoolteacher, uneasily bound to a woman many years his junior, Robert Mitchum gives a compelling, understated performance. Although he had frequently created a striking impression through his habitual laconic stillness in the midst of activity in many of his previous screen roles, here he exercises this unusual talent to its best advantage.

Reviews were mixed, perhaps inevitably so, and just as the film as a whole split the critics, so too did Mitchum's performance. Vincent Canby, in *The New York Times*, felt that his casting had been a 'terrible mistake'. Pauline Kael, in the *New Yorker*, suggested that 'at first he just naturally livens up the movie, but then he becomes as dull as his role'. Much more enthusiastic were Judith Crist, in *New York Magazine*, who considered this 'his finest performance in many years', and Derek Malcolm, in the *Guardian*, who wrote that 'Mitchum is simply and gloriously himself in spite of everything – one of the most powerful and expressive non-actors in the business. Even when off the screen … he casts his shadow. It makes everyone else, not least David Lean, look small.'

David Lean recognized this quality, remarking, 'Other actors act. Mitchum is. He has true delicacy and expressiveness but his forte is his indelible identity. Mitchum can, simply by being there, make almost any other actor look like a hole in the screen.'

Speaking of his own performance, Mitchum was equivocal: 'It's a film I can talk about without embarrassment, but I don't know whether I'll be able to sit through it. I might get a cramp in my butt.'

For all his dismissive comments, his performance is remarkable. There are numerous pitfalls for an actor in portraying a man with inherent weaknesses, especially those of a sexual nature. But Mitchum walks surefootedly through his role and at no time does the sensitivity of the character draw irritation, displeasure, or make him appear a man to be despised.

Perhaps it was a general weariness, more likely it was the long year of boredom sitting in Ireland waiting for David Lean to decide 'when the seagulls were in the right place', but when *Ryan's Daughter* was finished Mitchum finally did something he had been threatening to do. He retired.

No one took his announcement too seriously and after eight months he did what everyone, especially Dorothy, had expected and returned to the screen.

Mitchum's Talbot Productions, in collaboration with Herbert B. Leonard who would also direct, began work on *Going Home* (1971). A deal had been struck with MGM, under whose banner the film would appear, which gave the studio control over the final print. As things turned out, this was an unfortunate clause in the deal and it is difficult to arrive at any firm conclusion about what kind of a film *Going Home* might have been when confronted only with the truncated version which eventually reached the screen.

Going Home is the story of an uncomfortable and potentially lethal relationship between a father and his son. Thirteen years ago, Harry Graham (Mitchum) killed his wife in a drunken rage, an act which is observed by his six-year-old son. Now, having served a prison term for the killing, Harry is trying to make a new life for himself. His dead-end existence is briefly brightened by his relationship with a young divorcee, Jenny (Brenda Vaccaro), but then his son, Jimmy (Jan-Michael Vincent) turns up. Jimmy needs to understand what drove his father to commit the crime which has proved to be such a traumatic influence upon his own life. Harry tries hard to accommodate Jimmy, but the young man's frustration and anger continually spill over and he makes trouble for his father. Jenny, aware of the damage that all this is doing to Harry's precarious grasp on things, tells Jimmy to leave. In a fit of anger Jimmy rapes Jenny, then runs away, later calling his father to demand that they meet. When Harry learns what his son has done he beats him but stops short of another killing. Jimmy still wants to know why his mother was killed and, flatly, Harry tells him it was because he was drunk. With nothing resolved, Jimmy asks what will happen now. Harry tells his son, 'You get to be twenty.'

A bleak story, matter-of-factly told, *Going Home* has about it an air of defeated realism that fits well into the ethos of the times but there are some unaccountable deficiencies. The seemingly arbitrary acts of violence to which first the father, then the son, are prone are not explained. They simply exist as an inherent part of the make-up of the characters.

The driving forces of all three main characters are probably sexual but this assumption is based upon little on-screen evidence. That this is unclear is a result of some twenty minutes of cuts made by MGM who were striving to 'clean up' the movie. The chief result of these cuts is that the audience cannot begin to understand the characters and hence can see much of what happens as merely gratuitous sexual violence.

As Alvin H. Marill has reported, Herbert B. Leonard was moved to protest publicly at MGM's treatment of his film. By then, of course, it was too late.

All three principals perform their roles well but the film was generally poorly received. For the worst possible reasons, *Going Home* must be regarded as a notable 'miss' and one which, after the grandeur of *Ryan's Daughter*, must have given pause to hopes that Mitchum was pulling out of his dry patch.

His next film, which found him back in clerical garb, probably fuelled prognostications of doom. In *The Wrath of God* (1972) he is in an unnamed Latin American country in the 1920s. Not unlike his earlier screen clerics, his Father Van Horne mixes religion with substantial doses of his own brand of lethal fire and brimstone. The tools of Father Van Horne's trade are a revolver, a knife concealed in a crucifix and, to round it all off, a Thompson sub-machine gun for when the going gets really tough.

Along with an Irish revolutionary, Emmet Keogh (Ken Hutchison), and a British bootlegger, Jennings (Victor Buono), Van Horne attempts to free a village from the tyrannical domination of Tomas de la Plata (Frank Langella). In the process of freeing the villagers from the grasp of de la Plata, who is mentally unstable with homicidal inclinations, there is an attempted rape and numerous grisly deaths most of which are lingered over by a voyeuristic camera.

There is about *The Wrath of God* a curiously mixed air which suggests, as indeed does the title, that this was planned as a tale of violence with a message. Such a mixture was well within the grasp of director Ralph Nelson. Two years earlier, in 1970, he had made *Soldier Blue*, a film which used its sometimes sickening violence to powerful effect in transmitting an anti-violence message. This time, the delicate touch needed for such an effect had deserted Nelson and *The Wrath of God* is an uncomfortable mixture of violence that is supposed to be good because it is directed against the bad guys, violence that is bad because the good are the targets, and violence for its own sake.

Julian Fox, in *Films and Filming*, commented that Mitchum did 'wonders in a film whose supporting cast suffers chronically from an excess of "acting".' Most other reviewers didn't get down to detailed comments on individual performances, being content instead to deal with the whole offering. Clyde Jeavons, in *Monthly Film Bulletin*, remarked that the cast took 'an obvious delight in tossing off the more pretentious lines from an impossible script, and very sensibly send the whole thing up'. Arthur Knight, in *Saturday Review*, wrote that here was 'a director who manages to conceal the dubious morality of his theme in the flurry of incessant action'. Roger Greenspun, writing in *The New York Times*, managed to view *The Wrath of God* with sufficient detachment to observe, 'I cannot condemn a film in which the heroine, silent since she saw her parents killed, suddenly regains her speech to warn her lover of an assassin's bullet. Such miracles in this day and age bespeak a hokum beyond the reach of art.'

Mitchum's own view of the film was as off-handed as ever and he tacitly endorsed the bewilderment of many who saw it by declaring his reason for making the film: 'I'll do anything to get out of the house.'

Hindsight makes it possible to grant *The Wrath of God* a rather sad saving grace; this was the last-released film of Rita Hayworth who played the role of de la Plata's mother.

Mitchum's first three roles of the 1970s had been very different, even if his Father Van Horne did owe more than a passing nod to his earlier Jonathan Rudd in *Five Card Stud* (with a splash of Lee Arnold in *Villa Rides!*). But, just as he had done in *Ryan's Daughter*, for his fourth role of the new decade he trod new ground and to superb effect.

The Friends of Eddie Coyle (1973) contains many of the elements of the classic *films noirs* of the 1940s yet has a contemporary feeling of immorality which blends well into the gloomily cynical atmosphere of post-Vietnam, post-Watergate America.

Eddie Coyle (Mitchum) is a battered, bone-weary three-time loser on the brink of yet another prison term. This time he knows that if he goes down his wife and children will end up on welfare. Somehow, he has to figure a way to keep out of prison and at the same time continue to make a few illicit dollars. His solution is to juggle with his friendships, but Eddie's friends have no reciprocal feelings for this broken-down, small-time hoodlum. Eddie does a deal with a Treasury agent, Dave Foley (Richard Jordan), a man whose morality is no better than that of the criminals he seeks to capture. The deal they strike is for Foley to put in a good word for Eddie at his upcoming trial in exchange for which Eddie will inform on a group of criminals he is supplying with weapons.

Eddie plays the dangerous game and Foley makes an arrest but the government agent is after bigger fish. A team of bank robbers is operating in the district and Foley wants them. He tells Eddie that if he can nail the gang's leader, Scalise (Alex Rocco), then the court will certainly be lenient. Unwillingly but inevitably, Eddie begins to play this next stage of the game, aware that it is even more dangerous than the last.

Using a bartender named Dillon (Peter Boyle) as his contact with the bigger fish in the squalid underworld sink that lies beneath the city's tranquil surface, Eddie starts the final moves, but then uncompromising fate takes a hand. Before Eddie has a chance to finger Scalise and his gang, someone else tips off the authorities. Scalise's run is ended but time is also running out for Eddie. Dillon, who needs a few favours himself, has passed word along the line that Eddie is a squealer. Scalise's underworld colleagues assume it was Eddie who fingered their friend and order Dillon to kill him.

Despite the relationship he has with Eddie, an uneasy mixture of half trust and half-truths, Dillon agrees. He needs the approval of the gangs more than he needs Eddie's friendship. He takes Eddie out for a night's entertainment, a hockey game and a few beers. A few beers too many, in fact, for as they drive home Eddie passes out, exactly as Dillon intended. As Dillon's young assistant concentrates on driving the car, the bartender, with disquieting detachment, shoots Eddie through the head.

With Eddie's body left in a car parked outside a supermarket, Dillon meets Treasury Agent Foley. There the ultimate hypocrisy of Eddie's 'friends' is revealed. It was Dillon who gave Foley the tip that led to Scalise's arrest and thus inevitably to a contract being put out on Eddie, a contract which Dillon himself has just carried out. In gratitude for the arrest of Scalise, Foley agrees not to dig too deeply into the circumstances surrounding Eddie's death. Even before Eddie Coyle's body has been found, his scaly friends have forgotten him.

Directed by Peter Yates, an Englishman with a talent for

evoking the essence of urban America (San Francisco in *Bullitt*, New York in *John and Mary*), the setting for *The Friends of Eddie Coyle* is Boston. The film knowingly contrasts the seediness of the bars and parking lots in which much of Eddie's life is lived with the leafy open spaces of the parks where lethal deals are struck.

Effective use is made of other contrasts. Eddie Coyle's home is a cramped collection of tiny rooms into which he fits, but awkwardly. Here, his movements are correspondingly cramped and awkward, as if he is aware that momentary lack of caution will cause him to knock over a pile of dishes or crack his shin against a door. But, despite the grubby homeliness of this setting, Eddie is instantly more at ease in the huge, near-empty, echoing barn of a bar-room where Dillon works.

Then there is the contrast between the uptight evil enthusiasm of the younger criminals, men who see crime as a stepping-stone to riches and have no moral hang-ups over what they must do to succeed, and the weary acceptance of Eddie who is a criminal because he knows no other life and who is caught in an endless cycle. He can survive only by remaining a criminal and each crime he commits begets another. Unlike his younger associates, Eddie Coyle commits crimes to allow himself and his family to survive without falling on to welfare. Not that this should be seen as an apologia for Eddie's actions, and it most certainly is not put forward in that light in the film. Eddie is what he is; no more and no less. Yet, while his fellow criminals stridently dominate through the use of firearms and threats of physical violence and death, Eddie Coyle quietly avoids direct violence and goes on his way with stoic acceptance of his role in life. He doesn't seek a way out because, long ago, he learned that there is no way out.

From the outset, Eddie is doomed; for him there is no escape from an endless spiral of deal, double-deal and double-cross. No escape, that is, until death. The inevitability of the approaching end to his life is mirrored in every line of Eddie Coyle's time-battered face and in the broken and badly reset knuckles on his hands which are an ever-present memory of a past occasion when his 'friends' chose to give him a permanent reminder of how he had offended them.

The film is beautifully photographed by Victor Kemper, whose elegiac use of light in the park sequences, where Eddie and Foley meet, contrasts startlingly with the grim words of the characters. This superb use of sunlight and dappled shadow is one indication of how the movie's debt to *film noir* is evident less in its general appearance than in specific details. It is the manner in which director Peter Yates effects these details which lifts *The Friends of Eddie Coyle* into an altogether superior category.

There are no weak performances in *The Friends of Eddie Coyle*. All the minor roles, especially Steven Keats and Alex Rocco, bring understanding to their roles as criminals. Higher up the cast list, both Richard Jordan and Peter Boyle find precisely the right note of detached cynicism needed for the destroyers of Eddie Coyle.

But it is in Robert Mitchum's central performance that the film's main strength lies. In a role which could so easily have tipped over into pathos or even generated active dislike for a hardcore criminal, he brings to his beaten loser a quiet dignity that is always believable. Mitchum's powerful screen presence is used sparingly, in what is his most downbeat role, so that he never unbalances the film with the suggestion that all he needs do is flex those big shoulders and all will suddenly be well again. Yet Mitchum's importance to the film is such that the suspenseful sections which deal in sharp detail with the bank heists, and in which Eddie Coyle has no part to play, appear almost as unwanted intrusions. Conversely, the final scenes, after Eddie's death, are enhanced (much as were the closing moments of (*The Night of the Hunter*) by the shadow cast over them by Mitchum's absence.

Peter Cargin, in *Film*, called *The Friends of Eddie Coyle* 'a movie that demands an interest, needs attention [and] contains a fine performance from Robert Mitchum [who] conveys the sadness and tiredness with great feeling'. In *Films and Filming*, Gordon Gow observed that 'the film as a whole is heavily dependent on Robert Mitchum's key performance: the quality is diminished whenever he is off the screen ... Eddie Coyle is a really good role for him. He plays it with a quiet dedication, getting his teeth into some pithy lines by Paul Monash.'

Certainly Paul Monash's screenplay is a main strength, using George V. Higgins' remarkable first novel as his base, Monash effectively reproduces Higgins' fine ear for the clumsy, convoluted dialogue of the streets.

Monash was full of praise for Mitchum, declaring to Grover Lewis that he 'radiates a genuine presence. Above all, you can say about Mitchum that he *is*'. Higgins was similarly impressed but more with the off-screen Mitchum. 'I think he got into the wrong line of work. He should get himself a typewriter and stop fooling around with movie acting. He's a natural-born storyteller.'

For all such undoubted qualities, Mitchum chose to be much less than forthcoming to the movie's publicist who complained, 'the guy won't even *talk* to me'.

Undoubtedly, *The Friends of Eddie Coyle* is a major landmark in

Robert Mitchum's career. It marked his total emergence from the wasteland of the past decade or so and would have been an impressive high-water mark on which to leave the screen but, with the 1970s just halfway through, he still had many more movies to make. There would be another ten before the end of the decade alone. One of them was to prove another classic to rank with the best of his screen portrayals.

10 Travelling Star

I'm in demand because I don't waste the producers' money.

In the mid-1970s Robert Mitchum made more tabloid headlines over two movies he *didn't* make than over those he did.

He was announced as having signed for Terence Young's *Jackpot*, in which he was to co-star with Richard Burton. However, as a precaution over whether or not his salary would be forthcoming, he asked for payment up front. When the money failed to materialize he bowed out. The producers made quite a fuss over his non-appearance in Nice, where the film was to be shot, while carefully avoiding discussing his reasons.

With the benefit of hindsight he doubtless wished he could have avoided turning up to work on Otto Preminger's *Rosebud*. This extraordinary example of moviemaking is one of few such disasters to be fully documented. Coincidentally, American writer Theodore Gershuny had obtained permission from Preminger to sit in on pre-production conferences and to attend shooting in order to write a book which would be the most thoroughly detailed of any account written on the making of a film.

If *Rosebud* had been a good film, or even a mediocre one, Gershuny's book would have been important for anyone with an interest in film-making. That it turned out to be one of the biggest flops in the history of motion pictures made the book required reading.

As Gershuny reveals in *Soon to Be a Major Motion Picture*, the rot had begun to set in before Mitchum, accompanied by Dorothy, arrived on the Mediterranean island of Corsica where the production was located.

Mitchum was clearly edgy and, despite earlier suggestions that he was eager to work again with Otto Preminger, the star and the director were soon at loggerheads. It seems unlikely that any of the animosity that had existed between the two men back in 1952 during the filming of *Angel Face* still lingered; after all, they had got through *River of No Return* without conflict. Nevertheless, something was decidedly amiss and a few days into the shooting of *Rosebud* Mitchum exploded.

The account of the ensuing confrontation between Mitchum and Preminger revolves around the star's legendary capacity for alcohol. Over the years, stories about Mitchum's enthusiasm for a tipple have regularly appeared in the tabloids, and often in newspapers and magazines which customarily turn a deferentially shaded eye upon the excesses of famous people. He has never denied a liking for drink and over the years there have been enough well-documented tales to suggest he had a fearsome capacity for it. Nevertheless, although well publicized, Mitchum's drinking seems to have accounted for fewer days lost on movies than many other stars clocked up through head colds and tantrums.

More recently, following medical advice and a brief spell in the Betty Ford clinic in 1984, his drinking habits changed dramatically. At the time of the making of *Rosebud*, however, the wagon was still around a far-distant corner.

The final bust-up in Corsica occurred early one morning when Mitchum, who had been involved in some rather heavy partying which had merged into one long drinking session, turned up on the set a little before six o'clock. He was rather dishevelled, unshaven and clearly in a bad mood. The mood was partially induced by a hangover but was seriously exacerbated by having been called at the crack of dawn for the drive to the location only to discover that the driver didn't know the way. Eventually, late, dusty and with his hangover still firmly in place, Mitchum arrived on the set in an irritable frame of mind. What tipped his temper over the precarious edge on which it was balanced was the fact that the set wasn't ready.

He blew up, raging at everything and everyone in general and at the director in particular. As Gershuny recalls, Mitchum yelled at Preminger, 'You wake me up at four in the morning to watch 'em lay a fuckin' dolly track? Is that it?'

Preminger replied quietly, 'Bob, we cannot go on this way.'

After a brief debate, Mitchum turned and walked to his car and demanded to be taken back to his hotel.

Within hours, Mitchum and Dorothy were packed and ready to leave the beautiful island location. Then another argument with Preminger ensued, which helped cloud forever the issue of whether Mitchum had quit or was fired.

By the end of the decade the incident had faded sufficiently for it to be included in Mitchum's routine story-telling.

Interviewed in *Films Illustrated*, he said, 'One day the script had me looking beat-up and dishevelled, so I arrived on the set unshaven. "You are drunk," roared Otto, "and you cannot play this scene!" I argued with Otto saying how could I possibly be drunk at 5.30 in the morning, and pointed out the instructions on the script, but he wouldn't listen. "You are drunk and you are through!" he shouted. So I turned and yelled "Taxi!" and that was that. It really did break my heart.'

Whether it happened this way or, as seems probable, the way Gershuny reported it, Mitchum was off the picture.

Rosebud went ahead, of course, because no one in the motion picture business is irreplaceable. That the film subsequently bombed, becoming a disaster of mammoth proportions, suggests that Mitchum lost nothing by being out of it.

Later, Mitchum had a characteristic last word in an interview with United Press International's Vernon Scott: 'It's funny; Preminger objects to drinking actors, but he replaced me with Peter O'Toole. Hell, that's like replacing Ray Charles with Hellen Keller.'

Before the visit to Corsica, Mitchum had been in Japan filming a dark and complex tale that mixed the modern American gangster scene with ancient Japanese underworld traditions.

The Yakuza (1975) is a tale of violence and honour among thieves, and honourable violence between the good guys. The term *yakuza* means 'gambler' but is here portrayed as a cross between the Japanese *samurai* and the Italian *camorra*. These two traditions, the one arising from a warrior nobility, the other from men who turned to a life outside the law as a form of protest against poverty and oppression, evolve here into a group of individuals who bloodily wreak vengeance upon one another for impenetrable reasons that appear to them to be justified.

Harry Kilmer (Mitchum) had served in Japan during World War Two and returns there many years later at the request of an old army buddy, George Tanner (Brian Keith). Tanner's daughter, Louise (Lee Chirillo), has been kidnapped by a chieftain of the local *yakuza*, Tono Toshiro (Okado Eiji), who is dissatisfied with the way Tanner is conducting a business deal they have. Kilmer, a retired detective, agrees to help and arrives in Tokyo where he teams up with Tanaka Ken (Takakura Ken) whom he believes to be the brother of an old flame, Tanaka Eiko (Kishi Keiko).

At the end of the war Harry had left Eiko because Ken had objected to his sister's relationship with an American, but when they meet again it is clear that the flame still flickers.

Somehow, during the subsequent mayhem, Harry has time to

discover that Ken and Eiko are not brother and sister as he has always thought, but are husband and wife.

Among the dead who litter the scene after Harry and Ken have dealt with the enemy – including George Tanner – are Eiko's daughter and the son of Ken's older brother who is the chief arbiter of the code of the *yakuza*.

In penance for his nephew's death, Ken obeys the code by cutting off the little finger of one of his own hands and offering it to his brother. Before Harry Kilmer heads for the airport and his return flight to America, he repeats Ken's grisly action and cuts off his own little finger as penance for having lived, however inadvertently, with his wife during the war. The two men part with a curious bond of mutual respect between them.

Much of the plot is confused and a substantial part of the film is in the form of solid wedges of expository dialogue which recounts the historical background of the *yakuza*, presumably for the benefit of Occidental audiences.

Despite *The Yakuza* having an American director, Sydney Pollack, the film has that peculiar unevenness which characterizes many Japanese action movies. Bouts of frenzied and usually noisy action are intercut with moments of deep, silent, and presumably significant reflection upon honour and the meaning of life and death.

The leading Japanese player, Takakura Ken (in the role of Tanaka Ken), is a highly talented actor with great screen presence. Like Mitchum, he is an expert in the difficult screen art of silence and stillness.

Mitchum's performance is solid without being exceptional although the final scene between him and Ken, in which the finger-cutting gesture is made, is conducted with an impressive dignity which transcends the moment's improbability.

Many reviewers spent some of their space struggling with the plot but on performances they were generally favourable to Mitchum. Judith Crist, in *New York Magazine*, wrote that he 'goes beyond the macho moments to exhaustion and to a subtle depth of feeling. His scenes with Kishi Keiko … have a tender maturity to their silences and appreciations.' In the *New Yorker* Pauline Kael, never a wide-eyed Mitchum fan, conceded: 'He seems to be the only movie star who's becoming a more commanding figure as he ages.'

After *The Yakuza* Mitchum finally made his appearance in a role millions had waited for since his early *films noirs*. For thirty years his fans had asked why he had never played the role of Raymond Chandler's archetypal private eye, Philip Marlowe, and had speculated endlessly upon whether or not he would have been better than the other actors who had done so. When he finally put on Marlowe's trenchcoat and slouch hat, in *Farewell, My Lovely* (1975), three decades of speculation were over. This film, and *The Big Sleep* (1978), will be assessed in the next chapter together with some reflections on Mitchum as an icon of American *film noir*.

His next film was *Midway* (1976) in which he played the part of Admiral 'Bull' Halsey. Like two of his other war movies, *The Longest Day* and *Anzio*, this was a restaging of a real period of recent history into which were woven some fictional elements. This time the setting was the Pacific in 1942. Mitchum's role was necessarily brief as Halsey was hospitalized during the action being depicted. Having spent only one day on the set, and that lying in bed, Mitchum didn't bother to pick up his salary. Instead, he told the studio to send it to charity.

Then came another small role, this time in *The Last Tycoon* (1976), for which Mitchum voluntarily took a downward step on the status ladder to second male billing below the star, Robert De Niro.

The Last Tycoon is one of Hollywood's occasional hair-shirted attempts to lay the ghost of F. Scott Fitzgerald. Like practically all of Fitzgerald's work, *The Last Tycoon* (an unfinished novel) is concerned with the dreams and aspirations of individuals both idealistic and venal; in this case they are film-makers in Hollywood. The intensely personal mood, which Fitzgerald referred to as 'hauntedness', is sustained, but is upstaged by the overall effect of the film. In some respects *The Last Tycoon* suffers from having had so much money spent on it that the surface gloss has hardened to an impenetrable shell. In the end it is as if a succession of beautifully crafted Chinese boxes has been opened to reveal that the last one contains nothing of value.

Robert Mitchum, as Pat Brady, studio head and friend of Monroe Stahr (De Niro), does well enough with his role. Given that the character of Brady is based upon a combination of Carl Laemmle and Louis B. Mayer, well-laced with Fitzgerald's own invention (Stahr is based upon MGM's Irving Thalberg), there would seem to be room for strong characterization of a power-monster, but the weighting of the script in favour of the leading role makes this difficult.

Critical opinions on the film contained more than a hint of desperation at this repetition of Hollywood's previous failures to make a success out of an F. Scott Fitzgerald tale. Mitchum had his own comment: 'It's good, but dull. Still I got ten days' work and to wear a suit and speak with some authority. So what the hell.'

Having made a connection with the Japanese underworld in *The Yakuza*, Mitchum next tackled latter-day Chinese villains. *The Amsterdam Kill* (1977), which was made in Europe and the Far East, has a screenplay written with Mitchum in mind and expects of him little more than a reiteration of his customary world-weary persona.

Tacitly acknowledging the success of law enforcement officers in unseating the French connection from Marseilles, the film is concerned with drug trafficking between Hong Kong and Amsterdam.

Mitchum plays the role of Larry Quinlan, a disgraced former employee of the US Drug Enforcement Agency. To-ing and fro-ing between Hong Kong and Holland, Quinlan eventually uncovers a web of corruption at the heart of which are two of his former colleagues who still hold positions of authority in the DEA.

On-screen for much of the running time, Mitchum provides a strong central thread to a frequently confusing story-line. Some of the dialogue suggests that a non-too neat translator has been at work but there are flashes of the kind of thing at which Mitchum is so good; such as when he is confronted by a former colleague:

ODUMS: You could have been a bureau chief by now, if ...
QUINLAN: If. If my aunt were built differently she could've been my uncle. If!

Later Quinlan is with Odums again:

ODUMS: You've put us all between the rock and the hard place.
QUINLAN: I know the place. I've been living there for two years.

And when Quinlan leads his only trustworthy ally, Jimmy Wong (George Cheung), into the final confrontation with the bad guys, he tells him: 'Let's go stick our finger in somebody's eye.'

A considerable improvement over most of the multi-national, multi-lingual movies that litter the 1970s, *The Amsterdam Kill* may not be vintage Mitchum but it's not all bad. For all its flaws, and they are many, *The Amsterdam Kill* did not have the problem of a boxing kangaroo in the cast.

A boxing kangaroo? Yes, that is exactly what Matilda is in the movie which bears her name. *Matilda* (1978) is a comedy which appears to have the makings of a serious message buried deep inside its pouch. Unfortunately for everyone concerned, not least the kangaroo (and Gary Morgan, its sweating kangaroo-suited stand-in), the message vanished along with most of the jokes.

Mitchum plays the role of sports writer Duke Parkhurst who has long wanted to clean up the boxing game, and he thinks that Matilda, who is touring vaudeville fighting human boxers, can help him accomplish this.

Judging from the array of acting talent (the cast includes Elliott Gould, Lionel Stander and Harry Guardino) up against the less than formidable thespian qualities of the antipodean marsupial, it must be assumed that *Matilda* looked rather better at script stage than it does as a finished movie.

In 1978 the Mitchums moved house again. They not only sold the house in Bel-Air but also unloaded the ranch complete with the quarter-horses. Their new home was at Montecito, near Santa Barbara, about one hundred miles north of Los Angeles. Overlooking the Pacific Ocean, the comfortable two-bedroomed house, with pool, was about the right size for Robert and Dorothy and a large brown dog named Zimba. But as the decade rolled towards its end Mitchum had little time to enjoy the tranquillity of Montecito. Next, his professional wanderings took him north to Canada where he made *Agency* (1979).

The film takes as its starting point Paul Gottleib's novel but makes certain changes, almost all of which improve upon the original. In the novel the central theme is the use of subliminal television advertising as a means of causing malfunctions at spaceship launches; in the film the TV messages are used to manipulate the population.

Unfortunately, both script and direction are uncertain how to handle the material. Some scenes are played as comedy; some that are played straight turn out to be even funnier. In one scene a dead body, frozen into a sitting position with one arm outstretched, is carried away with the recalcitrant arm sticking out from the zipper of a yellow plastic body bag. Vaguely reminiscent of Captain Ahab, beckoning his shipmates from the back of Moby Dick, the scene owes an unfulfilled debt to Woody Allen.

The supporting acting leaves rather a lot to be desired but if the principals had been powerful enough the movie might have scrambled over its self-made hump. Unfortunately, despite Mitchum's top billing the leading roles are, in fact, taken by Lee Majors and Valerie Perrine. A popular television actor, Majors cannot carry the weight; Perrine, a gifted actress with such striking performances as those she gave in *Slaughterhouse Five* (1972) and *Lenny* (1974) to her credit, is here remarkably detached.

In a couple of scenes, Mitchum's old power is there but, unfortunately, such moments are too few. Indeed, some scenes in which he appears are shot silent with voice-over commentary from a minor character. Perhaps there were production reasons for this but with a potentially powerful role frittered away, Mitchum must have been aware of the film's lost potential. In an interview with Iain F. McAsh, in the April 1979 issue of *Films Illustrated*, he expressed his concern with the real-life harm possible through misuse of technology in the manner of the film's theme. He remarked that 'control of the examination of the audio-visual medium should be far more stringent than it is. We should have the right to know and not just be told what to know. The only information system we need is the one which deals with life and death – and then only trust the one that gets it right!'

Physically, Mitchum looks very sharp in *Agency*, slimmer than of late, unlined, tanned and smartly dressed. As he said to McAsh, 'My suit is so tight I have to stand up dead straight or I bust my clothes.'

Mitchum's last film of the 1970s was a relatively minor part in a production which gave Jaclyn Smith her first major screen role. As one of the three eponymous heroines in television's *Charlie's Angels* she had not had any opportunity to do anything other than look pretty. Giving her an entire feature to carry wasn't a very smart move, not that *Nightkill* (1979) places many demands on anyone. Although director Ted Post tries to wring some suspense from certain sequences, much of what happens is predictable and isn't helped by a central performance lacking in depth and confidence.

All the supporting players in *Nightkill* (and Mitchum takes fourth billing but has a cute little box around his name) go through the motions but have insufficient screentime to do much with their roles. Mitchum speaks his lines, manages to avoid looking threatening at any time, even though his role is that of a murderous private eye masquerading as a police officer, and gets it over with. In the final shot of him, as he rides an escalator up to a waiting aeroplane and escape, there is the faintest flicker of a smile behind his eyes.

In that same interview in *Films Illustrated* Mitchum expressed mild envy for the character actors in many of the movies in which he had played over the years: 'I'd like to have one of those character roles. I used to watch actors like Claude Rains come on to the set with their little paper bags and, two days later, they picked up the loot and left. Thirty-two days later, I was still there.'

Maybe that was what caused the flickering smile. Riding the escalator with a bag full of make-believe money must have seemed like an unconscious touch of reality in an otherwise improbable scenario.

In many respects the 1970s can be seen as the most rewarding of Robert Mitchum's four decades in motion pictures. Certainly, there were some moments which echoed the inferior quality of many of his films of the 1960s, and there were those that amounted to little more than cameo roles, but on balance there was much that vied with his best work.

There was his low-key performance in *Ryan's Daughter*; what remains of his original conception of the leading role in *Going Home*; a magnificent performance in *The Friends of Eddie Coyle*; and his long awaited and triumphant tackling of the role of Philip Marlowe in *Farewell, My Lovely*. These performances stretched him as an actor, and showed that anything he had so far chosen to tackle was well within his range.

Of particular pleasure to his fans was the fact that he had proved to the unbelievers that he had lost none of his screen presence and that given the right kind of role he could carry an indifferent movie upwards a few notches.

Just as *Out of the Past* and *The Night of the Hunter* belie their 1940s and 1950s origins when viewed today, so will *The Friends of Eddie Coyle* and *Farewell, My Lovely* be around to impress generations of moviegoers still unborn.

As the 1980s began, Mitchum was yet again in a position to sit back and take things easy. He chose not to do so, which, as it turned out, was just as well because the time was coming when he would *have* to work. Most important to his career was the way he chose to continue working in the 1980s. Not for him an easy ride of undemanding roles in inconsequential movies or a string of meaningless cameos. Instead, he decided to begin the new decade with head-on confrontations with challenges he had not yet faced.

Before examining his career in the 1980s, however, two of his films of the 1970s remain to be considered.

In *Farewell, My Lovely* and *The Big Sleep* he became the character millions had associated him with for more than thirty years, despite the fact that he had never played him. It was in these two films that Robert Mitchum finally became Philip Marlowe.

11 Mitchum as Marlowe

Creating another identity on the screen is fun.

In the mid-1940s film critics writing in the French magazine *Cahiers du Cinéma* drew attention to similarities between several films newly arrived from Hollywood and the kind of stories being printed in such French publications as *Série Noire*. In casting a searching light on these films, they coined a term for what they saw as a new category of motion pictures. *Film noir*, as they termed it, was not a simple genre as was, say, the earlier cycle of gangster movies. Within *film noir* can be found psychological dramas, westerns, and even films with a surface gloss of light-hearted comedy, but principally they are crime stories. However, they are crime stories of a very different type to the earlier gangster movie genre.

The new movement was decidedly unself-conscious as the makers of these films had not set out to create something new. Rather, they were holding up a mirror to reflect the times in which they lived; a mirror that produced a dark and pessimistic image quite unlike that which glowed brightly through the products of Hollywood's passing golden age.

Many elements went to form the distinctive products of the new movement. Some were contributed by the influence of the large number of German directors and cinematographers who left Europe in the years just before World War Two. Their techniques, founded in the Expressionist cinema of post-World War One Germany, included most notably gothic symbolism, morbidity, the striking use of dramatic camera angles and stark, angular sets. The development of improved light-sensitive film stock, suitable for night filming, lent a practical hand to the stylistic movement. Among the visual and aural effects encouraged by these artistic and pragmatic influences were such settings as rain-lashed streets, darkened rooms, and empty echoing buildings into which film-makers could introduce their

characters who would be lit with sharply contrasted melodramatic lighting.

Important though the appearance of the productions which
were tagged as *film noir* may be, similar importance must be
attached to the content of the stories told. Although they are
richly varied, there are certain recurring themes. The principal
character, almost always a man, is usually physically or mentally
isolated from his surroundings. He is often foredoomed and
carries a subconscious inarticulated awareness of his ultimate
fate with stoic resignation. He is bleakly fatalistic in his response
to what is being done around him and to him. Of great
importance to the movement is the *noir* hero's strongly defined
morality. His values may be very different from those of society
at large but they are frequently of a higher order. Out of step
perhaps, occasionally even against the law, but these
improbable heroes always answer to a sometimes idiosyncratic
but intensely moralistic view of what is right and what is wrong.

The hard-boiled school of American fiction produced many
writers of distinction in diverse fields. In the area of crime and
detection came men whose work appeared in *Série Noire* and it
was they who provided the French film critics with a positive
link to the movies they designated *film noir*. The most important
of these writers were Dashiell Hammett, Horace McCoy, James
M. Cain, Cornell Woolrich and Raymond Chandler.

Raymond Chandler was a self-confessed devotee of the work
of Dashiell Hammett, whose writing in *Black Mask* magazine was
the key to the changes which overcame crime fiction in the
1930s. Nevertheless, Chandler claimed that he did not base his
style on his spiritual mentor's and, while this might not be
entirely true of the earliest of his stories which were written for
Black Mask, the comment is certainly justified in respect of his
later stories and all his novels. In these later works Chandler can
be seen as an original talent with a sharp ear for memorable
dialogue and an even sharper eye for arresting descriptions of
his chosen locale.

The principal character in all the novels is Philip Marlowe and
the chief location is the city of Los Angeles. Marlowe, often
referred to as Chandler's 'White Knight', is a solitary man. He
has values which are his own and while they are different to
those of the society in which he exists, they are never less than
those of his peers. Indeed, most often, even when he steps
outside the law, Marlowe's standards of behaviour are
impeccably upright and honest. If it happens that they do not
concur with society's then it is society that is at fault, not
Marlowe. At his noble heart, Marlowe is the American

frontiersman updated to the 1940s and uprooted from the wilderness to be set down in the contemporary urban jungle. In terms of the morality of the heroic protagonist, the line which runs through American literature from James Fenimore Cooper's Hawkeye to Chandler's Marlowe is arrow-straight.

The nature of Raymond Chandler's creation, so close as it is to the heartfelt belief of many American men in their own characters, made the transference of Philip Marlowe to the screen inevitable. The fact that the setting of the novels was a contemporary Los Angeles made the movies that came along easy to stage. The techniques of *film noir* all lent themselves readily to a recreation on the screen of Chandler's work: dark, rain-slick streets; even darker, cheaply furnished offices and bars; the striking contrasts offered by the palatial homes of the super-rich up in the Hollywood Hills and the dilapidated houses and cheap hotels of downtown Los Angeles. Additionally, the narrative voice-over, which was a frequently used device in *film noir*, matched the fact that all the Marlowe novels were written in the first person.

The most serious problem for film-makers was who, out of all the many actors available to them, could play the part of Philip Marlowe?

In the first two efforts the problem was neatly sidestepped by simply changing the character to someone else. In *Time to Kill* (1942), which was based upon the novel, *The High Window*, Marlowe disappeared to become Michael Shayne, the popular hero of a number of B-pictures. Played here by Lloyd Nolan, there is nothing of Marlowe left; neither is there very much of Chandler. Similarly, an established screen detective adopted the Marlowe role in *The Falcon Takes Over* (1942), which was based upon *Farewell, My Lovely* and which starred George Sanders as the suavely sophisticated sleuth, the Falcon.

It was the novel used in the Falcon film which provided the vehicle for the first appearance of Philip Marlowe. *Farewell, My Lovely* (1945) starred Dick Powell as the world-weary private eye. Until this point in his career, Powell was known as a chubby-faced former dance-band singer who had strolled leisurely through various cheerful musicals of the past dozen years. In many of these films he had played the wide-eyed innocent juvenile lead, making them an unlikely training ground for an actor who was to be the first to tackle the character that millions of readers already had in their mind's eye. Yet, against all the odds, Powell slipped easily into the role. Even his face seemed to change, the rounded baby cheeks turning into tiredly-drooping jowls. For all the immediately obvious, if unexpected, validity of Powell's performance the makers of the film, ever-cautious, changed the title soon after release, so as not to shock any members of the audience who had wandered into a cinema in the belief that they were about to see a musical. American audiences thus went to see *Murder, My Sweet* (although British audiences were deemed to be less readily deceived and the original title was retained).

The opening moments of *Farewell, My Lovely* are among the most striking of the *film noir* genre. As Powell/Marlowe intones the depressing facts of his existence to the police, who suspect him of murder, the images merge into a riveting sequence which shows the detective staring out of his window at the neon-lit city. The sudden appearance alongside his reflection of Moose Malloy (Mike Mazurki) is a superb and memorable moment of cinema.

Next to try his hand at Marlowe was Humphrey Bogart in *The Big Sleep* (1946). Despite the convoluted screenplay, which never successfully untangles the equally distorted plot of the novel, this was an effective crime drama. Yet Bogart never becomes Marlowe. Not for one foot of the film does he take on the mantle of Chandler's Knight. Although Powell had managed it very well, Bogart doesn't even try. Instead, he brings to Chandler's Marlowe a considerable slice of the character he had adopted five years earlier for his role as Sam Spade in Dashiell Hammett's *The Maltese Falcon*. The problem with this characterization lies in the fact that, unlike Marlowe, Sam Spade does not lie in that same straight arrow-run between Hawkeye and Marlowe. Sam Spade, in something of the manner of his creator, is rebellious in the face of authority. Marlowe might have been out of step in his view of society, but he was never a rebel.

Two more attempts at Marlowe were made in the 1940s. In *The Brasher Doubloon* (1947), which is based upon *The High Window*, Marlowe is played by George Montgomery who never really gets to grips with the part, although the movie does have its share of enjoyable grotesques, a characteristic of many *films noirs*.

Robert Montgomery's attempt, *The Lady in the Lake* (1947), was rendered awkward and clumsy from the brave but ultimately foolhardy decision of Montgomery, who also directed, to use the camera as the personal eye of the central character. Even with today's small and relatively easily handled cameras this technique would be hard to sustain throughout one and three-quarter hours. With the technical limitations of the day adding to the inherent problems of expecting an audience to abandon its preconceived view of its own role in the cinema, *The Lady in the Lake* was doomed to failure. It is unfortunate that the gimmickry largely obscures Steve Fisher's literate script in which it is hard to see the joins between what is Fisher and what is Chandler's original material.

Hollywood let Chandler and Marlowe rest in the 1950s, leaving them to the mercy of television. An extremely violent series starring Phil Carey ran into problems and was soon dropped which was probably just as well, given the drastic and often substantial cuts that were made in Britain in response to demands for censorship.

Hollywood returned to the character in 1969 with *Marlowe* which was based upon *The Little Sister*. This time it was James Garner's turn to portray the legendary private eye. Garner's attempt was more than merely credible and in many respects this was the best Marlowe image to date. The problem with Garner as Marlowe lies in the fact that the actor frequently chooses to radiate a pleasing aura of naïve good humour which is ill-at-ease with the world-weary cynicism of Philip Marlowe.

Images were shattered when Elliott Gould played Marlowe in *The Long Goodbye* (1973). Leigh Brackett's screenplay, while deeply rooted in Chandler's novel, adopts a deliberately trendy late 1960s view of Southern California which makes its most obvious encroachment in the down-at-heel shabbiness of Gould's mannered hippy incarnation of Marlowe. This and the film's display of contemporary attitudes towards police and society makes an important shift from the feeling of Chandler's work.

Although greeted with enthusiasm by some reviewers, *The Long Goodbye* had much more to do with hippies and 'flower power' (an unfortunate choice since this was already a fast-fading trend by the time of the film's release) than with the essence of Chandler. It was thus as irrelevant to the genre as had been the sophisticated gentleman-crook in *The Falcon Takes Over* three decades earlier.

Given the unsatisfactory nature, in one respect or another, of its predecessors, the decision to make *Farewell, My Lovely* once again was a brave one. This becomes especially apparent when the film's makers decided that the ambience of a long-past Los Angeles should be recreated. In settling on this they acknowledged the importance of the city to the novels. Unlike the San Francisco of Hammett's *The Maltese Falcon*, Los Angeles is more than just a place where Chandler's action occurs. The city is integral to the characters who could not exist anywhere else in the world. It is possible to imagine Sam Spade searching for the Black Bird in any other major American city; New York or Chicago would serve just as well. But Los Angeles is never just a backcloth against which Marlowe and the people he meets play out their lives. They are *of* the city and the city affects the way they behave, how they think, the manner in which they connive and cheat and murder. Anywhere else and they probably wouldn't be in the kind of trouble they are in here. Almost as important as place is time. Chandler's novel was set at the end of the 1930s and while the slight step forward to the beginning of the 1940s does no harm at all, more drastic time changes upset the delicate balance.

The importance of the recreation of place and time were thus a significant burden upon the production designer for *Farewell, My Lovely* (1975). Fortunately, the responsibility was placed in the skilled and sensitive hands of Dean Tavolouris whose work was enhanced by the superb cinematography of John Alonzo, David Zelag Goodman's script takes much of Marlowe's novel, rightly omitting the unnecessary character of Anne Riordan, and makes certain other changes which help smooth the bumps caused by Chandler's one serious failing, his difficulty in writing convincing plots. Here, as in most of his novels, the plot betrays Chandler's economy-minded habit of taking pieces from earlier short stories and stringing them together. This practice created what might be termed a linear-plot in which Marlowe moves from character/event to character/event. Only rarely do his minor characters interact with one another. With a lesser writer the result could have been totally debilitating to the finished novel but Chandler's individual characters are usually so strong and the linking narrative so powerfully evocative that plot dificiencies fade into insignificance.

Dick Richard's direction is strong and if he is, for most of the time, noticeably paying homage to the *film noir* of the 1940s then, as a character of the genre might put it, so what? The fundamental feeling of affection for the central character, the locale and the era of the original story displayed by Richards throughout are essential to the film's mood. It is a mood which, while nostalgic, is sufficiently sharp-eyed to avoid falling into the trap of believing that the old days were always good. In adopting this attitude, the makers of this film are perhaps a little closer to the older more cynical Chandler who wrote *The Little Sister* than the Chandler of *Farewell, My Lovely*. In both novels there is a passage in which Marlowe recounts his view of Los Angeles, and especially of Hollywood. In *Farewell, My Lovely* he sees past the glittering façade of neon to the real tawdriness of the alleyways and clip joints but while mildly remonstrative he speaks with affection. In the later novel he is no longer prepared to accept the reality as a necessary part of his city. Marlowe dislikes what he sees, and says so. Clearly there is much of Chandler's own thinking here. *Farewell, My Lovely* pre-dates *The Little Sister* by a decade and it was a period which also saw the growth of Chandler's disenchantment with Hollywood. The cold dissecting of Hollywood in the later of these two novels corresponds in its ferocity to the view Nathaneal West took of Tinseltown in *The Day of the Locust* and that of F. Scott Fitzgerald in *The Last Tycoon*.

The casting of the 1975 version of *Farewell, My Lovely* doesn't always measure up to that of the earlier version although in some roles this movie is better served. But in any Marlowe movie the actor cast in the leading role is vital to whatever success the production might have. The unheard army of Robert Mitchum fans had known that their idol was right for the part for decades and, despite the fact that when he donned Marlowe's trenchcoat he was, at fifty-eight, some twenty-five years too old, they were soon proved to be ahead of Hollywood's decision makers. (In passing, when Bogart played Marlowe he was forty-six and was thus a dozen years past the right age but no one complained then either.)

The narrative thread of the film begins when Marlowe is hired by ex-convict Moose Malloy to find his former girlfriend Velma. Malloy (Jack O'Halloran) accidentally kills a man at the club where Velma once worked, then goes into hiding as Marlowe sets out to find the girl. At the same time the detective is hired by Lindsay Marriott (John O'Leary) to protect him when he attempts to buy back some stolen jewellery. Marlowe is knocked out during this mission and when he recovers consciousness Marriott is dead. The jewellery the dead man had been attempting to recover had been stolen from Helen Grayle (Charlotte Rampling) who now hires Marlowe to find Marriott's killer.

In quick succession Marlowe meets up with various unpleasant individuals including the madam of a brothel, Frances Amthor (Kate Murtagh), who is only one of several people to meet a sticky end in his wake. In the novel, as in the earlier film version, this character was a man, Jules Amthor, a phony psychic medium. The change to brothel-keeper is a concession to present-day movie mores which, while unnecessary, does not jar. As the body count increases, Marlowe meets gambling boss Laird Brunette (Anthony Zerbe) and is asked to bring Moose Malloy to the gambler's yacht which is a floating off-shore casino. Marlowe tries to contact Malloy through Jessie

Florian (Sylvia Miles), the alcoholic widow of the owner of the club where Velma sang but Jessie is murdered. Marlowe calls in the cops and does a deal with Police Lieutenant Nulty (John Ireland) who follows Marlowe when he takes Malloy to the yacht. There Marlowe confronts the gambler and Mrs Grayle who turns out to be the missing Velma. She had met Malloy when she was one of Frances Amthor's girls and had arranged for him to take the rap for a robbery she helped commit.

All the killings Marlowe has been stumbling through are part of Velma's attempts to prevent Malloy connecting her with the frame which sent him to prison. Velma shoots Malloy and is herself killed by Marlowe as the police come aboard the yacht to wrap up the proceedings.

While the film substantially simplifies the plot of the novel this surgery does not detract from the finished product. Indeed, in many respects it improves upon the original. As director Richards commented in an interview with Alexander Stuart in *Films and Filming*, 'I want a movie where people understand what happened. I don't want them to go out scratching their heads, claiming to know what happened just to be chic. I'd much rather explain as I go along.'

In the event the plot took second place to the characters who drift in and out of Marlowe's path. In itself, this is a sort of homage to Chandler for whom characters *always* took precedence over plot.

Among many good performances in these supporting roles are those of Walter McGinn, Sylvia Miles and John Ireland. McGinn plays Tommy Ray, former bandleader at Florian's club whose life and career have been destroyed by an inter-racial marriage. Miles, as the widow Florian, is superb in her portrayal of a crushed and weary woman approaching death as a release from the squalor in which she exists. (Miles was nominated for an Academy Award.) Ireland ably projects the weary cynicism that was a hallmark of a career that was never as good as it could have been if Hollywood had been more imaginative in their use of actors who were not regular, clean-cut all-Americans.

Robert Mitchum is, of course, simply and effortlessly Marlowe. The weariness inherent in the character had long been a hallmark of the actor and here he sits comfortably in a role which he had already made his own in other parts that were kin to Chandler's creation.

Screenwriter Goodman's opening to the movie neatly accommodates the fact that Mitchum's Marlowe is a little too old for the tasks he is to perform:

This past Spring was the first time that I'd felt tired and realized I was growing old. Maybe it was the rotten weather we'd had in LA. Maybe it was the rotten cases I'd had, mostly chasing a few missing husbands and then chasing their wives once I'd found them in order to get paid. Or maybe it was just the plain fact that I am tired … and growing old.

Later, Marlowe summarizes his place in the uncaring scheme of things to a disinterested Nulty who has offered a deal which will get the private eye off the hook:

Thanks, Nulty, but that's not what I need. What I need is another drink. I need a lot of life insurance. I need a home in the country. I need a vacation. I'm tired, Nulty. Everything I touch turns to shit. I've got a hat, a coat and a gun. That's it.

An admission of human warmth and sympathy for Tommy Ray, his wife and son (all are characters added to the story by Goodman) fits in well with Marlowe's state of mind as he tells Nulty:

Look, we've known each other for a long time, Nulty. You've got to let me go, otherwise that kid of Tommy Ray's is going to haunt me for the rest of my life for letting them kill his old man. He will, you know.

The death of Tommy Ray allows a neat wind up to the film. After gloomily observing that Joe DiMaggio's lucky streak has finally ended, Marlowe, tossing a baseball that has decorated his desk since God knows when, crosses the street towards the broken-down hotel where Ray's wife and son face a future made doubly uncertain by Tommy's murder.

I had two grand inside my breast pocket that needed a home and I knew just the place.

The film can thus end on a note which, while not exactly upbeat, is not quite as downbeat as might have been expected.

The obvious kinship Mitchum felt for Marlowe was enhanced by a curious coincidence the star revealed when interviewed for Thames Television's *South Bank Show* in December 1988. This edition of the show celebrated the 100th anniversary of Raymond Chandler's birth, and Mitchum recalled how he had tended bar at O'Sullivan's, an Irish pub, during his first spell in Los Angeles: 'Chandler came in a couple of times', but was perceived as not being one of the boys because he 'affected an English accent and he wore gloves'.

Most critics approved of *Farewell, My Lovely* and of Mitchum's performance as Marlowe, Martyn Auty, in *Movie*, wrote that 'Mitchum finally made the trip back to his origins and *became* Philip Marlowe. The part might have been written for him thirty years previously but he slipped into the baggy two-piece suit like he had never been away'. Richard Eder, in *The New York Times*, considered that after settling into the part Mitchum's 'performance drops away and he moves through the picture with force, humour and unexpected humility'. Tom Milne, in *Sight and Sound*, wrote that cameraman John Alonzo 'here embalms Marlowe's sleazy LA haunts in an amber shroud penetrated only by the scarlet neon signs of sin. Robert Mitchum (a stroke of casting genius) tucks his weary disillusionment, only a trifle double-chinned, cosily back into the soft felt hat and shabby raincoat that RKO have clearly been keeping in mothballs all these years.' Kathleen Carroll, in the New York *Daily News*, counselled her readers, 'If you are starved for entertainment, this is something you shouldn't miss. You certainly shouldn't miss Robert Mitchum who effortlessly sleepwalks through the role of Philip Marlowe.'

Jonathan Rosenbaum, writing in *Monthly Film Bulletin*, commented upon the many devices with which director Dick Richards had paid homage to the bygone age and genre that had created the cycle of *films noirs*. He pointed out that these devices 'paradoxically take up the equally dated brassy precision of Chandler's weary wisecracking prose and grant it an unlikely second life, letting its inventiveness shine and crackle through the actors' measured inflections like semi-abstract gibberish poetry flourishing for its own sake, inventing its own rules, and triumphantly outlasting the specific narrative circumstances, social portraits and ethical codes that it so painstakingly describes'.   There were few dissenters from the generally favourable view but most critics, like the millions of Marlowe and Mitchum devotees (often the two are interchangeable), were happy the event they'd waited for since the late 1940s had finally happened. Jenny Craven, writing in *Films and Filming*, summed up for all when she commented that Mitchum 'dominates the film, just as Marlowe dominates the book. He is Marlowe'.

The success of *Farewell, My Lovely* was such that a follow-up was almost guaranteed and three years later along came *The Big Sleep* (1978). At the time the idea of pursuing Mitchum as Marlowe doubtless seemed a good one but with the benefit of hindsight it is possible to see the flaws in this thinking. For one thing Mitchum was now past sixty and the fact that the new film was shot largely in bright and rather flat light made the age difference more noticeable.

The producers of *The Big Sleep* were the same as for *Farewell, My Lovely*, Elliott Kastner and Jerry Bick, while the director and writer was Michael Winner.

It has become something of a critical tradition in recent years to pan anything Winner does and especially when he allows his latent cynicism to rise to the surface of his films. Cynicism is by no means a serious failing in a film-maker, least of all one engaged in *film noir* or its latter-day equivalent, but some of the antipathy towards Winner might be explained by his sometimes relentless view which forces his audience into than total agreement with him.

In fact, in *The Big Sleep* Winner's cynicism is held well in check. This might have been an unfortunate choice of style but that doesn't help because an overriding decision to update the film to the late 1970s had already been taken and, worse still, the story had been transposed from Los Angeles to London. As the James Garner and Elliott Gould versions of Chandler's work had shown, updating was possible, if fraught with dangers, but moving Philip Marlowe out of his comfortably seedy milieu of Los Angeles to the Home Counties of England was a fundamental error. It overlooked that critical factor in Chandler's work, that his characters did not simply live in Los Angeles, they were an integrated part of the city's structure, and the city was ingrained in them. Take them out of their milieu and they gasp for breath for a while, then quietly expire. Sadly, this is what happens to *The Big Sleep*.

In this Marlowe tale the private eye is hired to sort out various problems in which the Sternwood family is immersed. General Sternwood (James Stewart) is a disillusioned old man whose daughters, Charlotte and Camilla (Sarah Miles and Candy Clark), have inherited his rebellious spirit but none of his fundamental goodness. Of the two, it is Camilla who has run into most trouble: she is being blackmailed by Arthur Geiger (John Justin), and while Marlowe tries to sort out that little problem Geiger is killed. Camilla is at the scene of the murder but in the 'spaced-out' condition in which Marlowe finds her she clearly could not be the guilty party. As Marlowe follows the trail from one crisis to the next, abetted but not always aided by Charlotte, he finds himself tangling with gambling boss Eddie Mars (Oliver Reed). Marlowe has to scramble long and wearily over several bodies before he can solve the case and discover who really killed Geiger and, more importantly, uncover a killing Camilla really did commit.

The storyline, while not as complicated as the 1946 version, to which the screenplay shows many similarities, has moments which still confuse. Some of the plot complications are resolved by chunks of exposition narrated by various characters. Characterizations are mostly undeveloped as people float into and then out of the story without time to make an impact. With a budget of the size needed to hire all the acting talent on view it seems a pity that some of the money wasn't spent on hiring a scriptwriter with the courage and skill of David Zelag Goodman. After what he had done with *Farewell, My Lovely* there seems little doubt that he might have finally solved the problems that existed in *The Big Sleep* from the moment it left Raymond Chandler's typewriter.

Nevertheless, there are moments to savour; among them Mitchum's delivery of a long speech at the end of the film in a scene with Sarah Miles, who puzzledly acknowledges that he doesn't appear to want money, which develops into a Chandleresque statement of the character's philosophy:

Oh, sure. All I itch for is money. I'm so greedy that for fifty pounds a day, plus expenses, on the days I work I risk my future, the hatred of the cops, of Eddie Mars and his pals. I dodge bullets, I put up with saps, I say thank you very much, if there's any further trouble please call me, I'll put my card here on the table. I do all that for fifty pounds and maybe just a bit to ... protect what little pride a sick and broken old man has in his family. So that he can believe his blood is not poisoned, that his little girls, though they may be a trifle wild, are not perverts and killers.

Mitchum is on screen almost continuously which means that, apart from cast members already mentioned, he is up against such acting threats as John Mills, Richard Boone, Colin Blakely, Don Henderson, Edward Fox and Joan Collins. He copes well with the competition, managing to be casually offhand while never appearing to be careless of what he is facing. For all the quality of his performance, however, and the talents of the others involved when *The Big Sleep* is set against *Farewell, My Lovely* there is not much to applaud.

On the credit side, Mitchum clearly got on well with Michael Winner and eagerly added the director to a growing list of masterly impersonations with which to entertain friends and, occasionally, public.

Fortunately, memories of *Farewell, My Lovely* were not affected by any of the faults which mar *The Big Sleep*, nor by those which afflicted the 1984 TV series, *Marlowe – Private Eye*, starring Powers Boothe. Although London Weekend Television (the British company which made the six episodes) did a superb job of the settings and the overall ambience, the forced jokiness of the scripts and a dull central performance scuttled the whole thing. The 1986 series which was made in Canada had nothing to add.

Without question, the Robert Mitchum version of *Farewell, My Lovely* offers the best of all incarnations of Philip Marlowe, and this film remains a superior adaptation of Raymond Chandler's work.

Farewell, My Lovely had challenged Mitchum to live up to the long-held expectations of many. It was a challenge he met so confidently that he delivered one of his finest and most memorable screen roles.

12 New Directions

Television is too much work. If I do that, I'll get more work.

Robert Mitchum's life and career were replete with a succession of challenges during the first half of the 1980s. Among them were a savage financial mauling which occurred when he discovered that he had been systematically robbed of millions of dollars; his decision to seek ways of combating the heavy drinking which was beginning to affect his health; and a series of career decisions which not only pitted him against a new and fast-rising breed of young screen actors but also brought him into television in the biggest way imaginable.

Perhaps fearing that Mitchum's days as a superstar might be numbered, the Los Angeles Film Critics Association gave him their Career Achievement Award in October 1980. In his acceptance speech he remarked on the fact that he still had to be granted that decidedly Hollywoodian form of recognition, a star on the sidewalk along Hollywood Boulevard. As for his career, he made it clear that he had no intention of quitting just yet: 'Hell, I'm like Lionel Barrymore, they'll wheel me out to play Scrooge when I'm eighty.'

One of the first Mitchum films to be granted a wide release in the new decade was, in fact, a hangover from 1979 when its release was severely limited. This was a World War Two tale entitled *Breakthrough* (1982) which picks up the exploits of Sergeant Steiner, a character from a 1976 film, *Cross of Iron*. The earlier production, zestfully directed by Sam Peckinpah, charted the service career of Steiner, a German soldier, during the major tank battles with the Russian army in 1943. With German soldiers as the principals, if not exactly the heroes, the movie enjoyed good business in Germany but met with mixed critical response elsewhere.

In *Breakthrough*, which takes place during the final disintegration of the Third Reich, Steiner (Richard Burton, replacing James Coburn who had played the role in the earlier film) is with the 71st Division on the Russian front at the moment of a large scale German withdrawal in the face of a massive enemy response.

Believing that Hitler will press on insanely with a lost cause, sacrificing his armies in the process, senior German officers plan to assassinate him. One of them, General Hoffman (Curt Jurgens), decides that Sergeant Steiner is the man to carry news of the plot against Hitler to the Americans. Colonel Rogers (Mitchum), newly arrived from North Africa, has a reputation as a hard man; as one soldier remarks to a comrade, 'He's mean, he's tough, and if there's one thing he hates more'n Krauts, it's Eye-talians.'

Rogers is captured by Sergeant Steiner who relays General Hoffman's message before releasing him. Rogers passes on the message to a highly sceptical Brigadier General Webster (Rod Steiger) and has to insist that word is sent to the American High Command.

When the plot against Hitler fails Hoffman shoots himself and the demoralized 71st Division prepares to tackle the Americans.

Steiner, by now totally disenchanted with the war, tries to prevent a massacre of civilians but is shot and wounded by a fellow German. Later, Rogers is once again saved as Steiner kills one of his own comrades. 'Too bad it didn't work out, Sergeant,' Rogers observes as Steiner salutes and walks away.

As an anti-war film *Breakthrough* almost works; as a straightforward action movie the fundamentally static nature of the heavy machinery involved keeps it bogged down when it should zip along.

Mitchum's performance in *Breakthrough* is competent, and his scenes with Rod Steiger interestingly show the manner in which widely contrasting acting styles complement the differences in the nature of the two characters. There is, however, a touch of ennui about Mitchum; he has been here before and it shows.

In most respects Mitchum's appearance in *Breakthrough* is akin to many of his lesser performances over the years. There is nothing to stretch and test him here and neither was there much to exercise him in a TV movie, *One Shoe Makes It Murder* (1983).

As Harold Schillmann, Mitchum dons an ill-fitting suit, an even wearier list than his customarily languid posture, and once more becomes a private eye. As an ex-cop, failed suicide and part-time alcoholic, the role of Schillmann presents few demands. This is, after all, another place he has been before.

Schillmann is hired to find the missing wife of a big-time Nevada gambling boss. He traces the missing woman easily enough, only to see her fall out of a high window. The fact that she takes the dive while wearing only one shoe convinces Schillmann that this is murder.

With the help and occasional hindrance of Fay Reid (Angie Dickinson), a hooker who knows more than she's telling, Schillmann blunders through in the expected style of any sub-Marlowe character. Unfortunately, the screenplay is also sub-Chandler by quite a margin and this, allied to some sloppy plotting and a jokey, pint-sized cop, Inspector Carmona (José Perez), provides too much of a burden. The customary flat lighting and straightforward camerawork demanded by television moguls doesn't help and neither does the rather flaccid direction.

As the ageing, seen-it-all-before loner, Mitchum doesn't exert himself but even so manages to bring to a routine TV movie a touch of class it doesn't really deserve.

Neither did Mitchum deserve the blow he was dealt in his private life when, at the end of November, his secretary of many years, Reva Frederick (who had married film producer Max Youngstein) suffered a stroke and was forced into retirement. For some years Dorothy Mitchum had been unhappy at certain aspects of the way in which her husband's career was managed, and she now took the opportunity to examine office records.

In the following months several legal proceedings were instituted, among them an action by Reva who sued for retirement benefits to which she claimed she was entitled. This action was eventually settled out of court.

The precise state of Mitchum's finances were never fully disclosed but it appears certain that the greater part of the fortune he had earned over the years had vanished. Instead of having a very comfortable retirement cushion, variously estimated at somewhere between $5 and $10 million, he was broke.

In his 1984 interview with *You* magazine's David Levin Mitchum stated that he had recently mortgaged his Montecito home and reflected that he had trusted people who had betrayed that trust. Although clearly disturbed by the discovery, as was his wife who was much less phlegmatic, he adopted a remarkably sanguine view: 'I have seen this sort of thing happen to too many people who have no way back. I can work. I do.'

And work he did. The offers he was receiving for TV movies were therefore no longer things to be cavalierly disregarded but a potential source of much-needed money.

Two years earlier, in the autumn of 1980, he had started work on a TV movie about Juan and Eva Peron in which he was to play the dictator. Had this come later, he might have decided that it was financially advisable to put up with unnecessary aggravation on the set. In the event, he had walked away after three days, leaving James Farentino to pick up the role of Peron in *Evita, First Lady* opposite Faye Dunaway in the title role. Of his premature departure, Mitchum observed. 'I walked in thinking I was the star and then found I was supposed to do everything the way she says. Listen, I'm not going to take temperamental whims from anyone ... I just take a long walk and cool off. If I didn't do that, I know I'd wind up dumping her on her derrière.'

There was an acceptable kind of confrontation for Mitchum when he went to work on *That Championship Season* (1982) where he was teamed with a formidable group of actors, most of whom are capable of single-handedly carrying a feature film.

That Championship Season is a powerful contemporary drama set in Scranton, Pennsylvania. Gathering there for their annual reunion are some former members of a suburban high school basketball team. In 1957, against all the odds, the team had become State Champions. Now, a quarter of a century on, the team members come together with their former coach to reminisce; but as the men talk together in the home of Coach Delaney (Mitchum) the easygoing camaraderie stretches, then snaps. The goals and ambitions of each, their fears and worries, spark long-forgotten enmities and jealousies. Delaney tries to hold the men together but revelations of old secrets and buried motives make this a difficult task.

As the evening wears on, enmity replaces friendship and old wounds are opened up alongside new ones. It eventually emerges that the one member of the winning team who never appears is the one man who objected to Coach Delaney's unfair and brutal match-winning methods; by implication he is a liberal and in this group's estimation this equates with abject weakness.

In the end, however, old enmities and petty jealousies and rivalries are smoothed over by Delaney who welds the team together again: 'Don't quit on yourselves, boys. Never. You won't lose, because I won't let you lose.'

Men like these typify the shallowness beneath success in a society in moral disrepair and whose lexicon begins with adultery, bigotry and corruption; unfortunately, perhaps due to the powerful personal characteristics of the individual actors (Bruce Dern, Stacy Keach, Martin Sheen and Paul Sorvino), all of whom give excellent performances, the overall impression the film creates is that these men are being held up for adulation.

Written and directed by Jason Miller and based upon his New York stage production, *That Championship Season* came to the screen with an impressive pedigree of theatrical success. First produced in 1972, the play won many awards including a Tony, the New York Drama Critics Award and a Pulitzer Prize. Perhaps the message was less clouded then, or maybe an irony existed which failed to transfer adequately to the screen. In the film, there is a pervading unpleasant odour as team members display acute racism, indulge in coke-sniffing, and show a marked over-fondness for hard liquor.

Although pivotal, Mitchum's role is the smallest of the five but, at sixty-five, he performs creditably with the younger men, all of whom have enviable reputations and powerful screen presences. It was a challenge he met head-on with considerable success.

Great as this challenge was, it did not prevent Mitchum from turning to a project which placed upon him much greater demands. It was also highly lucrative and in his new and unfamiliar state of financial embarrassment this may have been influential in his decision to sign on for the duration of an epic war story.

The sheer size of the project needed to bring Herman Wouk's best-selling novel, *The Winds of War*, to the television screen leads inevitably to the recounting of an impressive string of statistics. The script ran to 967 pages; there are almost 300 speaking roles; locations in America, England, Austria, Germany, Italy and Yugoslavia; the shooting schedule ran for slightly over twelve months; the cost was budgeted at $36 million (but came in $1 million under); the final running time was sixteen hours.

Produced by Pararmount for ABC, *The Winds of War* (1983) owes its existence on film largely to the vision and tenacity of Barry Diller and to the drive and enthusiasm of Dan Curtis.

Diller had wanted to film Herman Wouk's book from the moment he first read it but had to struggle against the author's reluctance to risk his major work to the vagaries of the motion-picture industry. Wouk felt that some of his other novels (*Youngblood Hawke, Marjorie Morningstar, The Caine Mutiny*) had been treated with considerable heavy-handedness. The novelist's initial intransigence generated financial problems for as time passed costs spiralled and Diller encountered serious difficulties in raising the rapidly increasing provisional budget.

Eventually, a deal was struck giving Wouk many approvals not normally granted a writer. He was even allowed to determine both the nature and the placing of the commercials in the breaks. A draft script was prepared by Jack Pulman, an Englishman with whom Wouk felt able to co-operate. Pulman's

previous adaptations of novels for television had included *I,
Claudius, Crime and Punishment* and *War and Peace*. Following
Pulman's sudden death in May 1979 Wouk took over all
responsibility for the script.

Meanwhile, Dan Curtis had been appointed as producer and
eventually as director too. To him fell the unenviable task of
masterminding the project and making sense of those statistics
which soon added up to the most important and prestigious
drama production in the history of American television. It was
Curtis who insisted from the start that the central role in the
story, that of Victor 'Pug' Henry, should go to Robert Mitchum.
Curtis felt that the fact that Mitchum was some fifteen years
older than the character in the novel was a small adjustment to
make to secure the services of a major actor with the necessary
ability, screen presence and drawing power.

Set during the three years leading up to America's entry into
World War Two, Wouk's novel traces the events of those
momentous years through the career of Pug Henry, a senior
officer in the United States Navy.

It has become commonplace for novelists to set their books in
recognizable and often recent historical periods and to fill them
with real people who are fully integrated into the fictitious
storyline. Wouk's novel was by no means the first to do this but
it is certainly one of the most technically successful. Rather than
thread reality through his fiction, Wouk chose to thread his
fictitious characters through historical fact.

A commander in the US Navy, Pug Henry (Mitchum), comes
to the attention of President Franklin D. Roosevelt (Ralph
Bellamy) who sends him on a series of missions to Europe.
Roosevelt, eager to ensure that he knows directly what is
happening across the Atlantic Ocean, wants Henry to be his
eyes and ears, and occasionally his spokesman.

The central thread of *The Winds of War*, traced by Pug Henry,
is only one aspect of Wouk's multi-faceted work. Henry's family
and his own personal life generate many sub-plots. Some of
these remain at a personal level, others spiral outwards to
become integrated with major events as the war in Europe
unfolds.

Despite the arduous complexities of Pug's duties on behalf of
the president, and the pressures these place on his personal life,
he allows further complications to develop when, on his first trip
to Germany, he meets a young Englishwoman, Pamela
Tudsbury (Victoria Tennant), and begins a doomed love affair.

But it is the love affair of Pug's youngest son, Byron
(Jan-Michael Vincent), which generates the main sub-plot of *The*

Winds of War. In Italy in 1939 Byron is employed by an elderly Jewish-American writer, Aaron Jastrow (John Houseman), and meets and falls in love with the old man's niece, Natalie (Ali MacGraw). In time Natalie, who is planning to marry an American diplomat, Leslie Slote (David Dukes), returns Byron's love but there is to be no happy future for the young couple. They marry in Lisbon when he is there on a fleeting visit as a member of the crew of a US submarine. Left behind in Lisbon, Natalie eventually returns to Italy and rejoins her uncle. Now pregnant, she is trapped there as Mussolini aligns himself and his nation with Hitler's ambitions. Desperate to avoid her baby being born in fascist Italy, Natalie tries everything to get herself and her uncle out. Eventually, after many troubled months during which the baby, Louis, is born, they board a ship in Naples in what will be a futile attempt to reach the safety of Palestine.

Pug Henry is torn by what is happening to his family and to himself, as he and Pamela part, and to the world which is fast descending into horror and chaos. Now risen to the rank of Admiral, he is at last given the opportunity to sail again – from Pearl Harbor.

The task of bringing to the screen this story and the momentous events it touches was clearly extraordinarily difficult but the good intentions of writer, director and production team, to say nothing of the huge budget and massive cast of talented actors, should have produced a high quality blockbuster. *The Winds of War* was certainly a blockbuster but the quality remained elusively inconsistent.

Location filming was mostly good, occasionally excellent with some effective set pieces (including a powerful evocation of the London blitz) although part of the $1 million under-budget might have been used to help create better water-borne model shots (admittedly a perpetual headache for special effects departments).

However, being made for television, it is upon the acting that a mini-series (a misnomer in this context) must depend for its strength. Here, the acting performances are something of a mixed bag. The impersonations of real people included a commendable Churchill, a cartoon Hitler, a cuddly bear Stalin with a bad case of pancake make-up, and an excellent Roosevelt from Ralph Bellamy, who had played the role before and had the mannerisms of the charismatic president off to a fine art.

The fictional roles sported an irritatingly petulant John Houseman making even more obvious than usual his penchant for stressing the wrong syllables in his words; Polly Bergen was movingly believable as the uncertain wife of Pug Henry whose behaviour vacillates between tragedy and vulgarity; Jan-Michael Vincent, having lost his bloom-of-youth good looks, which had for a while limited the roles he could tackle with conviction, was in fine, energetic form.

The actors and actresses in the roles of Pug Henry's other children and their associates were all competent while some of the lesser-known names included a very impressive David Dukes and Victoria Tennant (who was not only effective but also managed to collar most of the publicity in her native England).

The two leading roles presented contrasting images and came in for some criticism. Ali MacGraw was worst served by the press who, once a more daring colleague had drawn blood, fell upon her with savage glee. The fierce roasting she received over her performance as Natalie clearly had a seriously adverse effect upon the actress's career and also upon her as a person. In retrospect, it seems clear that she was miscast as the tragic Natalie, but to heap acrimonious insult upon her (and many critics appear to believe that they are honour-bound to be offensive about *someone* in a mega-buck TV series) was unfair and to some extent unjustified.

Robert Mitchum put very little obvious effort into his role (which means that he approached it like he approached everything else in his career) and strolled leisurely through most scenes, often standing stock-still when he could get away with it. Of course, this was what he usually did in movies but *The Winds of War* was largely commented upon by people who appeared to know little of his work over the previous forty years.

It must be conceded, however, that there were times when he appeared to have other, probably better, things on his mind. Maybe he was thinking about the payday at the end; this time it would need more than a paper bag to carry it home in. But overall, he achieved a remarkable consistency in a role which brought him face to face with historical figures, involved him in domestic crises of varying significance and, most of all, required him to serve as the on-screen lynch-pin for a massive undertaking. That he brought it off does him as much credit as is deserved by Dan Curtis who was his off-screen counterpart. Of Mitchum, Curtis remarked, 'He's a complete professional, a joy to work with.'

In interviews, Mitchum declared that *The Winds of War* gave him a million dollars and free lunches for a year. At least as far as interviews were concerned, he hadn't changed much.

The Winds of War enjoyed the third largest audience rating for a mini-series on American TV (after *Roots* and *The Thorn Birds*) with an estimated first-run audience of 140 millions.

By now, no one could be unaware that Robert Mitchum was still a major star. He was featured in numerous magazine and newspaper stories, most of which re-hashed his career complete with all the usual inaccuracies, and appeared on TV talk shows, where for the most part he repeated one or another of his tall stories, often embellishing them still further.

Late in 1983 the star was honoured when 5 October was declared to be Robert Mitchum Day in Los Angeles and two days later was awarded the Life Achievement Award of the American Theatre Arts. To some extent these honours compensated for the fact that he was not even nominated for an Emmy for his work on *The Winds of War* (almost a formality considering his role in such a massive enterprise). The Emmy snub might well have been a result of the fact that during the past year his behaviour in public had begun to give cause for concern. He behaved badly to some journalists at functions and to members of the public, and most of these incidents appear to have had at their root his drinking habits.

By far the worst incident was an interview he gave to Barry Rehfeld and which appeared in the February 1983 issue of *Esquire*. In this interview, in which Mitchum later asserted the journalist had missed the fact that he was playing the role of the bigoted Coach Delaney from *That Championship Season*, he ranged far and wide, making insulting references to individuals, nations and races. Most damaging were his comments about Jews which brought a rapid response from the Jewish Defence League and even death threats from some quarters.

Over the years some reports of his behaviour suggests a kind of intellectual chameleon; a man who takes on the characteristics of his surroundings and can thus switch from earthy crudity as one of the boys to deep sensitivity when in appropriate company. If this is the case then his immersion into the surroundings of his recent film role proved disastrous during the *Esquire* interview.

Mitchum's public behaviour continued to show unfortunate aspects (at this time the financial disaster which had overwhelmed the Mitchums and which must have contributed to his behaviour was not public knowledge) and then, in early May 1984, his lawyer, David Lafaille, announced that his client had entered Rancho Mirage, Palm Springs, the Betty Ford clinic for the rehabilitation of drug or alcohol abusers.

This delayed a planned visit to London for an appearance at

the National Film Theatre for one of the BFI's regular Guardian Lectures. He duly turned up, however, tanned, slimmer than of late, as fresh and sober as a glass of recently-squeezed orange juice, and held a capacity audience enthralled by his pertinent comments, and in stitches thanks to his astonishingly gifted mimicry (Michael Winner might be an easy target for other mimics but how many can also manage Joan Collins?).

Even with the substantial pay-packet generated by *The Winds of War* behind him there was still the need to earn money to try to put his financial life back on an even keel. Among the jobs he tackled was the lead in another TV movie, and important roles in a pair of feature films he made for the Cannon Group.

The TV movie was *A Killer in the Family* (1983). Gary Tison (Mitchum) is a small-time crook doing time, to the despair of his family. Two of his teenage sons, Ray and Ricky (Lance Kerwin and Eric Stoltz), plot their father's escape but their older brother, Donny (James Spader), urges them to rethink, fearing that they will either be killed or end up in the pokey alongside Dad. When Ray and Ricky insist on going ahead with their plan Donny decides to honour the dubious ties of blood and goes along. It quickly transpires that Donny's earlier caution was justified and soon the Tison kids realize that their father and his cellmate, Randy Greenwalt (Stuart Margolin), whom he brings along are vicious, unbalanced criminals with barely concealed homicidal tendencies.

Although generally predictable, the plot takes a nasty turn when the getaway vehicle breaks down and the Tisons commandeer the car of a young family. To the horror of the younger Tisons, their father and his evil comrade butcher the family in cold blood before continuing on their doomed way.

Based upon a real-life prison escape, in 1978, the movie made few demands on any of the participants but was effectively accomplished within the somewhat restricting framework of a production destined for showing on prime-time television.

When Burt Lancaster was hospitalized for heart surgery, Mitchum took over at short notice his role in Cannon's production of *Maria's Lovers* (1984). Set in the small Pennsylvanian town of Brownsville in the late 1940s, the story centres upon Ivan Struchka (John Savage) who is returning there after several years in a Japanese prisoner-of-war camp. Although he survived, the years in the camp were a severe psychological trauma for Ivan and he got through them by building a dream world into which he could escape but which he cannot now fully shake off. In his dream he has a perfect marriage to a perfect woman, his childhood sweetheart, Maria Bosic (Natassja Kinski).

War correspondent 'Dick Ennis' has his own battle plan for *Anzio* (1968) and Peter Falk can't quite believe it.

Relaxing with Dean Martin on the set of *Five Card Stud* (1968).

Time to leave and start life again in *Ryan's Daughter* (1970).
From right: 'Charles Shaughnessy', Trevor Howard,
Sarah Miles, John Mills.

On location for *The Yakuza* (1975) with director Sydney Pollack
and co-star Kishi Keiko.

'Pat Brady' at his desk while Ray Milland appears to have other things on his mind in *The Last Tycoon* (1976).

In *Farewell, My Lovely* (1975) 'Philip Marlowe' wearily surveys the seedy city down whose mean streets he must go.

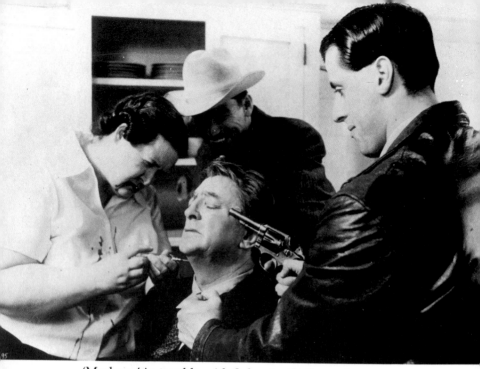

'Marlowe' in trouble with Sylvester Stallone, for once out-
muscled by tough Kate Murtagh in *Farewell, My Lovely* (1975).

'Marlowe' eavesdrops as shadowy Richard Boone prepares to
murder Colin Blakeley in *The Big Sleep* (1978).

Unfortunately for Ivan's plans, Maria's beauty attracts other men. Even Ivan's father (Mitchum) clings on to his own long-faded vitality through a despairing, unstated lust for Maria, a lecherous craving that even his approaching death cannot wholly dismiss.

Directed by Russian-born Andrei Konchalovsky (this being his first American film), *Maria's Lovers* was made at speed (the achieved shooting schedule was forty-one days) and is a moody work shot through with heavy symbolism which its rather thin fabric cannot always sustain. The performances are generally good although John Savage's method-style acting is not easy to accommodate among today's rather more laid-back styles. Natassja Kinski's talents are usually spoken of with bated (and rather hot) breath but there is little here to justify the awe in which she is held by many critics and filmgoers. Of the principals, Keith Carradine, as one of Maria's lovers, comes off best with a convincing portrait of casual immorality. Mitchum's stubbled old man, with wandering lecherous eyes, is a subtle performance of considerable depth and he achieves a strangely moving intensity for what is not, in fact, a particularly sympathetic role.

Mitchum's 'emergency' appearance in a supporting role in *Maria's Lovers* established him, temporarily at least, as resident father-figure at Cannon, the film company then controlled by Menahem Golan and Yoram Globus which had also produced *That Championship Season*.

Too often for comfort, and providing ammunition for its critics, the Golan-Globus stable turned out films which display signs that they were not thoroughly thought through, or were changed in mid-production. Among these signs are uneven narrative threads and sudden bursts of violence which shock for the sake of shocking.

Some of the best and the worst of Cannon's qualities appear in a film made back-to-back with *Maria's Lovers*. This was *The Ambassador* (1984), a tale of diplomatic intrigue in the Middle East.

Peter Hacker (Mitchum) is US Ambassador to Israel. Deeply concerned at the divisions and hatreds which make the region so unpredictable, Hacker attempts to mediate between the Israelis and the Palestine Liberation Organisation.

Hacker is beset by other problems, both professional and domestic. His right-hand man, Frank Stevenson (Rock Hudson), is also the local head of the CIA and is urged by Washington to keep the ambassador under tighter control. Hacker's marriage is on the rocks and his wife, Alex (Ellen Burstyn), is having an affair with Mustapha Hashimi (Fabio Testi). Outwardly a dealer in antiques, Hashimi is actually a senior official with the PLO. Although simplistic in its painting of the opposing sides of an impossibly complicated situation (there are several other story-lines running through the film including a kidnap attempt and the activities of a probing journalist), *The Ambassador* does try to show the good and bad in a clear light. Unfortunately, the simplistic approach renders some of the characterizations two-dimensional. For example, the motive for Hashimi's affair with Alex is insufficiently explored (the inference drawn is that he began the affair because she is the ambassador's wife but then fell in love). Stevenson, the CIA man, is another imprecise figure although, thankfully, not the cardboard cut-out bad guy that most latter-day movie CIA men have become.

As for the ambassador himself, he is given a characterization that simultaneously looks back to the liberal attitudes of the 1960s and forward to changes the film's makers can hardly have imagined would happen a few years on.

Acting performances in *The Ambassador* are generally sound, with a number of fine cameos from such distinguished performers as Donald Pleasance (as a high Israeli official) while the main supporting players, Hudson and Testi, do well in underwritten parts. Burstyn, as the wife seeking a final passionate encounter before sliding into bereft middle-age, is excellent. In his pleas for a peaceful solution to the region's problems, Mitchum is called upon to deliver several long pieces of polemic. In delivering such material, whatever its content, an actor faces the difficulties of getting the message across without alienating his audience who, by and large, are not there to be harangued but to be entertained. Most of the time Mitchum manages to overcome this inherent problem. Nevertheless, he is at his best in the scenes he plays with Burstyn. These moments have great depth and an unforced integrity which demonstrates that there was potential here for much more than the film eventually delivered.

With the 1980s only halfway through, Mitchum had already made a notable mark on his fifth decade in the motion-picture business. Whether or not the impetus was the financial loss he had suffered, he was showing few signs of slowing down and there was certainly no indication that he was prepared to settle for soft options. As the second half of the decade began it was clear that he still had professional challenges to face and the ambition to drive him on. What was also clear by now was that hardly anyone still clung on to the view that he lacked the technical prowess to achieve anything he sought to do.

This attitude contrasted with such past slights as the failure to receive an Emmy nomination for *The Winds of War* which was more than compensated for by the awards he did receive. One of these, celebrated on 25 January 1984, was that perennial peculiarity of tributes to the famous inhabitants of Tinseltown – a star on the sidewalk along Hollywood Boulevard. It was the 1775th star which suggests that, like the people who hand out Oscars, the organizers have a peculiar sense of priorities.

More important than any of this, the coming period would see a gradual emergence of a solid body of critical opinion that he was an actor deserving of accolades at the highest possible level, even if the material with which he had to work was growing steadily less likely to present him with opportunities to achieve that recognition.

13   Is There Life After Hollywood?

> I put people on all the time but they go away and say, 'Aw,
> what he *really* meant was ...' And they get it wrong.

For the past several years Hollywood has been the centre where much of the material needed by America's television networks is made. Studios labelled with still-famous names now echo to the frenetic laughter generated by game shows and sitcoms, the gunfire and violence (albeit toned down by the end of the 1980s) of weekly cop shows, and feature-length movies made for TV alongside megabuck mini-series. Of course, the studios are also fulfilling the needs of the home video markets and, sometimes seemingly by way of an unwilling afterthought, the movie theatres.

Of these three main strands of moviemaking in the late 1980s, two (those made for home viewing and those for theatrical release) are largely in the hands of young men and women, feature their contemporaries, and are aimed at their age-group.

Inevitably, the stories of such films slant in favour of actors at least one generation younger than Robert Mitchum's. Fortunately for actors of his age who are still willing to work, the third stream, TV movies and mini-series, have a different audience and it is in this area, therefore, that an older actor is most likely to find opportunities. Unfortunately, the demands of network television generally require much less adventurous themes and styles. Thus it is that although Mitchum has been offered (and has accepted) many roles he has rarely, if ever, found himself confronting challenges.

North and South (1985) tells a dramatic tale of two families, the Hazards and the Mains, caught up in the American Civil War. Inevitably, the greater conflict overshadows friendships, love and family loyalties as this mini-series progresses through to the conflict's end when all but the vestiges of southern plantation aristocracy are gone with the wind of civil war.

Mitchum's appearance was in one of several cameo roles.

Others were played by Gene Kelly, Elizabeth Taylor, Hal Holbrook and Robert Guillaume. The problem with these cameos was their lack of integration into the overall canvas. Neither were these special guest stars given the privilege of decent lines to speak. Mitchum, whose character was that of a surgeon-colonel of Irish origin, was required to remember at one point, 'Ah, yes, an amputation it was.'

Such minor matters aside, the overall problem, which proved to be insurmountable, was that the central theme of the series, the war between the states, became reduced to a simplistic conflict that no one wanted but for which all were to blame. John J. O'Connor, writing in *The New York Times*, drew attention to these failings, condemning the series as 'a monumental absurdity' and declaring it to be 'thoroughly reprehensible'.

Promises to Keep (1985) was very much a Mitchum family affair. In this TV movie, made for CBS, Robert Mitchum appeared as Jack Palmer, a man who returns to Santa Barbara after thirty years wandering the country to make amends to his wife and son whom he had abandoned on an irresponsible whim. The son, Tom, is played by Robert's son, Christopher, now aged forty-two, while Tom's son in the movie, Johnny, is played by Chris's own son Bentley.

Jack Palmer is heading from Wyoming to Los Angeles where he is to undergo an operation which may save his life, but his attempt to make amends to his family is fraught with difficulties. Even after all these years his wife (played by Claire Bloom) is still angry, while Tom is bitter and distracted by his failing fishing boat business and the fact that his son Johnny is showing the signs of wanderlust that led Jack Palmer to uproot himself and head for Wyoming. The family is eventually brought together by the improbability of a fistfight in which they band together to defeat a handful of local villains.

The potential for an emotionally powerful and dramatic tale was somehow lost and John J. O'Connor was quick to declare that 'Mitchum has been conveying the impression that he doesn't much care what he appears in these days as long as the money is good. He will no doubt understand if the rest of us don't care either.'

For many Mitchum fans the best moments came during the credit title sequence which featured home-movies of Robert and Christopher Mitchum.

Nancy Mills, writing in the *Los Angeles Times*, drew an interesting comment from Christopher Mitchum on the attitude of the press towards his father in the early years in Hollywood. By now a star of movies made in Asia and Spain but almost unknown to the home audience, Christopher recalled his childhood: 'I remember as a little boy answering the phone at home, and it would be Hedda Hopper asking about my father. I'd say, "Just a minute. I'll get him." She'd say, "Don't bother him. Just tell me what time he came home last night".'

Interestingly enough, for the amateur psychiatrist in all of us, the guard Robert Mitchum puts up is there even for those the outsider might think are closest to him. Interviewed by Leslie Bennetts for *The New York Times* while making *Promises to Keep* with his father, Christopher Mitchum remarked, 'I wanted him to be proud of me. Whether he is or not, God knows; he'll never tell me.'

On the subject of *Promises to Keep*, Robert Mitchum had his usual nonchalant last word, also to Leslie Bennetts in *The New York Times*. He claimed that the reason for playing in a movie with his son and grandson was because, 'It's cheaper than paying their room and board.'

The love affair between movie actress Marion Davies and newspaper tycoon William Randolph Hearst has long fascinated writers and film-makers. However, Orson Welles's *Citizen Kane* (1941) said so much with such powerful effect that very little was left to add except by way of passing reference. More than four decades after Welles, ABC television examined the story of this lasting love affair with *The Hearst and Davies Affair* (1985), starring Robert Mitchum as the ageing newspaper baron and Virginia Madsen as the film actress.

Filmed in Canada, the movie opens in 1937 when Hearst was in dire financial straits. Aware that the future may hold little for Marion he asks her if she wants to leave but she decides to stay, observing (and using the mode of address the actress sometimes used in real life), 'It's been one terrific ride, Mr Hearst.'

From here the movie flashes back to 1916 and tells their tale, touching only upon the highlights of their life together, a life which scandalized a nation which pretended shock while inwardly revelling in the juicier details. Unfortunately, perhaps once again due to the homogenizing effect of network television, this dramatic tale of two larger-than-life characters becomes just another soft-soap opera. The performances of the principals proved adequate without ever indicating the depths of passion that must have illuminated the lives of the real Hearst and Davies.

Neither does the movie make any attempt to restore Marion Davies's professional reputation. A gifted comedienne, her career deserved more critical attention that it was ever afforded by those critics who couldn't see past the façade unwittingly erected by her devoted lover.

In 1984 Mitchum visited England where he was doubtless delighted to be reunited with Deborah Kerr, an actress with whom he had enjoyed some of his happiest on-screen relationships. The result of this latest collaboration, *Reunion at Fairborough* (1986), is itself a tale of renewed friendships and rekindled past loves. Carl Hostrup (Mitchum) is among a party of World War Two veterans who come to the tiny East Anglian village from where they flew bombing missions over Germany. Among Carl's comrades are Jiggs (Red Buttons) and Nathan 'Ski' Barsky (Barry Morse). Jiggs is an alcoholic, Ski is still trying to live down the fact that during the war he was terrified of being thought a Jewish coward, while Carl himself is rich and lonely.

Although some of the veteran airmen see the reunion as an occasion for drinking and yarn-spinning and then more drinking, Carl is eager to find the woman with whom he had a brief wartime affair more than thirty years ago. With a disastrous private life behind him, which includes two failed marriages, Carl finds Sally Wells (Kerr) and the old embers begin to glow again. But it is only when he meets Sheila (Judi Trott) that Carl realizes just how much he really left behind. Sheila is Sally's granddaughter and it isn't long before he figures out the relationship the girl has to himself. When the war ended he had returned to America, unaware that Sally was pregnant. A daughter was born and many years later, by then married and with a baby girl, Sheila, she was killed in a road accident. Since then Sheila had been brought up by her grandmother.

Carl tries to forge a relationship with Sheila, an active anti-nuclear campaigner, but comes up against her political beliefs. He is more successful in his restored relationship with Sally as, tentatively at first, they begin to test the possibilities of rekindling their old romance. The veteran flyer proves his virility by taking off from the airfield in a rebuilt Flying Fortress. As the B-17 circles over Sally's cottage she too is convinced that there is still time left for a few years of happiness in their lives.

Gently undemanding of any of its performers, *Reunion at Fairborough* brings to the war years a pleasant, if slightly rose-tinted, romanticism. The 'old magic' which writers of advance publicity suggested would emerge from the reunion of Robert Mitchum and Deborah Kerr was certainly present but the chances are the pair could have brought no less a glow to a joint reading of the telephone directory.

Thompson's Last Run (1986), a TV movie made for CBS, teamed Mitchum with Wilford Brimley, a burly actor whose bit-part career only began to take serious shape in the 1980s when, already in late middle age, he found a comfortable niche as a supporting player in numerous high-quality dramas.

In *Thompson's Last Run* Brimley plays Detective Red Haines, a lawman fast approaching retirement. Haines' last job before handing in his badge is to take habitual criminal John Thompson (Mitchum) from Leavenworth Prison, Kansas, to the prison at Huntsville. A safe-cracker fallen on hard times, Thompson has known Haines since childhood when they were pals and even though their lives since then have placed them in opposition their old friendship proves a still-potent bond. Concerned more with friendship and loyalty than with crime and punishment, *Thompson's Last Run* is told engagingly, and thanks to solid central performances it proves rather better than most TV movies of its time.

The ending, when Thompson, having escaped from Haines, returns to aid his old friend when he is stricken with a heart attack, may be a trifle sentimental but it fits the mood of the piece and the nature of the relationship the movie has allowed to develop.

In 1987 Mitchum stepped into an unlikely breach when British actor Edward Woodward, star of an American TV series, CBS's *The Equalizer*, was felled by a heart attack. While Woodward was recovering, a two-part episode was hastily created in which Robert McCall (Woodward's character) is kidnapped and the only man capable of finding him is his old comrade-in-arms Richard Dyson (Mitchum). Needless to say (and, indeed, thankfully, because Woodward was soon fit for work), Dyson was successful.

The script showed signs of haste and the performances were decidedly uneven and replete with unconvincing Slavonic and European accents. Mitchum took it all with his customary equanimity, and probably enjoyed riding around in his character's Rolls Royce.

Around this same time Mitchum was called in to deputize for another sick man, John Huston, whose mark is upon *Mr North* (1988) even though he died before the production was up and running.

Based upon Thornton Wilder's novel, *Theophilus North*, the film was co-written by Huston, who was also executive producer and intent upon playing the role of James Bosworth. Although Huston's final illness and death intervened, his son, Danny, directed and his daughter, Anjelica, takes a leading role. Aware that he would be unable to take the role of Bosworth, Huston asked Mitchum to step in and play what is a fairly minor part in this whimsical tale of small-town America.

Set at Newport, Rhode Island, in 1926, *Mr North* centres upon a young man, T. Theophilus North (Anthony Edwards), who constantly startles and impresses the people he meets through the charges of static electricity which are conducted through his body. North earns a little money as a reader and is hired to read the Bible to wheelchair-bound James McHenry Bosworth (Mitchum). In fact, the old man is not really sick but is kept immobile by the plotting of his daughter, Sarah (Tammy Grimes), and Dr Angus McPherson (David Warner). North strikes up a cautious friendship with the old man and is also attracted to Bosworth's granddaughter, Persis (Anjelica Huston), a widow.

Discovering that Bosworth is not the only old man Dr McPherson is conniving to keep in ill-health, North takes on the wrong-doers. Restoring old Bosworth's vitality to him, he helps send McPherson packing.

In the end, having charmed the community and cured it of its aberrations, North looks set to form a lasting relationship with Persis and hold an important position at an academy which Bosworth plans to open on the estate of a philosopher the old man admires.

A lightly satirical piece of whimsy, *Mr North* is not the powerfully resonant work many might have wanted to be the last to bear John Huston's name, but it is charming and unpretentious and leaves a pleasant afterglow recalling a past age of popular cinema before sex, violence and four-letter words took over the minds of many moviemakers.

Mitchum turned up in another piece of engaging whimsy, playing a cameo role in *Scrooged* (1988), a film which attempted to update Charles Dickens's *A Christmas Carol*. The tale winds around the heartless young president of a television company, Francis Xaviar Cross (Bill Murray), who learns the error of his ways thanks to ghostly visitations from past, present and future. Mitchum lends his presence only briefly, as Preston Rhinelander, owner of the TV company, sharing screentime with a string of other cameo players including Buddy Hackett, Lee Majors, Robert Goulet and John Houseman, several of whom appear as 'themselves'. Sensibly, no one wasted time suggesting to Mitchum that he should do such a thing.

When Mitchum had finished making *The Winds of War* he was eager to declare that he would not be interested in working on the sequel if it ever came to be. Equally unwilling to commit himself to another long and arduous haul was producer-director Dan Curtis who, as he entered the twelfth and final month of shooting on *The Winds of War*, was asked if he would be interested in working on the sequel. 'No, thank you,' he said.

Time, however, can change most things and when the sequel became not merely talk but a reality Curtis was persuaded to change his mind. 'Deep down inside me,' he admitted, 'I know I've always wanted to finish the story.' It was important for ABC to have the assurance that Curtis's presence brought. After all, an investment of $110 million is no mean commitment, especially when the money was intended for a venture that would be largely one of prestige since the chances of turning a profit were known to be slightly less than zero. Prestige would, of course, be supplemented by extensive worldwide headlines to say nothing of substantial advertising revenue.

When Curtis committed himself to *War and Remembrance* (1988) he was unsure about Mitchum reprising his role as Admiral Henry. For one thing, Mitchum had been fifteen years too old for the role in *The Winds of War* and was now five years older still. For another, Curtis was aware that when *The Winds of War* was released Mitchum had openly expressed his lack of interest in the sequel (and had, anyway, been less than complimentary about the original). Mitchum's visit to Rancho Mirage must also have been on the minds of everyone connected with the new venture, especially as the experience had not been a 100 per cent success although it had certainly put the actor back in control.

In the event, Paul Newman, James Coburn and Gene Hackman were approached before Mitchum came barrelling in to the act declaring that the part was his if he wanted it and, dammit, he did. (The London *Daily Mail* reported in May 1986 that the star even went to the extent of an 'eye job' although there were no discernible signs of any such tampering with nature's course.)

Whatever the pre-production hassles might or might not have been, when shooting began on *War and Remembrance* (which picks up the action precisely where *The Winds of War* left off) Robert Mitchum was back in command as Admiral Pug Henry, adviser to the president.

Several of the leads in the original series returned for their roles: Polly Bergen and Peter Graves as Rhoda Henry and her lover Palmer Kirby, Victoria Tennant as Pamela Tudsbury, with whom Pug had been in love, Chaim Topol as Berel Jastrow, Jeremy Kemp as General Armin Von Roon (a German army fictional equivalent to Henry who moved in high government circles), and David Dukes as diplomat Leslie Slote, the young man who was still in love with the ill-fated Natalie.

Admiral Henry's long-awaited return to active duty comes just as Pearl Harbor is attacked and he takes command of the

Northampton which is part of the surviving American fleet. Also with the fleet, on board the carrier *Enterprise*, is Pug's son Warren (Michael Woods) while elsewhere in the Pacific is the submarine on board which Byron (Hart Bochner) is torpedo officer.

Although he is an exemplary officer, Byron's thoughts are always with his wife, Natalie (Jane Seymour), who is still trapped in Italy with their tiny son, Louis, and Natalie's uncle Aaron Jastrow (John Gielgud). Despite a chance to escape to Palestine on board a boat carrying refugees, Natalie and Aaron have stayed behind in the hope of securing freedom from detention.

Pug Henry's private life is in turmoil as his wife, Rhoda (Bergen), continues her affair with Palmer Kirby (Graves) while Pamela Tudsbury (Tennant) continues to convince him, by her letters, that there is still fire in the embers of their love for one another.

The war in the Pacific piles horror upon horror for the admiral as he watches helplessly when his son, Warren, dies as his aircraft crashes in flames into the sea and the carrier he is supposed to protect is sunk. Then, when he disobeys fleet orders and attacks the Japanese, Pug Henry's own ship is hit and sunk.

Rescued and returned to Washington, Henry is asked by President Roosevelt (Ralph Bellamy) to resume his previous role as globe-trotting adviser. Thus, Pug Henry is once again a welcome guest of heads of state across the world and, once more, he is able to renew his previously uneasy love affair with Pamela.

Henry travels to Moscow where he chances to meet Leslie Slote (Dukes) who asks him to help Pamela obtain permission to visit the city. This is one of Slote's last acts in the diplomatic service. Angry and frustrated over his government's refusal to act on the matter of what is being done to the Jews in Europe, Slote quits and joins the Office of Strategic Services. It is as an agent of the OSS that Slote is later parachuted into France to help establish links with the Resistance but is killed.

Meanwhile, Natalie and Aaron are among many Jews being shunted from place to place and eventually transported to Theresienstadt in Czechoslovakia, the showplace to which the Germans bring the Red Cross and others inquiring into the treatment of concentration camp inmates.

For Natalie, the past months have turned her actively back to her religion and she contrives to smuggle her son out of Theresienstadt but there is no escape for herself and Aaron and soon they are shipped to Auschwitz where the old man goes to the gas chamber. In time Natalie and Byron are reunited and eventually they find Louis. Although suffering from severe psychological damage, the child is alive.

The actors in *War and Remembrance* are generally sound although, as in *The Winds of War*, the enormous canvas upon which the story is painted is often too large to allow even the most gifted performers to make an impact.

Inevitably, given the bad publicity received by Ali MacGraw in the role of Natalie in *The Winds of War*, a great deal of attention was directed at Jane Seymour. Not known for her ability in roles as demanding as this one, she comes through remarkably well and what must have been something of a career gamble appears to have paid off handsomely.

Robert Mitchum also came in for a mixed reception the first time around and his return to the role of Admiral Pug Henry attracted a substantial share of the publicity. As he had done in *The Winds of War* (and, for that matter, in just about every other role in his long career) he strolls effortlessly through his central performance, endowing it with the characteristics needed to help bind together this massive thirty-hour series.

Just as the statistics of *The Winds of War* had bent the mind so those of *War and Remembrance* are numbing in their extent and complexity: 358 speaking roles, more than 2,200 bit parts and over 40,000 extras, a shooting schedule of 21 months for a 1,488-page script covering 2,070 scenes (including some actually filmed at Auschwitz, the first time such permission had been granted to the makers of a feature film).

Despite such an impressive array of statistics, however, the demands placed upon Mitchum by *War and Remembrance* were those of endurance rather than of acting. In this respect, his role resembles so many that he had performed during the 1980s.

As he had previously been with *The Winds of War*, Mitchum was dismissive of his work on *War and Remembrance* (although he did appear as host in a TV trailer for the series). To Tom Green in *USA Today* he remarked that had he not done it, he 'probably would have done a lot of smaller things that were far less nourishing'. Asked if he would watch it, he repeated, almost word for word, his reply to similar questions about *The Winds of War*: 'I'll probably see part of it if I'm in the vicinity.'

That all this work which required great physical endurance but was undemanding of his acting talents should come at a time when most critics were ready to accept him as one of the greatest of screen actors is unfortunate. In order to justify such claims it was necessary for them to hark back to earlier performances, often generously reappraising work which was condemned or ignored by their critical predecessors.

Mitchum's appearance in *War and Remembrance* was far from being the last shot in his locker for the 1980s. As 1988 ended he completed work on yet another TV mini-series. This one, *The Brotherhood of the Rose* (1989), although set in several countries, was made in New Zealand.

Mitchum plays the role of CIA spymaster John Eliot. Many years ago, Eliot took two boys from an orphanage, brought them up as his own, but turned them into spies and killers.

Now, Saul Grisman (Peter Strauss) and Chris Kilmoonie (David Morse) are pitted against one another as Eliot attempts to destabilize his own government. Saul and Chris, code-named Romulus and Remus, join forces and with Saul's ex-girlfriend, Israeli agent Erika Bernstein (Connie Selecca), in a bloody campaign to separate right from wrong and bring the guilty to book.

As so often happens in such dramas, the victors are those who manage to kill most of their opponents. Right doesn't appear to have much to do with it.

Early in 1989 Mitchum was scheduled to start work in Canada on *Smoke Bellew*, a movie based upon Jack London's novel (which had been made into a silent film in 1929 as a starring vehicle for Conway Tearle). And, towards the end of the year, he was slated to play the lead in *Jake Spanner: Private Eye* and in yet another TV mini-series, *A Family for Joe*, in which he plays the part of an old man who adopts four young runaways as his grandchildren.

As the 1980s ended and the 1990s began he was quite clearly intent on working as long as offers came in. And offers did, even if one, for a TV commercial for shampoo, was rejected along with its $250,000 fee.

It would seem therefore that, contrary to his oft-quoted remarks, money isn't always everything.

Afterthoughts

Looking back on Robert Mitchum's career from the standpoint of the early 1990s it is clear that while his activity during the last few years has been extensive it was aimed at something other than the achievement of artistic excellence. At best, this is an unfortunate decision on his part; nevertheless, it can be seen as entirely typical of his attitude towards his work.

Over the years his self-defensive put-downs of his ability as an actor have caused him frequently to decry his talent. Indeed, most often he denies that he has any because to do so would be an admission that he is doing anything for the camera other than be himself. Yet this runs counter to his oft-proclaimed determination to retain a shield between himself and his public persona. The last thing a man as private as he would do is play himself on the screen.

This paradox is only one of many which make Robert Mitchum an interesting man. He writes poetry, for his eyes only, yet has proved himself capable of decking a couple of sailors and a soldier or two in bar-room fistfights. He wrote and directed plays for children at the age of 21, yet refuses to direct a film on the grounds that it means getting up too early in the morning. He can be sensitive in a part, bringing a poet's delicacy to a role; then, in the very next film, he can somnambulate through it with total disdain for the words in his mouth.

Personal interviews with him prove unhelpful in determining what makes him tick. Those he gives are almost always filled with self-deprecatory comments, and overflow with remarks that can scarcely be taken seriously (yet often are by interviewers). He cheerfully contradicts himself from interview to interview, thus confounding those who would seek to discover from the man's own lips that jealously guarded secret self.

Accepting that any attempt to summarize the man is fraught with difficulties, it is easier to assess him as an actor. Easier, but by no means easy.

Including the twenty-five films in which he appeared as an

extra or bit-part player, he has made well over a hundred motion-pictures. These include some which are poor but in which he is always watchable. In many that are themselves watchable, if only average entertainment, he could, when the role so moved him, lift the production a notch or two upwards on the critical scale. In some, he slotted into his role as if it were the most natural place in the world for him to be and accordingly enhanced such films. Among this last group are some films which rank among the finest in motion-picture history.

In *The Story of GI Joe* he brought warmth and compassion to the role of Lieutenant Walker, making the character the true heart of the film. In *Out of the Past* he played the role of Jeff Bailey in a manner which made him forever afterwards the classic male icon of American *film noir*.

For *The Lusty Men* he found a touch of sadness which never degenerates into pathos, a characteristic which he rightly saw would sit ill upon the shoulders of a tough rodeo rider. In *The Night of the Hunter* he became the personification of evil and sustained a bravura performance quite unlike anything he had done before (and which he was never seriously asked to do again). To *Heaven Knows, Mr Allison* he brought exactly the right measure of embarrassed awkwardness to blend into the character of the otherwise self-sustaining marine. In *The Enemy Below* he was the epitome of the single-minded military commander all the while avoiding the pitfalls of caricature. To *The Wonderful Country* he gave to what might well have otherwise been an ordinary western an extra dimension that allowed the storyline to match the scenic splendour of the movie's setting.

In *The Sundowners* he risked touching upon a characteristic of his real self and made Paddy Carmody the man Robert Mitchum might have been, given an existence in another time and place. *The Good Guys and the Bad Guys* allowed him to express a feeling for times past which matched the nostalgic recollections of many who had never in fact experienced the changing times the film displayed.

In *Ryan's Daughter* he helped bridge the gap between the two artistic halves of director David Lean: the vast canvas on which the film was boldly stretched and the tight, delicate, personal tragedy at its core were held together by Mitchum's presence. In *The Friends of Eddie Coyle* he showed himself unafraid to look old and beaten. Tackling the role of a three-time loser at this stage in his career was a brave decision and one which no one can now regret. *Farewell, My Lovely* reinforced his status as a *film noir* icon and placed on film what proved to be the definitive screen interpretation of Chandler's Marlowe.

That Championship Season gave him the challenge of working with powerful actors of another generation in a role which called for him to project a personality at least as commanding as that of his colleagues. *The Winds of War* allowed him to enter television in the leading role in an epic of super-blockbusting proportions, repeating the enterprise in spectacular fashion in *War and Remembrance*.

In this selection of films his roles have been richly varied and should disprove forever charges that he is essentially a one-role player. There is no doubt that to each of these he has brought a highly individual and very different characterization.

Intriguingly, in all these roles, at odd moments, something of the real man shows through in tantalizing and potentially misleading glimpses.

As to the nature of that real man, Julie Kirgo, writing in *Film Noir*, described Mitchum's Philip Marlowe in *Farewell, My Lovely* thus: 'Mitchum's shell may be ... tough ... but within he is a turmoil of unspoken passions and lost dreams. The hooded eyes in the life-creased face may seem remote at first glance; but they are fastened on idealistic dreams and veil a hidden vulnerability.' She might easily have been writing about Robert Mitchum himself.

So where does Robert Mitchum go in the 1990s? Despite the quality of the films listed in the foregoing few paragraphs and the extreme watchability of many dozens more, there is still the impression that as a performer (a term he probably prefers to 'actor') he has not been stretched anywhere close to his limits. Perhaps he doesn't want to allow himself to be placed upon the rack of a really testing film because to do so might endanger his personal privacy. If that is so then no one can really argue with him. It is, after all, his life. But it is also cinema's loss.

Nevertheless, for many millions of Mitchum fans throughout the world who have remained steadfastly faithful to their idol throughout artistically thin times (and thus helped prevent those times from becoming financially thin too), it would prove a memorable and fascinating experience to discover just how far Robert Mitchum could go if stretched.

Maybe, if he would try it, the experience would prove to be just as memorable and just as fascinating to the man himself.

It would be rather nice, if fruitlessly sentimental, to hope that something will come along that might fulfil that demand of his quoted earlier: 'If you want my interest, interest me. If you just want my presence, pay me.'

Maybe, if someone could come along with a script that really interested him he might just decide to turn in the kind of performance of which is so eminently capable and which would allow his Hollywood peers to grant him an Academy Award, that missing accolade he has richly deserved on at least four occasions: *The Story of GI Joe, The Friends of Eddie Coyle, Farewell, My Lovely* and, perhaps most deserving of all, *The Night of the Hunter.*

It may well be that among the films currently being offered to him not many are in the same exalted category as these four but surely, somewhere in the world, there is at least one.

After all, there is still time. But only just.

Filmography

As indicated earlier, the chronology of motion pictures can be complicated by often extreme differences between the sequence in which films are released and that in which they are shot. For example, *Aerial Gunner* and *Minesweeper* were made back-to-back but released many months apart becoming respectively Mitchum's fifth and fourteenth film appearances. Similarly, *Cry Havoc* was kept on the shelf for more than a year; although this was Mitchum's third screen role it was twelfth to be released. The following list adopts the chronology of release dates.

I would like to express by gratitude to Dave Dalton for his painstaking researches; however, any errors which may occur are my responsibility.

B.C.

BORDER PATROL (1943)
UA: 64 minutes.
Producer: Harry Sherman. *Director*: Lesley Selander. *Screenplay*: Michael Wilson. *Photographer*: Russell Harlan (b&w). *Leading players*: William Boyd, Andy Clyde, Jay Kirby, Claudia Drake, Bob Mitchum.

HOPPY SERVES A WRIT (1943)
UA: 67 minutes.
Producer: Harry Sherman. *Director*: George Archainbaud. *Screenplay*: Gerald Geraghty. *Photographer*: Russell Harlan (b&w). *Leading players*: William Boyd, Andy Clyde, Jay Kirby, Victor Jory, George Reeves, Bob Mitchum.

THE LEATHER BURNERS (1943)
UA: 66 minutes.
Producer: Harry Sherman. *Director*: Joseph Henabery. *Screenplay*: Jo Pagano. *Photographer*: Russell Harlan (b&w). *Music: Samuel Kaylin*. *Leading players*: William Boyd, Andy Clyde, Jay Kirby, Victor Jory, Bob Mitchum.

THE HUMAN COMEDY (1943)
MGM: 118 minutes.
Producer: Clarence Brown. *Director*: Clarence Brown. *Screenplay*: Howard Estabrook based upon material by William Saroyan.

Photographer: Harry Stradling (b&w). *Music*: Herbert Stothart. *Leading players*: Mickey Rooney, James Craig, Frank Morgan, Van Johnson, Ray Collins, Marsha Hunt, Donna Reed, S.Z. Sakall, Bob Mitchum.

AERIAL GUNNER (1943)
Paramount: 78 minutes.
Producers: William Pine, William Thomas. *Director*: William Pine. *Screenplay*: Maxwell Shane. *Photographer*: Fred Jackman Jr (b&w). *Music*: Daniele Amfitheatrof. *Leading players*: Chester Morris, Richard Arlen, Lita Ward, Bob Mitchum.

FOLLOW THE BAND (1943)
Universal: 73 minutes.
Producer: Paul Malvern. *Director*: Jean Yarbrough. *Screenplay*: Warren Wilson, Dorothy Bennett. *Photographer*: Woody Bredell (b&w). *Music*: Charles Previn. *Leading players*: Eddie Quillan, Mary Beth Hughes, Leon Errol, Anne Rooney, Leo Carrillo, Frances Langford, Bob Mitchum.

COLT COMRADES (1943)
UA: 67 minutes.
Producer: Harry Sherman. *Director*: Lesley Selander. *Screenplay*: Michael Wilson. *Photographer*: Russell Harlan (b&w). *Music*: Irving Talbot. *Leading players*: William Boyd, Andy Clyde, Jay Kirby, Victor Jory, George Reeves, Bob Mitchum.

BAR 20 (1943)
UA: 54 minutes
Producer: Harry Sherman. *Director*: Lesley Selander. *Screenplay*: Michael Wilson, Norman Houston, Morton Grant. *Photographer*: Russell Harlan (b&w). *Leading players*: William Boyd, Andy Clyde, George Reeves, Victor Jory, Dustine Farnum, Bob Mitchum.

WE'VE NEVER BEEN LICKED (UK: TEXAS TO TOKYO) (1943)
Universal: 103 minutes.
Producer: Walter Wanger. *Director*: John Rawlins. *Screenplay*: Norman Reilly Raine, Nick Grinde. *Photographer*: Milton Krasner (b&w). *Music*: Frank Skinner. *Leading players*: Richard Quine, Anne Gwynne, Martha O'Driscoll, Noah Beery Jr, William Frawley, Bob Mitchum. (Reissued in 1949 as FIGHTING COMMAND)

CORVETTE K-225 (UK: THE NELSON TOUCH) (1943)
Universal: 99 minutes.
Producer: Howard Hawks. *Director*: Richard Rosson. *Screenplay*: Lt. John Rhodes Sturdy. *Photographer*: Tony Gaudio (b&w). *Music*: David Buttolph. *Leading players*: Randolph Scott, Barry Fitzgerald, James Brown, Ella Raines, Andy Devine, Noah Beery Jr, Charles McGraw, Robert Mitchum.

THE LONE STAR TRAIL (1943)
Universal: 57 minutes.
Producer: Oliver Drake. *Director*: Ray Taylor. *Screenplay*: Oliver Drake.

Photographer: William Sickner (b&w). *Music*: Hans J. Salter. *Leading players*: Johnny Mack Brown, Tex Ritter, Fuzzy Knight, Jennifer Holt, Bob Mitchum.

CRY HAVOC (1943)
MGM: 97 minutes.
Producer: Edwin Knopf. *Director*: Richard Thorpe. *Screenplay*: Paul Osborne (from the play 'Proof Through the Night' by Allan R. Kenward). *Photographer*: Karl Freund (b&w). *Music*: Daniele Amfitheatrof. *Leading players*: Margaret Sullavan, Ann Sothern, Joan Blondell, Fay Bainter, Marsha Hunt, Ella Raines, Bob Mitchum.

FALSE COLORS (1943)
UA: 65 minutes.
Producer: Harry Sherman. *Director*: George Archainbaud. *Screenplay*: Bennett Cohen. *Photographer*: Russell Harlan (b&w). *Leading players*: William Boyd, Andy Clyde, Jimmy Rogers, Claudia Drake, Douglas Dumbrille, Bob Mitchum.

MINESWEEPER (1943)
Paramount: 67 minutes.
Producers: William Pine, William Thomas. *Director*: William Berke. *Screenplay*: Edward T, Lowe, Maxwell Shane. *Photographer*: Fred Jackman Jr (b&w). *Music*: Mort Glickman. *Leading players*: Richard Arlen, Jean Parker, Russell Hayden, Guinn Williams, Bob Mitchum.

BEYOND THE LAST FRONTIER (1943)
Republic: 57 minutes.
Producer: Louis Gray. *Director*: Howard Bretherton. *Screenplay*: John K. Butler, Morton Grant. *Photographer*: Bud Thackery (b&w). *Music*: Mort Glickman. *Leading players*: Eddie Dew, Smiley Burnette, Lorraine Miller, Ernie Adams, Bob Mitchum.

THE DANCING MASTERS (1943)
TCF: 63 minutes.
Producer: Lee Marcus. *Director*: Malcolm St Clair. *Screenplay*: W. Scott Darling. *Photographer*: Norbert F. Brodine (b&w). *Music*: Arthur Lange. *Leading players*: Stan Laurel, Oliver Hardy, Trudy Marshall, Margaret Dumont, Robert Bailey, Bob Mitchum.

DOUGHBOYS IN IRELAND (1943)
Columbia: 61 minutes.
Producer: Jack Fier. *Director*: Lew Landers. *Screenplay*: Howard J. Green, Monte Brice. *Photographer*: L. W. O'Connell (b&w). *Leading players*: Kenny Baker, Jeff Donnell, Lynn Merrick, Bob Mitchum.

RIDERS OF THE DEADLINE (1943)
UA: 68 minutes.
Producer: Harry Sherman. *Director*: Lesley Selander. *Screenplay*: Bennett

Cohen. *Photographer*: Russell Harlan (b&w). *Leading players*: William Boyd, Andy Clyde, Jimmy Rogers, Frances Woodward, Richard Crane, Bob Mitchum.

GUNG HO! (1943)
Universal: 88 minutes.
Producer: Walter Wanger. *Director*: Ray Enright. *Screenplay*: Lucien Hubbard. *Photographer*: Milton Krasner (b&w). *Music*: Frank Skinner, Hans J. Salter. *Leading players*: Randolph Scott, Grace MacDonald, Alan Curtis, Noah Beery Jr, J. Carroll Naish, Bob Mitchum.

MR WINKLE GOES TO WAR (UK: ARMS AND THE WOMAN) (1944)
Columbia: 80 minutes.
Producer: Jack Moss. *Director*: Alfred E. Green. *Screenplay*: Waldo Salt, George Corey, Louis Solomon (from the novel by Theodore Pratt). *Photographer*: Joseph Walker (b&w). *Music*: Carmen Dragon, Paul Sawtell. *Leading players*: Edward G. Robinson, Ruth Warrick, Ted Donaldson, Bob Haymes, Jeff Donnell, Bob Mitchum.

GIRL RUSH (1944)
RKO: 65 minutes.
Producer: John Auer. *Director*: Gordon Douglas. *Screenplay*: Robert E. Kent. *Photographer*: Nicholas Musuraca (b&w). *Music*: Gene Rose. *Leading players*: Wally Brown, Alan Carney, Frances Langford, Vera Vague, Robert Mitchum.

JOHNNY DOESN'T LIVE HERE ANYMORE (1944)
Monogram: 77 minutes.
Producers: Maurice and Frank King. *Director*: Joe May. *Screenplay*: Philip Yordan, John H. Kafka. *Photographer*: Ira Morgan (b&w). *Music*: W. Franke Harling. *Leading players*: Simone Simon, James Ellison, William Terry, Minna Gombell, Robert Mitchum.
(alternative title: AND SO THEY WERE MARRIED)

NEVADA (1944)
RKO: 62 minutes.
Producers: Sid Rogell, Herman Schlom. *Director*: Edward Killy. *Screenplay*: Norman Houston (from the novel by Zane Grey). *Photographer*: Harry J. Wild (b&w). *Music*: Paul Sawtell. *Leading players*: Robert Mitchum, Anne Jeffreys, Guinn Williams, Nancy Gates.

WHEN STRANGERS MARRY (1944)
Monogram: 67 minutes.
Producers: Maurice and Frank King. *Director*: William Castle. *Screenplay*: Philip Yordan, Dennis Cooper. *Photographer*: Ira Morgan (b&w). *Music*: Dimitri Tiomkin. *Leading players*: Dean Jagger, Kim Hunter, Robert Mitchum, Neil Hamilton.
(alternative title: BETRAYED)

THIRTY SECONDS OVER TOKYO (1944)
MGM: 139 minutes.
Producer: Sam Zimbalist. *Director*: Mervyn LeRoy. *Screenplay*: Dalton

Trumbo. *Photographers*: Harold Rossen, Robert Surtees (b&w). *Music*: Herbert Stothart. *Leading players*: Spencer Tracy, Van Johnson, Robert Walker, Phyllis Thaxter, Robert Mitchum.

WEST OF THE PECOS (1945)
RKO: 66 minutes.
Producer: Herman Schlom. *Director*: Edward Killy. *Screenplay*: Norman Houston (from the novel by Zane Grey). *Photographer*: Harry J. Wild (b&w). *Music*: Paul Sawtell. *Leading players*: Robert Mitchum, Barbara Hale, Richard Martin, Thurston Hall.

THE STORY OF GI JOE (UK: WAR CORRESPONDENT) (1945)
UA: 108 minutes.
Producer: Lester Cowan. *Director*: William A. Wellman. *Screenplay*: Leopold Atlas, Guy Endore, Philip Stevenson (from the novel by Ernie Pyle). *Photographer*: Russell Metty (b&w). *Music*: Ann Ronell, Louis Applebaum, Louis Forbes. *Leading players*: Burgess Meredith, Robert Mitchum, Freddie Steele, Wally Cassell.
(alternative title GI JOE)

TILL THE END OF TIME (1946)
RKO: 105 minutes.
Producer: Dore Schary. *Director*: Edward Dmytryk. *Screenplay*: Allen Rivkin (from the novel 'They Dream of Home' by Niven Busch). *Photographer*: Harry J. Wild (b&w). *Music*: Leigh Harline. *Leading players*: Dorothy McGuire, Guy Madison, Robert Mitchum, Bill Williams, Tom Tully.

UNDERCURRENT (1946)
MGM: 114 minutes.
Producer: Pandro S. Berman. *Director*: Vincente Minnelli. *Screenplay*: Edward Chodorov (from the story 'You Were There' by Thelma Stradel). *Photographer*: Karl Freund (b&w). *Music*: Herbert Stothart. *Leading players*: Katharine Hepburn, Robert Taylor, Robert Mitchum, Edmund Gwenn, Marjorie Main.

THE LOCKET (1946)
RKO: 86 minutes.
Producer: Bert Granet. *Director*: John Brahm. *Screenplay*: Sheridan Gibney. *Photographer*: Nicholas Musuraca (b&w). *Music*: Roy Webb. *Leading players*: Laraine Day, Brian Aherne, Robert Mitchum, Gene Raymond.

PURSUED (1947)
WB: 101 minutes.
Producer: Milton Sperling. *Director*: Raoul Walsh. *Screenplay*: Niven Busch. *Photographer*: James Wong Howe (b&w). *Music*: Max Steiner. *Leading players*: Robert Mitchum, Teresa Wright, Judith Anderson, Dean Jagger, Alan Hale, Harry Carey Jr.

CROSSFIRE (1947)
RKO: 86 minutes.
Producer: Adrian Scott. *Director*: Edward Dmytryk. *Screenplay*: John Paxton (from the novel 'The Brick Foxhole' by Richard Brooks). *Photographer*: J. Roy Hunt (b&w). *Music*: Roy Webb. *Leading players*: Robert Young, Robert Mitchum, Robert Ryan, Gloria Grahame, Sam Levene, Steve Brodie, Paul Kelly.

DESIRE ME (1947)
MGM: 91 minutes.
Producer: Arthur Hornblow Jr. *Directors*: Arthur Hornblow Jr (George Cukor, Jack Conway, Mervyn LeRoy all uncredited at own request). *Screenplay*: Marguerite Roberts, Zoe Atkins, Casey Robinson (from the novel 'Karl and Anna' by Leonhard Frank). *Photographer*: Joseph Ruttenberg (b&w). *Music*: Herbert Stothart. *Leading players*: Greer Garson, Robert Mitchum, Richard Hart, Morris Ankrum, George Zucco.

OUT OF THE PAST (UK: BUILD MY GALLOWS HIGH) (1947)
RKO: 97 minutes.
Producer: Warren Duff. *Director*: Jacques Tourneur. *Screenplay*: Daniel Mainwaring under nom-de-plume Geoffrey Homes (from his own novel 'Build My Gallows High'). *Photographer*: Nicholas Musuraca (b&w). *Music*: Roy Webb. *Leading players*: Robert Mitchum, Jane Greer, Kirk Douglas, Richard Webb, Steve Brodie, Virginia Huston, Paul Valentine, Rhonda Fleming.

RACHEL AND THE STRANGER (1948)
RKO: 92 minutes.
Producers: Richard H. Berger, Jack L. Gross. *Director*: Norman Foster. *Screenplay*: Waldo Salt (from the novel 'Rachel' by Howard Fast). *Photographer*: Maury Gertsman (b&w). *Music*: Roy Webb. *Leading players*: Loretta Young, William Holden, Robert Mitchum, Tom Tully.

BLOOD ON THE MOON (1948)
RKO: 88 minutes.
Producer: Sid Rogell, Theron Warth. *Director*: Robert Wise. *Screenplay*: Lillie Hayward (from the novel 'Gunman's Choice' by Luke Short). *Photographer*: Nicholas Musuraca (b&w). *Music*: Roy Webb. *Leading players*: Robert Mitchum, Barbara Bel Geddes, Robert Preston, Walter Brennan, Phyllis Thaxter, Frank Faylen.

THE RED PONY (1949)
Republic: 89 minutes.
Producer: Lewis Milestone. *Director*: Lewis Milestone. *Screenplay*: John Steinbeck (from his own novel). *Photographer*: Tony Gaudio (Technicolor). *Music*: Aaron Copland. *Leading players*: Myrna Loy, Robert Mitchum, Louis Calhern, Shepperd Strudwick, Margaret Hamilton, Peter Miles, Beau Bridges.

THE BIG STEAL (1949)
RKO: 71 minutes.
Producer: Jack J. Gross. *Director*: Don Siegel. *Screenplay*: Geoffrey

Homes, Gerald Drayson Adams (from the story 'The Road to Carmichael's by Richard Wormser). *Photographer*: Harry J. Wild (b&w). *Music*: Leigh Harline. *Leading players*: Robert Mitchum, Jane Greer, William Bendix, Patric Knowles, Ramon Novarro.

HOLIDAY AFFAIR (1949)
RKO: 87 minutes.
Producer: Don Hartman. *Director*: Don Hartman. *Screenplay*: Isobel Lennart (from the story 'Christmas Gift' by John D. Weaver). *Photographer*: Milton R. Krasner (b&w). *Music*: Roy Webb. *Leading players*: Robert Mitchum, Janet Leigh, Wendell Corey.

WHERE DANGER LIVES (1950)
RKO: 84 minutes.
Producer: Irving Cummings Jr. *Director*: John Farrow. *Screenplay*: Charles Bennett. *Photographer*: Nicholas Musuraca (b&w). *Music*: Roy Webb. *Leading players*: Robert Mitchum, Faith Domergue, Claude Rains, Maureen O'Sullivan.

MY FORBIDDEN PAST (1951)
RKO: 81 minutes.
Producers: Robert Sparks, Polan Banks. *Director*: Robert Stevenson. *Screenplay*: Marion Parsonnet (from the novel 'Carriage Entrance' by Polan Banks). *Photographer*: Harry J. Wild (b&w). *Music*: Frederick Hollander. *Leading players*: Robert Mitchum, Ava Gardner, Melvyn Douglas.

HIS KIND OF WOMAN (1951)
RKO: 120 minutes.
Producer: Robert Sparks. *Director*: John Farrow (and Richard Fleischer uncredited). *Screenplay*: Frank Fenton, Jack Leonard. *Photographer*: Harry J. Wild (b&w). *Music*: Leigh Harline. *Leading players*: Robert Mitchum, Jane Russell, Vincent Price, Raymond Burr, Tim Holt, Charles McGraw.

THE RACKET (1951)
RKO: 89 minutes.
Producer: Edmund Grainger. *Director*: John Cromwell. *Screenplay*: W. R. Burnett, William Wister Haines (from the play by Bartlett Cormack). *Photographer*: George E. Diskant (b&w). *Music*: Paul Sawtell, Roy Webb. *Leading players*: Robert Mitchum, Lizabeth Scott, Robert Ryan, Ray Collins, William Talman, Robert Hutton, William Conrad.

MACAO (1952)
RKO: 80 minutes.
Producer: Alex Gottlieb. *Directors*: Joseph von Sternberg (and Nicholas Ray uncredited). *Screenplay*: Bernard C. Schoenfeld, Stanley Rubin. *Photographer*: Harry J. Wild (b&w). *Music*: Anthony Collins. *Leading*

players: Robert Mitchum, Jane Russell, William Bendix, Gloria Grahame, Thomas Gomez.

ONE MINUTE TO ZERO (1952)
RKO: 105 minutes.
Producer: Edmund Grainger. *Director*: Tay Garnett. *Screenplay*: Milton Krims, William Wister Haines. *Photographer*: William E. Snyder (b&w). *Music*: Victor Young. *Leading players*: Robert Mitchum, Ann Blyth, William Talman, Charles McGraw.

THE LUSTY MEN (1952)
RKO: 112 minutes.
Producers: Jerry Wald, Norman Krasner. *Director*: Nicholas Ray. *Screenplay*: David Dortort, Horace McCoy. *Photographer*: Lee Garmes (b&w). *Music*: Roy Webb. *Leading players*: Robert Mitchum, Susan Hayward, Arthur Kennedy, Arthur Hunnicutt.

ANGEL FACE (1952)
RKO: 90 minutes.
Producer: Otto Preminger. *Director*: Otto Preminger. *Screenplay*: Frank Nugent, Oscar Millard. *Photographer*: Harry Stradling (b&w). *Music*: Dimitri Tiomkin. *Leading players*: Robert Mitchum, Jean Simmons, Mona Freeman, Herbert Marshall, Leon Ames.

WHITE WITCH DOCTOR (1953)
TCF: 95 minutes.
Producer: Otto Lang. *Director*: Henry Hathaway. *Screenplay*: Ivan Goff, Ben Roberts. *Photographer*: Leon Shamroy (Technicolor). *Music*: Bernard Herrmann. *Leading players*: Robert Mitchum, Susan Hayward, Walter Slezak, Timothy Carey.

SECOND CHANCE (1953)
RKO: 82 minutes.
Producers: Edmund Grainger, Sam Wiesenthal. *Director*: Rudolph Maté. *Screenplay*: Oscar Millard, Sydney Boehm. *Photographer*: William E. Snyder (Technicolor and 3-D). *Music*: Roy Webb. *Leading players*: Robert Mitchum, Linda Darnell, Jack Palance.

SHE COULDN'T SAY NO (UK: BEAUTIFUL BUT DANGEROUS) (1954)
RKO: 89 minutes.
Producer: Robert Sparks. *Director*: Lloyd Bacon. *Screenplay*: D. D. Beauchamp, William Bowers, Richard Flourney (from Beauchamp's story 'Enough For Happiness'). *Photographer*: Harry J. Wild (b&w). *Music*: Roy Webb. *Leading players*: Robert Mitchum, Jean Simmons, Arthur Hunnicutt, Edgar Buchanan, Wallace Ford (released in UK in 1953).
(alternative title: SHE HAD TO SAY YES)

RIVER OF NO RETURN (1954)
TCF: 91 minutes.
Producer: Stanley Rubin. *Director*: Otto Preminger. *Screenplay*: ˙Frank

Fenton. *Photographer*: Joseph LaShelle (Technicolor and CinemaScope). *Music*: Cyril Mockridge. *Leading players*: Robert Mitchum, Marilyn Monroe, Rory Calhoun, Tommy Rettig.

TRACK OF THE CAT (1954)
WB: 102 minutes.
Producers: John Wayne, Robert Fellows. *Director*: William A. Wellman. *Screenplay*: A. I. Bezzerides (from the novel by Walter Van Tilburg Clark). *Photographer*: William H. Clothier (WarnerColor and CinemaScope). *Music*: Roy Webb. *Leading players*: Robert Mitchum, Teresa Wright, Beaulah Bondi, Philip Tonge, Diana Lynn, Tab Hunter, William Hopper, Carl Switzer.

NOT AS A STRANGER (1955)
UA: 135 minutes.
Producer: Stanley Kramer. *Director*: Stanley Kramer. *Screenplay*: Edna and Edward Anhalt (from the novel by Morton Thompson). *Photographer*: Franz Planer (b&w). *Music*: George Antheil. *Leading players*: Robert Mitchum, Olivia de Havilland, Frank Sinatra, Charles Bickford, Gloria Grahame, Broderick Crawford, Myron McCormick, Harry Morgan, Lee Marvin.

THE NIGHT OF THE HUNTER (1955)
UA: 93 minutes.
Producer: Paul Gregory. *Director*: Charles Laughton. *Screenplay*: James Agee (from the novel by Davis Grubb). *Photographer*: Stanley Cortez (b&w). *Music*: Walter Schumann. *Leading players*: Robert Mitchum, Shelley Winters, Lillian Gish, James Gleason, Peter Graves, Billy Chapin, Sally Jane Bruce, Don Beddoe.

MAN WITH THE GUN (UK: The Trouble Shooter) (1955)
UA: 84 minutes.
Producer: Samuel Goldwyn Jr. *Director*: Richard Wilson. *Screenplay*: N. B. Stone Jr, Richard Wilson. *Photographer*: Lee Garmes (b&w). *Music*: Alex North. *Leading players*: Robert Mitchum, Jan Sterling, Karen Sharpe, Henry Hull, Emile Meyer, Barbara Lawrence.

FOREIGN INTRIGUE (1956)
UA: 106 minutes.
Producer: Sheldon Reynolds. *Director*: Sheldon Reynolds. *Screenplay*: Sheldon Reynolds. *Photographer*: Bertil Palmgren (Eastman Color). *Music*: Paul Durand. *Leading players*: Robert Mitchum, Genevieve Page, Ingrid Tulean (Thulin), Eugene Deckers, Frederick O'Brady.

BANDIDO! (1956)
UA: 92 minutes.
Producer: Robert L. Jacks. *Director*: Richard Fleischer. *Screenplay*: Earl Felton. *Photographer*: Ernest Laszlo (DeLuxe Color and CinemaScope). *Music*: Max Steiner. *Leading players*: Robert Mitchum, Ursula Thiess, Gilbert Roland, Zachary Scott.

HEAVEN KNOWS, MR ALLISON (1957)
TCF: 107 minutes.
Producers: Buddy Adler, Eugene Frenke. *Director*: John Huston. *Screenplay*: John Lee Mahin, John Huston (from the novel by Charles Shaw). *Photographer*: Oswald Morris (DeLuxe Color and CinemaScope). *Music*: Georges Auric. *Leading players*: Robert Mitchum, Deborah Kerr.

FIRE DOWN BELOW (1957)
Warwick-Columbia: 116 minutes.
Producers: Irving Allen, Albert R. Broccoli. *Director*: Robert Parrish. *Screenplay*: Irwin Shaw (from the novel by Max Catto). *Photographers*: Desmond Dickinson, Cyril Knowles (Technicolor and CinemaScope). *Music*: Arthur Benjamin, Kenneth V. Jones, Douglas Gamley. *Leading players*: Robert Mitchum, Rita Hayworth, Jack Lemmon, Herbert Lom, Bernard Lee, Anthony Newley, Bonar Colleano Jr.

THE ENEMY BELOW (1957)
TCF: 98 minutes.
Producer: Dick Powell. *Director*: Dick Powell. *Screenplay*: Wendell Mayes (from the novel by Cmdr. D. A. Rayner). *Photographer*: Harold Rossen (DeLuxe Color and CinemaScope). *Music*: Leigh Harline. *Leading players*: Robert Mitchum, Curt Jurgens, Al (David) Hedison, Theodore Bikel.

THUNDER ROAD (1958)
UA: 92 minutes.
Producer: Robert Mitchum. *Director*: Arthur Ripley. *Screenplay*: James Atlee Phillips, Walter Wise. *Photographers*: Alan Stensvold, David Ettenson (b&w). *Music*: Jack Marshall. *Leading players*: Robert Mitchum, Gene Barry, Jacques Aubuchon, Keely Smith, James Mitchum.

THE HUNTERS (1958)
TCF: 108 minutes.
Producer: Dick Powell. *Director*: Dick Powell. *Screenplay*: Wendell Mayes (from the novel by James Salter). *Photographer*: Charles G. Clarke (DeLuxe Color and CinemaScope). *Music*: Paul Sawtell. *Leading players*: Robert Mitchum, Robert Wagner, Richard Egan, May Britt, Lee Phillips.

THE ANGRY HILLS (1959)
MGM: 105 minutes.
Producer: Raymond Stross. *Director*: Robert Aldrich. *Screenplay*: A. I. Bezzerides (from the novel by Leon Uris). *Photographer*: Stephen Dade (b&w and CinemaScope). *Music*: Richard (Rodney) Bennett. *Leading players*: Robert Mitchum, Stanley Baker, Elisabeth Mueller, Gia Scala, Theodore Bikel, Sebastian Cabot, Donald Wolfit, Kieron Moore.

THE WONDERFUL COUNTRY (1959)
UA: 96 minutes.
Producer: Chester Erskine. *Director*: Robert Parrish. *Screenplay*: Robert

Ardrey (from the novel by Tom Lea). *Photographers*: Floyd Crosby, Alex Phillips (Technicolor). *Music*: Alex North. *Leading players*: Robert Mitchum, Julie London, Gary Merrill, Jack Oakie, Albert Dekker, Pedro Armendariz, Charles McGraw, Leroy 'Satchel' Paige.

HOME FROM THE HILL (1960)
MGM: 150 minutes.
Producer: Edmund Grainger. *Director*: Vincente Minnelli. *Screenplay*: Harriet Frank Jr, Irving Ravetch (from the novel by William Humphrey). *Photographer*: Milton Krasner (Metrocolor and CinemaScope). *Music*: Bronislau Kaper. *Leading players*: Robert Mitchum, Eleanor Parker, George Peppard, George Hamilton, Everett Sloane, Luana Patten.

THE NIGHT FIGHTERS (UK: A TERRIBLE BEAUTY) (1960)
UA: 88 minutes.
Producer: Raymond Stross. *Director*: Tay Garnett. *Screenplay*: Robert Wright Campbell (from the novel 'A Terrible Beauty' by Arthur Roth). *Photographer*: Stephen Dade (b&w). *Music*: Cedric Thorpe-Davie. *Leading players*: Robert Mitchum, Anne Heywood, Cyril Cusack, Dan O'Herlihy, Richard Harris.

THE SUNDOWNERS (1960)
WB: 133 minutes.
Producer: Gerry Blattner. *Director*: Fred Zinnemann. *Screenplay*: Isobel Lennart (from the novel by Jon Cleary). *Photographer*: Jack Hildyard (Technicolor). *Music*: Dimitri Tiomkin. *Leading players*: Robert Mitchum, Deborah Kerr, Michael Anderson Jr, Peter Ustinov, Glynis Johns, Dina Merrill, John Meillon, Mervyn Johns, Ronald Fraser.

THE GRASS IS GREENER (1960)
Universal: 104 minutes.
Producer: Stanley Donen. *Director*: Stanley Donen. *Screenplay*: Hugh and Margaret Williams (from their own stage play). *Photographer*: Christopher Challis (Technicolor and Technirama). *Music*: Noël Coward. *Leading players*: Cary Grant, Deborah Kerr, Jean Simmons, Robert Mitchum, Moray Watson.

THE LAST TIME I SAW ARCHIE (1961)
UA: 98 minutes.
Producer: Jack Webb. *Director*: Jack Webb. *Screenplay*: William Bowers (from the novel 'Archie' by Rodney Carlisle). *Photographer*: Joseph MacDonald (b&w). *Music*: Frank Comstock. *Leading players*: Robert Mitchum, Jack Webb, Martha Hyer, France Nuyen.

CAPE FEAR (1962)
Universal: 105 minutes.
Producer: Sy Bartlett. *Director*: J. Lee Thompson. *Screenplay*: James R. Webb (from the novel 'The Executioners' by John D. MacDonald). *Photographer*: Sam Leavitt (b&w). *Music*: Bernard Herrmann. *Leading*

players: Robert Mitchum, Gregory Peck, Polly Bergen, Martin Balsam, Jack Kruschen, Telly Savalas, Lori Martin, Barrie Chase.

THE LONGEST DAY (1962)
TCF: 180 minutes.
Producer: Darryl F. Zanuck. *Directors*: Andrew Marton, Ken Annakin, Bernhard Wicki (and Gerd Oswald, Darryl F. Zanuck uncredited). *Screenplay*: Cornelius Ryan (from his own novel) with additional scenes by Romain Gary, James Jones, David Pursall, Jack Seddon. *Photographers*: Jean Bourgoin, Henri Persin, Walter Wottitz (b&w and CinemaScope). *Music*: Maurice Jarre. *Leading players*: John Wayne, Robert Mitchum, Henry Fonda, Robert Ryan, Rod Steiger, Robert Wagner, Richard Beymer, Mel Ferrer.

TWO FOR THE SEESAW (1962)
UA: 119 minutes.
Producer: Walter Mirisch. *Director*: Robert Wise. *Screenplay*: Isobel Lennart (from the play by William Gibson). *Photographer*: Ted McCord (b&w and Panavision). *Music*: André Previn. *Leading players*: Robert Mitchum, Shirley MacLaine.

THE LIST OF ADRIAN MESSENGER (1963)
Universal: 98 minutes.
Producer: Edward Lewis. *Director*: John Huston. *Screenplay*: Anthony Veiller (from the novel by Philip MacDonald). *Photographer*: Joe MacDonald (b&w). *Music*: Jerry Goldsmith. *Leading players*: George C. Scott, Dana Wynter, Clive Brook, Gladys Cooper, Herbert Marshall, Kirk Douglas with cameo roles by Robert Mitchum, Tony Curtis, Burt Lancaster, Frank Sinatra.

RAMPAGE (1963)
WB/Seven Arts: 98 minutes.
Producer: William Fadiman. *Director*: Phil Karlson (and Henry Hathaway uncredited). *Screenplay*: Robert I. Holt, Marguerite Roberts (from the novel by Alan Caillou). *Photographer*: Harold Lipstein (Technicolor). *Music*: Elmer Bernstein. *Leading players*: Robert Mitchum, Elsa Martinelli, Jack Hawkins, Sabu.

MAN IN THE MIDDLE (1964)
TCF: 94 minutes.
Producer: Walter Seltzer. *Director*: Guy Hamilton. *Screenplay*: Keith Waterhouse, Willis Hall (from the novel 'The Winston Affair' by Howard Fast). *Photographer*: Wilkie Cooper (b&w and CinemaScope). *Music*: Lionel Bart, John Barry. *Leading players*: Robert Mitchum, Keenan Wynn, Sam Wanamaker, Trevor Howard, France Nuyen, Barry Sullivan, Alexander Knox.

WHAT A WAY TO GO! (1964)
TCF: 111 minutes.
Producer: Arthur P. Jacobs. *Director*: J. Lee Thompson. *Screenplay*: Betty

Comden, Adolph Green. *Photographer*: Leon Shamroy (DeLuxe Color and CinemaScope). *Music*: Nelson Riddle. *Leading players*: Shirley MacLaine, Paul Newman, Robert Mitchum, Dean Martin, Gene Kelly, Bob Cummings, Dick Van Dyke.

MISTER MOSES (1965)
UA: 113 minutes.
Producer: Frank Ross. *Director*: Ronald Neame. *Screenplay*: Charles Beaumont, Monja Danischewsky (from the novel by Max Catto). *Photographer*: Oswald Morris (Technicolor and Panavision). *Music*: John Barry. *Leading players*: Robert Mitchum, Carroll Baker, Ian Bannen, Alexander Knox, Raymond St Jacques, Orlando Martins.

EL DORADO (1966)
Paramount: 126 minutes.
Producer: Howard Hawks. *Director*: Howard Hawks. *Screenplay*: Leigh Brackett (from the novel 'The Stars in Their Courses' by Harry Brown). *Photographer*: Harold Rossen (Technicolor). *Music*: Nelson Riddle. *Leading players*: John Wayne, Robert Mitchum, James Caan, Arthur Hunnicutt.

THE WAY WEST (1967)
UA: 122 minutes.
Producer: Harold Hecht. *Director*: Andrew V. McLaglen. *Screenplay*: Ben Maddow, Mitch Linderman (from the novel by A. B. Guthrie). *Photographer*: William H. Clothier (DeLuxe Color and Panavision). *Music*: Bronislau Kaper. *Leading players*: Robert Mitchum, Kirk Douglas, Richard Widmark, Lola Albright.

ANZIO (UK: THE BATTLE FOR ANZIO) (1968)
Columbia: 117 minutes.
Producer: Dino De Laurentiis. *Director*: Edward Dmytryk. *Screenplay*: Harry A. L. Craig (from the novel by Wynford Vaughan Thomas). *Photographer*: Giuseppe Rotunno (Technicolor and Panavision). *Music*: Riz Ortolani. *Leading players*: Robert Mitchum, Peter Falk, Arthur Kennedy, Robert Ryan, Earl Holliman, Mark Damon.

VILLA RIDES! (1968)
Paramount: 125 minutes.
Producer: Ted Richmond. *Director*: Buzz Kulik. *Screenplay*: Robert Towne, Sam Peckinpah (from the novel 'Pancho Villa' by William Douglas Lansford. *Photographer*: Jack Hildyard (Technicolor and Panavision). *Music*: Maurice Jarre. *Leading players*: Robert Mitchum, Yul Brynner, Charles Bronson, Grazia Buccella.

FIVE CARD STUD (1968)
Paramount: 103 minutes.
Producer: Hal B. Wallis. *Director*: Henry Hathaway. *Screenplay*: Marguerite Roberts (from the novel 'Glory Gulch' by Ray Gaulden).

Photographer: Daniel L. Fapp (Technicolor). *Music*: Maurice Jarre. *Leading players*: Robert Mitchum, Dean Martin, Inger Stevens, Roddy McDowall.

SECRET CEREMONY (1968)
Universal: 109 minutes.
Producer: John Heyman, Norman Priggen. *Director*: Joseph Losey. *Screenplay*: George Tabori. *Photographer*: Gerald Fisher (Technicolor). *Music*: Richard Rodney Bennett. *Leading players*: Elizabeth Taylor, Mia Farrow, Robert Mitchum, Pamela Brown, Peggy Ashcroft.

YOUNG BILLY YOUNG (1969)
UA: 88 minutes.
Producer: Max E. Youngstein. *Director*: Burt Kennedy. *Screenplay*: Burt Kennedy (from the novel 'Who Rides with Wyatt' by Will Henry). *Photographer*: Harry Stradling Jr (DeLuxe Color). *Music*: Shelly Manne. *Leading players*: Robert Mitchum, Angie Dickinson, Robert Walker Jr, David Carradine, Jack Kelly.

THE GOOD GUYS AND THE BAD GUYS (1969)
WB/Seven Arts: 90 minutes.
Producers: Ronald M. Cohen, Dennis Shryack. *Director*: Burt Kennedy. *Screenplay*: Ronald M. Cohen, Dennis Shryack. *Photographer*: Harry Stradling Jr (Technicolor and Panavision). *Music*: William Lava. *Leading players*: Robert Mitchum, George Kennedy, Martin Balsam, David Carradine, Lois Nettleton, Dick Peabody, John Davis Chandler.

RYAN'S DAUGHTER (1970)
MGM: 206 minutes.
Producer: Anthony Havelock-Allan. *Director*: David Lean. *Screenplay*: Robert Bolt. *Photographer*: Freddie Young (Metrocolor and Super Panavision). *Music*: Maurice Jarre. *Leading players*: Robert Mitchum, Sarah Miles, Trevor Howard, John Mills, Christopher Jones, Leo McKern, Barry Foster.

GOING HOME (1971)
MGM: 97 minutes.
Producer: Herbert B. Leonard. *Director*: Herbert B. Leonard. *Screenplay*: Lawrence B. Marcus. *Photographer*: Fred Jackman (Metrocolor). *Music*: Bill Walker. *Leading players*: Robert Mitchum, Jan-Michael Vincent, Brenda Vaccaro.

THE WRATH OF GOD (1972)
MGM: 111 minutes.
Producer: Ralph Nelson. *Director*: Ralph Nelson. *Screenplay*: Ralph Nelson (from the novel by James Graham). *Photographer*: Alex Phillips Jr (Metrocolor and Panavision). *Music*: Lalo Schifrin. *Leading players*: Robert Mitchum, Rita Hayworth, Frank Langella, Victor Buono, Ken Hutchison, John Colicos.

THE FRIENDS OF EDDIE COYLE (1973)
Paramount: 102 minutes.
Producer: Paul Monash. *Director*: Peter Yates. *Screenplay*: Paul Monash
(from the novel by George V. Higgins). *Photographer*: Victor J. Kemper
(Technicolor and Panavision). *Music*: Dave Grusin. *Leading players*:
Robert Mitchum, Peter Boyle, Richard Jordan, Steven Keats, Alex
Rocco.

THE YAKUZA (1975)
WB: 112 minutes.
Producer: Sydney Pollack. *Director*: Sydney Pollack. *Screenplay*: Paul
Schrader, Robert Towne. *Photographers*: Okazaki Kozo, Duke Callaghan
(Technicolor and Panavision). *Music*: Dave Grusin. *Leading players*:
Robert Mitchum, Takakura Ken, Kishi Keiko, Brian Keith, Richard
Jordan, Herb Edelman.
(alternative title: BROTHERHOOD OF THE YAKUZA)

FAREWELL, MY LOVELY (1975)
EK/ITC: 96 minutes.
Producers: George Pappas, Jerry Bruckheimer. *Director*: Dick Richards.
Screenplay: David Zelag Goodman (from the novel by Raymond
Chandler). *Photographer*: John A. Alonzo (Technicolor and Panavision).
Music: David Shire. *Leading players*: Robert Mitchum, Charlotte
Rampling, Sylvia Miles, John Ireland, Anthony Zerbe, Walter McGinn,
Jack O'Halloran, Harry Dean Stanton, Kate Murtagh.

MIDWAY (UK: The Battle of Midway) (1976)
Universal: 132 minutes.
Producer: Walter Mirisch. *Director*: Jack Smight. *Screenplay*: Donald S.
Sanford. *Photographer*: Harry Stradling Jr (Technicolor and Panavision).
Music: John Williams. *Leading players*: Charlton Heston, Henry Fonda,
Glenn Ford, James Coburn, Hal Holbrook, Toshiro Mifune, Robert
Mitchum, Cliff Robertson, Robert Wagner.

THE LAST TYCOON (1976)
Paramount: 123 minutes.
Producer: Sam Spiegel. *Director*: Elia Kazan. *Screenplay*: Harold Pinter
(from the novel by F. Scott Fitzgerald). *Photographer*: Victor Kemper
(Technicolor and Panavision). *Music*: Maurice Jarre. *Leading players*:
Robert De Niro, Tony Curtis, Robert Mitchum, Jeanne Moreau, Jack
Nicholson, Ray Milland, Dana Andrews, Donald Pleasence.

THE AMSTERDAM KILL (1977)
Golden Harvest: 93 minutes.
Producer: André Morgan. *Director*: Robert Clouse. *Screenplay*: Robert
Clouse, Gregory Teifer. *Photographer*: Alan Hume (Technicolor and
Panavision). *Music*: Hal Schaffer. *Leading players*: Robert Mitchum,
Bradford Dillman, Richard Egan, Leslie Nielsen, Keye Luke, George
Cheung.
(alternative title: QUINLAN MUST DIE)

THE BIG SLEEP (1978)
UA: 99 minutes.
Producer: Elliott Kastner, Michael Winner. *Director*: Michael Winner. *Screenplay*: Michael Winner (from the novel by Raymond Chandler). *Photographer*: Robert Paynter (DeLuxe Color). *Music*: Jerry Fielding. *Leading players*: Robert Mitchum, Sarah Miles, Richard Boone, Candy Clark, James Stewart, Edward Fox, Harry Andrews, John Mills, Oliver Reed, Joan Collins, Colin Blakely, Don Henderson.

MATILDA (1978)
AI/FFG: 105 minutes.
Producer: Albert S. Ruddy. *Director*: Daniel Mann. *Screenplay*: Albert S. Ruddy, Timothy Galfas (from the novel by Paul Gallico). *Photographer*: Jack Woolf (Movielab/Fujicolor). *Music*: Jerrold Immel. *Leading players*: Robert Mitchum, Elliott Gould, Lionel Stander, Harry Guardino, Clive Revill, Karen Carlson.

AGENCY (1979)
RSL/Canadian Film Dev. Co: 82 minutes.
Producer: Robert Lantos, Stephen J. Roth. *Director*: George Kaczender. *Screenplay*: Noel Hynd (from the novel by Paul Gottlieb) *Photographer*: Miklos Lente (Eastmancolor). *Music*: Lewis Furey. *Leading players*: Robert Mitchum, Lee Majors, Valerie Perrine, Saul Rubinek.

NIGHTKILL (1979)
Cine-Artist: 95 minutes.
Producers: Richard Hellman, David Gil. *Director*: Ted Post. *Screenplay*: Joan Andre. *Photographer*: Anthony Richmond (Movielab Color). *Music*: Gunther Fischer. *Leading players*: Jaclyn Smith, Mike Connors, James Franciscus, Robert Mitchum.

BREAKTHROUGH (1982)
Globe Film Alliance/IMPC: 111 minutes.
Producer: Ted Richmond. *Director*: Andrew V. McLaglen. *Screenplay*: Tony Williamson. *Photographer*: Tony Imi (Technicolor and Panavision). *Music*: Peter Thomas. *Leading players*: Richard Burton, Rod Steiger, Robert Mitchum, Curt Jurgens, Michael Parks, Helmut Griem. (this film had a limited release in 1979 as SERGEANT STEINER).

ONE SHOE MAKES IT MURDER (1982)
Lorimar: 96 minutes.
Producer: Mel Ferrer. *Director*: William Hale. *Screenplay*: Felix Culver (from the novel 'So Little Cause for Caroline' by Eric Bercovici). *Photographer*: Terry K. Meade (color). *Music*: Bruce Broughton. *Leading players*: Robert Mitchum, Angie Dickinson, Mel Ferrer, José Perez, Howard Hesseman.

THAT CHAMPIONSHIP SEASON (1983)
Cannon: 110 minutes.
Producer: Menahem Golan, Yoram Globus. *Director*: Jason Miller.

Screenplay: Jason Miller (from his own stage play). *Photographer*: John Bailey (colour). *Music*: Bill Conti. *Leading players*: Robert Mitchum, Martin Sheen, Bruce Dern, Stacy Keach, Paul Sorvino.

THE WINDS OF WAR (1983)
Paramount for ABC: 16 hours.
Producers: Dan Curtis, Barbara Steele. *Director*: Dan Curtis. *Screenplay*: Herman Wouk, Jack Pulman (from Wouk's novel). *Photographer*: Charles Correll (color). *Music*: Robert Cobert. *Leading players*: Robert Mitchum, Ali McGraw, Jan-Michael Vincent, Polly Bergen, Victoria Tennant, David Dukes, Chaim Topol, John Houseman, Ben Murphy, Lisa Eilbacher, Deborah Winters, Jeremy Kemp, Peter Graves, Michael Logan.

A KILLER IN THE FAMILY (1984)
Sunn Classic/Taft for ABC/WB/Seven Arts: 90 minutes.
Producer: Stan Margulies. *Director*: Richard T. Heffron. *Screenplay*: Sue Grafton, Stephen Jeffrey. *Photographer*: Hanania Baer (color). *Music*: Gerald Fried. *Leading players*: Robert Mitchum, James Spader, Lance Kerwin, Eric Stoltz, Stuart Margolin, Salome Jens, Lynn Carlin, Catherine Mary Stewart.

THE AMBASSADOR (1984)
Cannon: 95 minutes.
Producers: Menahem Golan, Yoram Globus. *Director*: J. Lee Thompson. *Screenplay*: Max Jack (suggested by novel '52 Pick-Up' by Elmore Leonard). *Photographer*: Adam Greenberg (TVC color). *Music*: Dov Seltzer. *Leading players*: Robert Mitchum, Ellen Burstyn, Rock Hudson, Fabio Testi, Donald Pleasence.

MARIA'S LOVERS (1984)
Cannon: 109 minutes.
Producers: Menahem Golan, Yoram Globus. *Director*: Andrei Konchalovsky. *Screenplay*: Gerard Brach, Andrei Konchalovsky, Paul Zindel, Marjorie David. *Photographer*: Juan Ruiz Anchia (MGM color). *Music*: Gary S. Remal. *Leading players*: John Savage, Natassja Kinski, Keith Carradine, Robert Mitchum, Anita Morris, Bud Cort.

NORTH AND SOUTH (1985-6)
ABC/Warner/David Wolper: 24 x 50 mins.
Producers: Robert Papazian, Paul Freeman. *Directors*: Kevin Connor, Richard T. Heffron. *Screenplay*: Douglas Heyes and others (from the novel by John Jakes). *Leading players*: Lesley-Anne Down, David Carradine, Jean Simmons, Patrick Swayze, Lewis Smith, Jonathan Frakes with cameos by Robert Mitchum, Gene Kelly, Robert Guillaume, James Stewart, Elizabeth Taylor.

PROMISES TO KEEP (1985)
CBS: 90 minutes.
Producer: Sandra Harmon. *Director*: Noel Black. *Screenplay*: Phil

Penningroth. *Photographer*: Dennis A. Dalzell (color). *Music*: Michel Legrand. *Leading players*: Robert Mitchum, Christopher Mitchum, Bentley C. Mitchum, Claire Bloom, Tess Harper, Merritt Butrick, Jane Sibbett.

THE HEARST AND DAVIES AFFAIR (1985)
ABC: 90 minutes.
Producer: Paul Pompian. *Director*: David Lowell Rich. *Screenplay*: Alison Cross, David Solomon. *Photographer*: Charles Wheeler (color). *Music*: Laurence Rosenthal. *Leading players*: Robert Mitchum, Virginia Madsen, Fritz Weaver, Doris Belack, Laura Henry, Caroline Yeager.

REUNION AT FAIRBOROUGH (1985)
HBO: 105 minutes.
Producer: William Hill. *Director*: Herbert Wise. *Screenplay*: Albert Ruben. *Photographer*: Tony Imi (color). *Music*: Nigel Hess. *Leading players*: Robert Mitchum, Deborah Kerr, Red Buttons, Judi Trott, Shane Rimmer, Ed Devereaux, Barry Morse.

THOMPSON'S LAST RUN (1986)
CBS: 95 minutes.
Producer: Jennifer Faulstitch. *Director*: Jerrold Freedman. *Screenplay*: John Carlen. *Photographer*: Hal Trussell (color). *Leading players*: Robert Mitchum, Wilford Brimley, Kathleen York, Guy Boyd, Royce Wallace, Tony Frank, Susan Tyrell.

THE EQUALIZER: MISSION McCALL (1987)
CBS: 2 x 50 minutes.
Producers: Marc Lamb, Daniel Lieberstein. *Director*: Alan Metzger. *Screenplay*: Ed Walters, Scott Shepherd, Robert Eisele. *Photographer*: Geoffrey Erb (color). *Music*: Stewart Copeland. *Leading players*: Robert Mitchum, Richard Jordan, Frankie R. Falson, Robert Lansing.

MR NORTH (1988)
Columbia-Tri-Star/Heritage: 93 minutes.
Producer: Steven Haft, Skip Steloff. *Director*: Danny Huston. *Screenplay*: Janet Roach, John Huston, James Costigan (from the novel 'Theophilus North' by Thornton Wilder). *Photographer*: Robin Vidgeon (Metrocolor). *Music*: David McHugh. *Leading players*: Anthony Edwards, Robert Mitchum, Lauren Bacall, Harry Dean Stanton, Anjelica Huston, David Warner.

SCROOGED (1988)
Columbia-Tri-Star/Heritage: 101 minutes.
Producers: Richard Donner, Art Linson. *Director*: Richard Donner. *Screenplay*: Mitch Glazer, Michael O'Donaghue (suggested by the novel 'A Christmas Carol' by Charles Dickens). *Photographer*: Michael Chapman (Technicolor). *Music*: Danny Elfman. *Leading players*: Bill Murray, Karen Allen, John Forsythe, John Glover, Bobcat Goldthwait, David Johansen, Carol Kane, Robert Mitchum.

WAR AND REMEMBRANCE (1988)
ABC (Paramount): 30 hours.
Producers: Dan Curtis, Barbara Steele. *Director*: Dan Curtis. *Screenplay*: Herman Wouk, Dan Curtis, Earl Wallace (from Wouk's novel). *Leading players*: Robert Mitchum, Jane Seymour, Hart Bochner, Polly Bergen, Victoria Tennant, David Dukes, Chaim Topol, John Gielgud, Michael Woods, Leslie Hope, Sharon Stone, Jeremy Kemp, Peter Graves, Robert Morley.

THE BROTHERHOOD OF THE ROSE (1989)
TV mini-series, 300 minutes.
Leading players: Robert Mitchum, Peter Strauss, David Morse, Connie Selecca, James B. Sikking, M. Emmet Walsh.

Scheduled productions for 1990:

SMOKE BELLEW; JAKE SPANNER: PRIVATE EYE; A FAMILY FOR JOE.

Bibliography

Among the following books are some to which I have referred (and these are mentioned in the text) and others which readers of this book might find interesting and worthy of study.

Agee, James, *On Film* vol. 2 (Peter Owen, London, 1965).
Belton, John, *Robert Mitchum* (New York: Pyramid, 1976).
Douglas, Kirk, *Ragman's Son* (New York: Simon and Schuster, 1988)
Downing, David, *Robert Mitchum* (W. H. Allen, London, 1985).
Eells, George, *Robert Mitchum: a Biography* (London: Robson, 1984).
Gershuny, Theodore, *Soon To Be a Major Motion Picture* (New York: Holt, Rinehart and Winston, 1981).
Gish, Lillian, *The Movies, Mr Griffith and Me* (New Jersey: Prentice-Hall, 1969).
LeRoy, Mervyn, *Take One* (London: W. H. Allen, 1974).
Lewis, Grover, *Academy All The Way* (San Francisco: Straight Arrow, 1974).
Malcolm, Derek, *Robert Mitchum* (Tunbridge Wells: Spellmount, 1984).
Marill, Alvin H., *Robert Mitchum on Screen* (New York: A. S. Barnes, 1978).
Mayersberg, Paul, *Hollywood the Haunted House* (London: Allen Lane, Penguin, 1967).
Mitchum, John, *Them Ornery Mitchum Boys: the Adventures of Robert & John Mitchum* (Pacifica, California: Creatures at Large Press, 1989).
Peary, Gerald, and Roger Shatzkin eds., *The Modern American Novel and the Movies* (New York: Frederick Ungar, 1978).
Silver, Alain, and Elizabeth Ward eds., *Film Noir* (London: Secker & Warburg, 1980).
Tomkies, Mike, *The Robert Mitchum Story* (London: W. H. Allen, 1972).

Magazine references are made in the text but special mention should be given to *Emmy*, *Films and Filming*, *Films Illustrated*, *Monthly Film Bulletin*, *The New York Times*, *Variety* and the many film critics whose work has appeared in these journals over the years. In particular, the acerbic comments of my near-namesake, Bosley Crowther of the *NYT*, have provided much insight and amusement even if I have usually disagreed profoundly.

B.C.

Index